PERSPECTIVES ON THE HISTORY
OF ECONOMIC THOUGHT
VOLUME I

CLASSICAL AND NEOCLASSICAL
ECONOMIC THOUGHT

Perspectives on the History of Economic Thought
Volume I

Classical and Neoclassical Economic Thought

Selected Papers from the History
of Economics Society Conference,
1987

Edited by
Donald A. Walker

Published for the History of Economics
Society by
Edward Elgar

Published by
Edward Elgar Publishing Limited
Gower House
Croft Road
Aldershot
Hants GU11 3HR
England

Gower Publishing Company
Old Post Road
Brookfield
Vermont 05036
USA

British Library Cataloguing data

Perspectives on the history of economic thought:
    Selected papers from the History of Economics
    Society Conference 1987.
    Vol. 1: Classical and neoclassical economic
    thought.
    1. Economics, to 1986
    I. Walker, Donald A. (Donald Anthony) 1934–
    II. History of Economics Society.
    330'.09

ISBN 1 85278 131 9

Printed and bound in Great Britain by
Anchor Press Ltd, Tiptree, Essex

Contents

v

Introduction

Donald A. Walker

In the last two years the sentiment has grown in the History of
Economics Society that some of the best papers given at its annual
meeting should be published under the sponsorship of the Society in an
annual series that recognizes and draws attention to the work of the
Society. This has now been made possible by arrangement with Edward
Elgar Publishing Ltd. The name of the series is *Perspectives on the
History of Economic Thought*. The first two volumes in the series
comprise papers given at the 1987 meeting of the Society, which was
held at the Harvard School of Business, 19–22 June 1987. The publication of the first two volumes thus marks the beginning of an annual
event and of another stage in the development of the projects under-
taken by the History of Economics Society. There is a rich variety of
papers given at the Society from which to draw the publications in this
series – at the 1987 conference, for example, there were 156. The series
will make available to a wide readership some of the achievements of
those who attend the Society's meetings. It will provide another vehicle
for revealing the intellectual vitality and excellent quality of the work
that is being done by scholars in the field of the study of the history of
economic thought.

The reader will see that the papers in the first two volumes correct
errors of perspective and interpretation. They indicate some of the
many ways in which economic theory has been applied to real problems.
They show the importance of studies of the history of economic thought
for an understanding of its influence on our conceptions of the world
and on economic, social and political behaviour.

Volume 1 contains papers on the classical and neoclassical schools of
economic thought. The first group of papers are presented in a section
entitled 'Early Classical Economics'. This does not mean that they are
all confined to the study of the work of classical economists. Indeed,
what is striking about the papers is the way in which they relate classical
economics to subsequent developments. Salim Rashid indicates the
surprising extent to which non-academic writers in England during the
mid-eighteenth century developed ideas which were important in the

subsequent development of economics. These writers, he demonstrates, have been unjustly neglected in favour of the academic economists of the period. Edd S. Noell contrasts the work of Edward Coke and Adam Smith on occupational regulation, a matter of modern concern. Coke is seen to be an exponent of the common law approach and of the Tudor concept of public good, whereas Smith is shown to have adopted the contrasting criterion of economic efficiency. Noell's paper is a useful contribution to our understanding of the history of different attitudes towards the question of occupational regulation and the goals that it should achieve. Bruce D. Larson reappraises Nicholas-François Canard's work on price determination, showing that there are more substantial reasons for admiring his work than were recognized by his contemporaries, and demonstrating that he was a precursor of a number of neoclassical ideas on that topic. Marco Bianchini performs a similar task regarding the work of the Italian eighteenth-century economists. He explains their contributions to a scientific treatment of exchange and money, and reveals their use of algebra and calculus in application to economic questions.

The second group of papers deals with nineteenth-century classical thought. Royall Brandis examines the classical doctrine of the approach to a stationary state and discusses its characteristics. He shows that W. S. Jevons also adhered to the doctrine of the stationary state, but did not base it upon the classical ideas. Brandis then draws attention to the disappearance of the doctrine from economic theory, and offers an explanation for why that happened. Fyodor I. Kushnirsky and William J. Stull write on productive and unproductive labour and the related definitions of the treatment of material and non-material output. Their concern is to determine whether the ideas of Adam Smith and Karl Marx on these topics were adopted by the national income accountants of the communist nations. Giovanni Caravale examines David Ricardo's analysis of pricing and production in the light of the subsequent work of Piero Sraffa. Caravale's objective is to investigate the question of whether or not there has been continuity in economic thought on that matter. Gary Mongiovi makes clear that the classical economists were concerned with the role of demand in the economic system, and analyses the limitations of their analysis. Like the contributions of Larson and Salerno, Mongiovi's paper is intended to provide a more accurate account of economic thought during the liberal period.

The third group of papers deals with writers of the neoclassical school. Peter de Gijsel investigates how Léon Walras utilized his theory of general equilibrium, which in itself is neutral on the issue of social justice, in his normative theory of a just society. This requires de Gijsel to explain Walras's theory of the latter and to analyse how Walras used his positive theory of general equilibrium as a means of substantiating the feasibility of his normative views. Hans Brems examines the work of Knut Wicksell and Gustav Cassel, two writers who were greatly influenced by Walras. Brems is concerned to show that Wicksell made a number of important contributions that were subsequently to be developed by the Swedish school and economists generally. Brems also shows that Cassel was a more original thinker than we have been accustomed to believe, making contributions in both microeconomic and macroeconomic work on growth theory, and anticipating some of the elements of the theory of revealed preference. Orhan Kayaalp informs us about Italian neoclassical contributions to the theory of public finance. The economists with whom he deals are Maffeo Pantaleone, Ugo Mazzola and Antonio De Viti. Kayaalp provides interesting comparisons between the Italian contribution and English-speaking economists in the field of public finance, revealing the Italian work to be a manifestation of the marginalist revolution and showing its bases in Italian social theory. Arnold Heertje analyses the work of N.G. Pierson, who lived from 1839 to 1909. Pierson was Professor of Economics, President of the Dutch Central Bank, Minister of Finance, and Prime Minister of the Netherlands. His economic thought spanned the late classical school and the work of the neoclassical economists, and was influenced especially by W.S. Jevons. He was able through his many publications to influence theoretical developments in the Netherlands. Nahid Aslanbeigui contrasts Alfred Marshall's and A.C. Pigou's policy recommendations on the topics of unemployment, socialism and inequality, and reveals fundamental differences between their outlook and prescriptions. She thus adds to the accumulating evidence that Pigou emancipated himself in a number of important respects from Marshall's thought, which is not to say that he necessarily had sounder thoughts on the topics. Pigou is increasingly revealed to be one of the group of influential British thinkers who 'took a leaf from the book of Soviet Russia'. The reader can judge for himself or herself whether Marshall was an advocate of outmoded and useless ideas on the topics, or a wise precursor of the views of those modern economists who would undo some of the machinery of the welfare state.

Contributors

Nahid Aslanbeigui, Department of Economics, Tulane University, New Orleans, LA

Marco Bianchini, Istituto di Storia Economica, Università degli Studi di Parma, Italy

Royall Brandis, Department of Economics, University of Illinois at Urbana-Champaign, Champaign, IL

Hans Brems, Department of Economics, University of Illinois at Urbana-Champaign, Urbana-Champaign

Giovanni Caravale, Department of Economic Theory, and Quantitative Methods, University of Rome, Rome, Italy

Peter de Gijsel, Department of Economics, Rijksuniversiteit Limburg, Maastricht, The Netherlands

Arnold Heertje, Department of Economics, University of Amsterdam, Naarden, The Netherlands

Orhan Kayaalp, Department of Economics and Accounting, Lehman College, Bronx, New York

Fyodor I. Kushnirsky, Department of Economics, Temple University, Philadelphia, PA

Bruce D. Larson, Department of Economics, University of North Carolina, Ashville, NC

Gary Mongiovi, Department of Economics and Finance, St John's University, Jamaica, New York

Edd S. Noell, Department of Economics and Business, Westmont College, Santa Barbara, CA

Salim Rashid, Department of Economics, University of Illinois, Urbana-Champaign, Champaign, IL

William J. Stull, Department of Economics, Temple University, Philadelphia, PA

Donald A. Walker, Department of Economics, Indiana University of Pennsylvania, Indiana, Pennsylvania.

PART I

EARLY CLASSICAL TOPICS

1 English financial pamphleteers of the mid-eighteenth century: the last phase of pragmatic political economy

Salim Rashid[1]

I

In his exposition of the Quantity Theory of Money in 1801, Walter Boyd referred to the theory itself as 'the alphabet or first principle of every financier and merchant for above a century'. That merchants theorized about economic problems is familiar to all students of the period, but *financiers*? There seems to be a gap in our study of eighteenth-century economics.[2] It is only natural that academic economists should look to academia for the origins of their profession; it is equally natural for us to identify the publication of comprehensive treatises as marking the recognizable beginnings of the subject. However justifiable these biases may be, in the case of eighteenth-century economics they have served to magnify the contributions of Sir James Steuart and Adam Smith and to minimize the writings of the eighteenth-century financial pamphleteers.

It is no secret to students of the period that English economics grew largely through pamphlets written for particular economic issues. While this phase of economic thought has traditionally been known as 'Mercantilism', it is better called 'Pragmatic Political Economy'.[3] I begin by a brief sketch of the growth of Pragmatic Political Economy in order to emphasize that, by 1730, the English pamphleteers were dealing with a commercially mature and rich economy. As a result, the primary economic questions were financial – relating to taxes and the national debt. Focus upon these issues meant that an economy-wide viewpoint was increasingly taken. In particular, concern with the balance of trade was quite limited.

The financial pamphleteers were 'political' economists in that their pamphlets were frequently interspersed with comments on party politics. Sometimes this took the form of comments on the monied versus the landed interest, at others on Whigs versus Tories. The pamphlets sold very well and some of the best-selling pamphlets of the period 1740–67 were concerned with finance. Because of the close link of finance with war, the analysis of several of these pamphlets has been passed over because of their ostensible politics. One might not expect an analysis of the lagged effects of an inflow of gold into a country in a pamphlet such as Malachy Postlethwayt's *Great Britain's True System*.[4] None the less, such is the case.

The financial writers of this period have not been much studied with a view to seeing how they exemplify the growth of economic thought. E.R.A. Seligman's *Incidence of Taxation*, originally published in 1899, took a first step in classifying the pamphlet literature according to their views on incidence. William Kennedy's *English Taxation 1640–1799* is more valuable in that it places the issues in their political context and deals with the growth of ideas. Joseph Schumpeter's monumental *History of Economic Analysis* has several insightful remarks, but Schumpeter's knowledge of the primary literature was not extensive and his desire to find a variety of European provisions for Adam Smith's views on public finance gives his work a peculiar perspective. While I have drawn on each of these sources, the selection and arrangement of matter is perhaps new.[5]

II

British economic thought in the two centuries before Adam Smith was predominately policy-oriented. The practical bent of the English mind is so pronounced that a student of the Civil War period is led to remark that, 'When Englishmen are driven to imitate their continental neighbours, and leave the well-ploughed fields of practical activity for the less secure heights of theory and first principles, it is a severe sign that something is very rotten in the state.'[6] Of the thousands of pamphlets written in this period those concerned primarily with an intellectual understanding of trade can be counted on both hands. The overwhelming majority of pamphlets had some immediate practical end in view. Thus John Locke, the philosopher, wrote to support recoinage at the old par: Sir Josiah Child, Director of the East India Company, wrote to support a reduction in the rate of interest; and Henry Martyn, Inspector General of the Customs wrote to support the free import of East India textiles. Such pamphlets were written by men from all walks of life – economics had not yet adopted a professional attitude and a jargon to scare away amateurs. One of the richest sources for the economic thought of these centuries consist of the speeches of Members of Parliament. It is instructive to see the issues raised by Sir Edwin Sandys while attacking grants of Monopoly by the Crown (only the first, fourth and fifth reasons are quoted).[7]

I.   Natural Right, the first Reason for a free Trade.

IV. Increase of Wealth, a fourth Reason for a free Trade.
V. Equal Distribution, a fifth Reason for a free Trade.

There does not appear to be any claim for a monopoly as being generally beneficial in the subsequent literature. Hereafter, anyone who wished for monopoly privileges had always to show that special circumstances justified such privileges.

Since the most oppressive monopolies were those obtained by a charter from the monarch, often in return for a monetary equivalent, the debates over monopolies led naturally into questions over taxes. These debates continued for the first half of the seventeenth century and the basic principles of taxation were widely recognized by this time. When Sir William Petty came to write *A Treatise on Taxes* in the 1660s he was not originating a subject but elaborating upon widely accepted ideas. The difference in the two periods lies rather in the different political climate of the early and late seventeenth century. Until after the Restoration of Charles II in 1660, but not entirely successfully until the Glorious Revolution of 1688, the King's personal finance constituted the main worry in thinking about Public Finance. After 1688 Parliament took control of the purse, and Public Finance became visibly a *public* concern. Shortly thereafter, other concomitant features of a modern financial system – the Bank of England, a reformation of the coinage and a National Debt – made their prominent appearance.

The English economy of the early seventeenth century was heavily dependent upon trade and upon the woollen trade in particular. This dependence was not so much a question of the proportion of the GNP derived from trade as upon the volatility and importance of this branch of the economy. Lord Keynes expressed well the sort of relationship the mercantilists were concerned with while defending the choice of investment as the crucial macroeconomic variable.[8]

> Given the psychology of the public, the level of output and employment as a whole depends upon the amount of investment. I put it in this way, not because this is the only factor on which aggregate output depends, but because it is usual in a complex system to regard as the *causa causans* that factor which is most prone to sudden and wide fluctuation.

The failure of the cloth trade from about 1615 led to a disastrous depression in the 1620s and to the appointment of a Commission to investigate the causes and remedies of the stagnation. Thomas Mun, a merchant of the East India Company, was a member of this Commission and his subsequent pamphlets arose directly from his experience on it. Mun's most famous work, *England's Treasure by Foreign Trade*, not only emphasized the Balance of Trade, the feature it has become notorious for, but was also a plea for England to diversify its industry away from a precarious dependence upon wool:[9]

> But first, I will deliver my opinion concerning our CLOTHING, which although it is the greatest Wealth and best Employment of the Poor of this Kingdome, yet nevertheless we may peradventure employ our selves with better Safety, Plenty, and Profit in using more Tillage and Fishing, than to tryest so wholly to the making of cloth.

The depression of the 1620s was brought on, to some extent, by the attempt of the English to displace the Dutch as the finishers of English raw cloth exports. The first half of the seventeenth century shows the English consumed by both admiration for Dutch industry and jealously at their success. In subsequent years these feelings led to the Navigation Acts and to three Dutch wars which ended with the Dutch, literally, beaten out of the field.

Now it was the turn of the French to be both hated and admired. The economic policies of Colbert could not but attract English attention and the power and purse of France was constantly on English minds. The fact that Charles II was quietly receiving money from Louis XIV helped the English to concentrate on these issues. France however was not a naval power and did not directly enter into a contest for naval and commercial supremacy. Whenever the question of closer economic ties with France arose, the Balance of Trade reared its head. This was as true in the 1660s as in the 1720s. The Tories supported the King and therefore more free trade with France. William Ashley has written perceptively on how early free trade policy was frequently supported by the Tories,[10] and political factors seem to provide the explanation for this division.

Having become undisputed masters of the shipping lanes by 1690, the English were faced with the problem of deciding whether to continue along the Dutch model, with its emphasis on free trade, or strike out along a new path. The question of industrialization gripped the energies of British economists between 1695 and 1720. As may be expected, the cloth industry was still the centrepiece of the show but now it was the competition from Indian textiles that exercised the English. The decision to adopt a protective attitude towards domestic cloth manufacturers was a monotonous one and was considerably aided by the activities of workers who feared unemployment if free importation was permitted. A student of these debates has conjectured that without such protection the British cotton industry might not have developed.[11] And without cotton, the question arises of how successful the Industrial Revolution would have been. The increased emphasis upon industry also led to an increased concern for employment. It can be shown that there was a steady change of emphasis between 1650 and 1750 upon the primary means by which to achieve growth – in 1650 a favourable balance of trade was most desired; by 1750 full employment had become the dominant goal.

The overarching features of British economic policy and thought were thus set by the 1720s. This of course did not mean that economic controversy ended. Mandeville produced a considerable stir with his thesis that Private Vices could be Public Benefits in his *Fable of the Bees* (1726). George Blewitt and Francis Hutcheson however satisfactorily shows that Mandeville's support of consumption for any and every purpose was both misplaced and unnecessary. At about the same time a brilliant group of Anglo-Irish writers, whom Jonathan Swift joined every so often, analysed the faults of British imperialist policy in Ireland. Some of the most penetrating treatments of economic development in a poor country (it should be remembered that England was the richest country in Europe well *before* the Industrial Revolution) are to be found in the writings of the Anglo-Irish school.[12] None the less, these issues did not dominate the pamphlet literature. Financial issues did. Nor is this surprising – a country that is rich and growing and has settled its general trade and commercial policy really has only taxation and the National Debt as its primary worries.

III
Adam Smith begins his treatment of Taxation by stating four maxims, whose truth he takes to be readily apparent, which should guide tax policy.[13]

I.   The subjects of every state ought to contribute . . ., as nearly as possible, in proportion to their respective abilities.   [equality]
II. The tax which each individual is bound to pay ought to be certain, and not arbitrary.   [uncertainty]
III. Every tax ought to be levied at the time, or in the manner, in which it is most likely to be convenient for the contributor to pay it.   [convenience of payment]
IV. Every tax ought to be so contrived as both to take out and to keep out of the pockets of the people as little as possible, over and above what it brings into the public treasury of the state.   [economy]

Smith takes no credit for these maxims, but, with excessive generosity, states that they are all well known:[14] 'The evident justice and utility of the foregoing maxims have recommended them more or less to the attention of all nations.' He then goes on to examine how far various taxes that have been imposed in different countries do satisfy these

criteria. Smith's modesty and clear admission that he is an expositor in
the theory of taxation have not prevented his admirers from crediting
Smith with pathbreaking originality.[15] Smith was right in claiming the
maxims of taxation that he elaborated upon were well known. Indeed,
the development of the rules of taxation from the guidelines for just laws
seems to have been little noticed hitherto.

In 1599, Thomas Milles, a customs officer, states the following
general principles at the beginning of his pamphlet on the customs:[16]

> All Common Wealths are established and maintained by Lawes. The life of
> Law is Reason. Reason is making Lawes aymes at Equitie. Equitie is guided
> by Certainitie and Indifference, the two Ballances of Justice.

The twin themes of equity and certainty are to be repeated many times
in the subsequent literature.

In 1628, Bishop Sibthorpe preached a sermon that has become
notorious because of its defense of the royal authority to tax. In the
course of this sermon he laid down a guide for the manner in which the
king should exercise this right.[17]

> The Dutie therefore of the Law and Interpreters of the same is
>
> First; to be just, without tyranny . . .
> Secondly; Equall without partialitie . . .
> Thirdly; they must be moderate without extremity . . .
> Fourthly; they must be plain without ambiguitie . . .

An anonymous pamphleteer of the 1690s virtually anticipates all Smith's
maxims in his dicta for good taxes:[18]

> Could the whole present Want of this Nation be raised by some one way, and
> that way be more frugal, expedite and certain, than any one, or all, or any
> select number of Ways now in use no one can deny this assertion that we
> ought to use that way only, unless such Inconveniences necessarily attend
> that way, as would appear to equal, if not exceed the benefits it promised
> from the forementioned Qualities (viz.), Thrift, Equality, Expedition and
> Certainity in respect of the sum to be raised.

During the Walpole administration, the criteria for good taxes were
often raised during debates on the salt-tax in 1732 as well as those on the
excise scheme of 1733.[19] The government based its case for the salt duty
upon the grounds that both rich and poor contributed as their means
permitted,

> Of all the taxes I ever could think of, there is not one more general, nor one
> less felt, than that of the duty upon Salt. The duty upon Salt is a tax that
> every man in the nation contributes to according to his circumstances.

The opposition retorted that a tax which reached those who were barely
able to subsist was not their idea of equity:[20]

It is not always a certain maxim, that those taxes which are most general are least burthensome; upon the contrary, it holds true in all countries, and at all times, that those taxes which are laid upon the luxuries of mankind are the least burthensome.

The authority of John Locke was frequently used during economic debates of the 1730s and 1740s, especially on issues of taxation, and it is worth considering Locke's analytics because his approach was later adopted by Adam Smith as well as by the Physiocrats.

Locke's argument is so deceptively simple that a few words may help the reader. Locke assumes that all workers are earning a bare subsistence and that the rate of profit in all lines must be equal due to competition. If a tax is laid upon wages, the workers must pass it on or die; if laid upon a commodity, the dealers in that good must raise prices so that their profit rate equals that of other merchants. Hence neither wages nor profits can be made to some to bear the burden of taxes. It follows that all taxes must be borne by rents, and so a rational tax system would only tax the landed class.[21]

Let us see now who, at long-run, must pay this quarter, and where it will light. It is plain, the merchant and broker neither will nor can; for, if he pays a quarter more for commodities than he did, he will sell them at a price proportionably raised. The poor labourer and handicraftsman cannot: for he just lives from hand to mouth already, and all his food, clothing, and utensils costing a quarter more than they did before, either his wages must rise with the price of things, to make him live, or else, not being able to maintain himself and family by his labour, he comes to the parish; and then the land bears the burthen a heavier way.

The merchant (do what you can), will not bear it, the labourer cannot, and therefore the landholder must: and whether he were best to do it, by laying it directly where it will at last settle, or by letting it come to him by the sinking of his rents, which, when they are once fallen, every one knows are not easily raised again, let him consider.

Adam Smith's treatment of taxation is very much in accord with the accepted wisdom of his contemporaries. He praises Walpole's proposed excise scheme on the well-worn grounds that it would force down the costs of labour and lower the costs of collection, and notes that the scheme failed due to party politics. His analytics are based so heavily upon the assumption of a fixed real wage for labour that there is nothing to admire in Smith after having read Locke and Decker. His treatment of other issues varies considerably in quality. Thus, he correctly argues that a tax on a particular species of profit cannot fall on the entrepreneurs in that industry because competition will ensure that all trades earn the same rate of profit. Agriculture, however, is made an exception on the basis of the following curious argument:[22]

> But when a tax is imposed upon the profits of stock employed in agriculture, it is not the interest of the farmers to withdraw any part of their stock from that employment. Each farmer occupies a certain quantity of land, for which he pays rent. For the proper cultivation of this land a certain quantity of stock is necessary: and by withdrawing any part of this necessary quantity, the farmer is not likely to be more able to pay either the rent or the tax. In order to pay the tax, it can never be his interest to diminish the quantity of his produce, nor conseqently to supply the market more sparingly than before. The tax, therefore, will never enable him to raise the price of his produce, so as to reimburse himself by throwing the final payment upon the consumer. The farmer, however, must have his reasonable profit as well as every other dealer, otherwise he must give up the trade. After the imposition of a tax of this kind, he can get this reasonable profit only by paying less rent to the landlord. The more he is obliged to pay in the way of tax, the less he can afford to pay in the way of rent.

On other occasions, Smith's argument is made correct by the use of a questionable *ceteris paribus*. Consider his treatment of the incidence of a tax on wages:[23] 'A direct tax upon the wages of labour . . . could not properly be said to be even advanced by him; at least if the demand for labour and the average price of provisions remained the same after the tax as before it.' What requires justification in such cases is the proviso that the demand for labour and the price of provisions remains the same.

On the whole, Smith's analysis of taxation is plausible rather than penetrating; it provides a modest and sober account of the state of economic thought on taxation in the mid-eighteenth century. William Kennedy's perceptive assessment is worth repeating:[24]

> It has sometimes been supposed that the publication of the *Wealth of Nations* brought to the world a new revelation of the principles of taxation, and that it immediately affected the policy of the Chancellors of the Exchequer. But this is a serious misconception; the only respect in which it bears some relation to the facts is on the subject of trade policy in the Customs. Apart from that, what Adam Smith did was to expand the commercial view of tax questions which we have been following, and to attempt to systematize and rationalize it by bringing it into relation with the distributive theory of the seventeenth century which Walpole expressed. He gave a wider intellectual sanction to a set of opinions already very influential.

IV

It is time to provide a more detailed account of the financial writers. The pamphleteers I shall refer most often to are Joseph Massie and Malachy Postlethwayt. Each of them wrote several works and Postlethwayt in particular was quite prolific. Unfortunately, not much biographical information is available for either of them. This is also true of a more famous figure, Sir Mathew Decker, who has not been rescued from obscurity by Adam Smith's praise. The main pamphlets involved are: J. Massie, *Observations upon Mr. Fauquier's Essay on Ways and Means* (London, 1756), M. Postlethwayt, *Great Britain's True System* (London, 1756), Sir M. Decker, *Serious Considerations on the High Duties* . . . (London, 1743). In addition, the following anonymous works are of interest: *An Essay upon Publick Credit* (London, 1745), and *Remarks on the Present State of the National Debt* (London, 1764). If I have referred to a pamphlet only once, the quote has been provided from a secondary source, such as Kennedy or Seligman. The selection of financial pamphleteers is not complete by any means: some very able men, like Sir John Bernard, have been ignored, as have lesser men like William Knox and several anonymous pamphleteers.[25]

The first point worth noting about this literature is its firm grounding in a demand–supply explanation of price:[26]

'It is the plenty, or Scarcity of any Commodity, in Proportion to its Vent and Demand, which must always rule in these Cases, and by which the Trade will make more or less Profit in his Dealings.'

'Everyone admits,' says the author, 'that Quantity and Vent give a Price to any Commodity; it is therefore to be considered in what Cases the Quantity can be commanded or ascertained, in proportion to the Vent, and in what Cases it cannot; for where it can, the Duties will lie on the Consumer; but where it cannot, it will evidently lie on the Producer or Maker as often as the Quantity exceeds the Vent.'

With this basis, they went on the provide canons of taxation.[27]

As the benefits of taxes to the public results only from the clear income, and the evil to individuals extends not only to the gross produce but to every other expense and loss incident and consequential; that tax is most beneficial to the public and least hurtful to the subject which produces a large sum through a cheap collection and which is free from every other eventual charge.

There are three Things necessary to be considered before this or any other proposed Tax is laid; and these are,

I.   Whether it can be paid or not.
II. What Effect the Payment of it will have upon other Taxes.
III. Whether the Money to be raised by such Tax can be raised in any other manner that will be less prejudicial to the landed and trading interests of the nation.

Some writers explicitly distinguished between types of tax policy.[28]

All Taxes ought to be laid for one or both of these Purposes. Either it is a Tax of Revenue, the view of which is to supply the Necessities of the Publick, or it is a Tax of Police, intended to operate as a Restraint; for Instance, on the Importation or Consumption of foreign Manufacturers, to the Prejudice of our own, or on some Article of Luxury prejudicial to the Publick.

While others argued that taxes should be laid on the final consumer to minimize distortions in the economy:[29]

> 'that all Taxes should be laid as near as possible in the last Instance, and upon the immediate Consumer, and in proportion only to what he consumes there being nothing more unjust or absurd, than that a Man should pay a Tax for what he does not consume.' He bases his conclusion in favour of taxing the consumer, rather than the producer or importer, largely on the argument that taxes accumulate with each transfer and 'consequently draw with them, through their whole Progress, a Profit on the Tax, as well as upon their first value or prime cost.'

Concern over the incidence of taxation had led John Locke to provide a rudimentary general equilibrium account of this issue, which proved highly influential well into the eighteenth century.

While Locke has already established the analysis of long-run equilibrium, together with a *ceteris paribus* clause, later financial writers emphasized the method of real analysis for clarifying several issues.[30]

> It is evident, as we have before observed, throughout this Tract, that the Introduction of Money into Commerce has not any Ways altered the nature of that Commerce. It still conflicts in an Exchange of Commodities for Commodities; or, in the Absence of those which are wanted, for Money, which is the Representation of them.
>
> Now the case, as above stated, appears in all the simplicity it will admit of; but when we suppose that money, according to the custom and practice of latter ages, is made use of in traffic, and allowed to pass in exchange for commodities, it renders our ideas somewhat more complex and intricate. But every difficulty will immediately vanish, if we only consider them as equivalents.

Providing for the National Debt was one of the important stimulants for discussions of taxation. This divided pamphleteers into two groups – those who believed the burden of the debt to be negligible in so far as the debt remained a domestic debt, and those who argued that the taxes needed to finance the debt were ruining trade. A second concern was the availability of adequate specie to permit all the transactions to be made.

On the first issue, those who supported a continued debt argued that it merely involved payments from the right hand to the left, a viewpoint said to arise from the Prime Minister, Walpole:[31]

> If Sixty Millions of [the Debt] be the Property of the People of Great Britain it seems to me very plain that we are not the richer nor the poorer for that part of the Debt because if the Taxes be collected from the People of Great Britain, the Money arising from those Taxes is paid to the Proprietors of the Public Funds in the Dividends or Interest, which circulating again to purchase the necessaries and Superfluities of Life, enable the farmer to pay

his Rent, the Landlord his Taxes, helps to support the Industrious and to consume the Produce of their Labour.

Those who opposed this position, such as Postlethwayt, believed the increased taxation would raise prices and ruin England's ability to export. The argument that the National Debt was in fact the source of England's Public Credit was ignored by such writers.

The money obtained as debt could just as easily have been obtained through taxes. The emphasis here is on the circulation of money:[32]

> To make a right Judgment of this Matter, it may be previously necessary to inquire, where all the Money raised by the Parliament to carry on the War, may actually center and circulate; for that Proportion which is spent in the Kingdom, will not impoverish the Nation, so as to disable her from raising some considerable Part, at least, if not the Whole of the Supplies within the Year.

The Balance of Trade now comes to be discussed as a means of providing enough coin to make the payments of taxes feasible:[33]

> For, if our national debt should keep continually increasing, and our stock of cash should not keep pace with it, . . . we must inevitably stop payment when this happens to be the case. For these fifty or sixty years back, however, our exports have brought in more cash considerably, than what is only just sufficient to answer this purpose.
>
> Therefore our taxes are nothing more, in fact, than a general muster of our circulating cash, whereby a kind of estimate is taken of it, as it were to see whether it is equal or not to the total amount of the annual interest of our national debt. While we are able to collect taxes amongst us to this amount, it is very evident that there can be no necessity to stop payment. And this we have not as yet failed to do.

Since the value of stocks depended upon the general state of confidence and since this in turn depended partially upon the state of the National Debt, financial writers were naturally led to discussing banking. It is remarkable how closely some of these discussions anticipate issues of the later Bullion Debate:[34]

> In our present situation, everybody knows that there must be Remittances abroad to pay the Army and to support our Allies; and it is not improbable that so near the Time of opening the Campaign, as this is, the Balance of Drawing and Remitting may be against us; and the Consequence must follow, that Goods, or foreign Specie, must be exported, to answer that balance, whether you do, or do not discount Bills of Exchange.

The author even goes on to argue for compensatory actions on the part of the Bank of England during such times of stress, much as Henry Thornton was to urge some fifty years later:[35]

> I must further observe to you, Sir, that the Business of private Bankers is, to keep Cash, and Bank Notes, what is sufficient to answer their current

Demand, and to employ the remaining Part for their particular Benefit. But the Case of the Bank of England differs widely; because they are sure of having all the Cash deposited with them, that is not absolutely necessary to carry on Trade and Business, and to supply the Necessaries of Life; so that Bank Notes are a kind of real Specie, which are current in all forts of payment; and therefore so long as there is Property in the Kingdom, they are sure of a more than sufficent Quantity of Cash, to answer any Demand.

Postlethwayt is generally considered one of those economists whose objectives differ most widely from those of Adam Smith. Recent scholarship has portrayed Postlethwayt as the most perceptive economist dealing with the importance of the African slave trade to Britain's colonial system. It is instructive to see how closely Postlethwayt developed the notion that competition is valuable.

[I]t is proper to be acquainted with what is the most active Principle of useful Commerce: I mean Rivalship. All other Principles may be ranked under this: they emane from it, and without it would have no Vigour. It is the Life and Spirit of Industry; for which Reason it would be dangerous to check it: but as every Kind of Industry is not equally useful and necessary, to Emulation or Rivalship may be encouraged more or less in Proportion. This Difference is not an Exception; if it be thought such, it is the only one that the Application of this Principle will admit of.

Competition is based on self-interest and leads to society becoming richer: 'Hope of Advantage, of some Kind or other, is undoubtedly the Source of Rivalship; its Preservation depends on the real Utility that is found in aspiring at preference; and its general Effect is to multiply the Objects of Preference.' Such competition, or rivalry, is the principal means of commercial success and should form the rule of all domestic trade:

Emulation in Work between the Subjects: it conflicts in each of them being allowed to employ himself, in what he thinks most lucrative, or what is most pleasing to him, provided that Employment be useful to Society. It is the chief Basis of Freedom in Trade; and alone contributes more than any other Means to procure a Nation that foreign Rivalship by which she grows rich and powerful.

The difference between Adam Smith and his 'Mercantilist' predecessors lies not in their grasp of economic principles but rather on the extent to which politics and economics were considered independently. The same Postlethwayt who extolled competition so highly refused to allow it to override political considerations. This is abundantly clear in his statement of the principles guiding foreign trade:[36] 'The Balance of Trade, I cannot too often repeat it, is in Fact the Balance of Power.'

V

When we gather together the insights obtained by the financial writers of the mid-eighteenth century we find several items of value. Malachy

Postlethwayt, for example, was nearly obsessed with the idea of raising supplies by taxation within the year so that future taxes would not burden future trade. How can supplies be raised without imposing some current taxes which will burden current trade? Postlethwayt came to grips with this issue by noting that his first preference would be a poll tax, even though it is not politically viable. He appears to have recognized that the only way to get a non-distortionary tax is to have a lump-sum tax and the poll tax was the closest approximation he could find. This shows a fair amount of theoretical insight. Joseph Massie, as another example, argued that Portugal deserved special treatment for the following reason: Portuguese consumption of English goods was more elastic with respect to Portuguese revenue than was the consumption of English goods by the French, with respect to French revenue. Joseph Schumpeter has aptly remarked that such a statement is theoretically interesting, regardless of its correctness. There appears to have been a friendly rivalry between the two men: Postlethwayt attacked the residence of landlords in London and Massie, without naming names, provides a sharp critique of this position.[37]

Pragmatic political economy can lay claim to a considerable achievement in positive economics. A statement of their ideas in general theoretical terms flattens them somewhat but it is worth making for emphasis. Cogent use of demand and supply in analysis of market equilibrium awareness of the *ceteris paribus* clause needed for the validity of results as well as the distinction between long- and short-run analysis. A firm faith in competition as the basis of efficiency in the market as well as a capacity to assess the nature of distortion minimizing taxes. If their normative principles, particularly on political issues, differed from those of the classical economists, this should not blind us to their positive analysis.

Taxes are the one economic subject that cannot be usefully discussed if they are not practicable. The unwritten rules for a viable tax scheme are those of sufficiency and feasibility – the taxes must raise the required revenue and they must be implementable. The tax debates of the 1730s and 1740s frequently raised such practical issues as the difficulty of assessment, the costs of collection, as well as the quasi-political argument that some tax schemes, such as the excise, would lead to an 'intolerable' multiplication of revenue officials. The Public Choice school is sometimes traced back to Adam Smith for such views, but it will be seen that Smith himself is part of a much older tradition:[38]

> One of the greatest evils of a salt tax, I may say the greatest, because it strikes at our constitution, is the great number of officers which must be employed in collecting that small branch of the revenue.

All taxes which require a multitude of officers to be employed in collecting them, and which give thereby both occasion and pretence to quarter numbers of useless subjects on the labour and industry of others, become so changeable and oppressive, that they are hardly borne in the most arbitary governments.

Perhaps the most interesting, and most neglected, feature of this age is the attempt to introduce something very close to free trade. Walpole's bonded warehouse scheme was quite explicit in this regard, and Walpole himself is reported as having claimed that the scheme would ease other forms of taxation and London would quickly become a 'free-port, and by consequence, the market of the world'.[39] This policy received increased support in the following decades and the two best-selling pamphlets of the 1740s were concerned with minimizing taxes and making England a free port. Decker's views are somewhat obliquely phrased in a pamphlet purportedly supporting a tax on houses, while Richardson's views are quire clear even in his preface.[40]

The consideration of our numerous monopolies naturally led to an inquiry into the nature of a free-port trade, as well as the strong prejudices now subsisting against it. . . . Perhaps it may seem strange that no bounty should be proposed as a means to restore trade; but if a free-port will gain us all those trades we are naturally capable of; it will appear to be itself the greatest bounty, and in endeavouring to force nature, the expence is certain, but the success doubtful.

The English seemed unaware of the value of gathering together and systematizing the knowledge they had gathered from so much policy debate. No professorships of trade and commerce were endowed and young men in the universities had no chance to learn from the past. The curious thing is that people were fully aware of the importance of trade and commerce. In the Harleian miscellany, in Lord Somers' tracts, in the collections made by William Patterson or by Joseph Massie, we see a continual growth of sustained interest in economics. The situation undoubtedly says something about the English character at this period, but someone with more knowledge than myself will have to develop this theme. It persisted throughout the eighteenth century, and as a result, the systematic pedagogy of the Scots aroused attention out of proportion to its merits.

Notes
1. I am grateful to the participants at the History of Economics Meeting, Boston, 1987, for their comments and especially to R.D.C. Black, Mark Blaug, James Earley and Michael Perelman.
2. J. Hollander (1928), 'The Dawn of a Science', in *Adam Smith 1776–1926* (Chicago: University of Chicago) has perceptive comments on this issue.
3. R.C. Wiles has suggested that 'Mercantilism' was concerned with economic develop-

ment or 'progress'. There is substantial truth in this claim. 'The Development of Mercantilist Economic Thought', in *Pre-Classical Economic Thought,* ed. S. Todd Lowry (Boston: Kluwer, 1986), pp. 147–74. Also see C. Wilson (1965), *England's Apprenticeship 1603–1763* (London: Longman).

4. M. Postlethwayt (1757), *Great Britain's True System,* reprinted by Augustus M. Kelley (New York, 1967), pp. 205–12. In view of Postlethwayt's unacknowledged borrowings in 1751 from Richard Cantillion's unpublished *Essai sur la nature du commerce en général* such analysis displays a keen eye for recognizing good economic reasoning rather than originality.

5. E.R.A. Seligman (1917), *Incidence of Taxation* (New York: Columbia University Press, 5th edn). W. Kennedy, *English Taxation 1640–1799* (1913), (London: Bell). J.A. Schumpeter (1954), *History of Economic Analysis* (New York).

6. M. James (1966), *Social Problems and Policy During the Puritan Revolution* (New York), p. 105.

7. As quoted by Josiah Tucker in his privately printed (1931), *Elements of Commerce,* reprinted in R.L. Schuyler (ed.), *Josiah Tucker* (New York), pp. 200–5. The similarity with the arguments of Althusius suggest a possible link with Calvinism. R. de Roover (1951), 'Monopoly Theory Prior to Adam Smith', *Quarterly Journal of Economics,* p. 500.

8. J.M. Keynes (1937), 'The General Theory', *Quarterly Journal of Economics,* reprinted in S.E. Harris (ed.) (1947), *The New Economics* (New York), p. 191.

9. T. Mun (1666), *England's Treasure by Foreign Trade,* reprinted in J.R. McCulloch (1954), *Early English Tracts on Commerce* (Cambridge), p. 193.

10. W. Ashley (1900), 'The Tory Origin of Free Trade Policy', in *Surveys, Historic and Economic* (London), pp. 268–303.

11. P.J. Thomas (1926), *Mercantilism and the East India Trade* (London).

12. S. Rashid (1986), 'Mandeville's *Fable:* Laissez-Faire or Libertinism', *Eighteenth Century Studies,* pp. 313–30. S. Rashid (1984), 'The Irish School of Economic Development: 1720–1750', Working Paper, BEBR, University of Illinois.

13. Adam Smith (1976), *An Inquiry into the Nature and Causes of the Wealth of Nations,* ed. R.H. Campbell and A.S. Skinner (Oxford, OUP), II, p. 741. Referred to hereafter as WN.

14. Ibid., 756.

15. E. Roll (1976), 'The Wealth of Nations 1776–1976', *Lloyds Bank Review,* reprinted in J.C. Wood (1983), *Adam Smith Critical Assessments,* p. 150.

16. T. Milles (1599), *The Customer's Apologie,* p. 1. The maxims can be traced even to Nicole Oresme (1360?), as quoted by A.E. Monroe (1848), *Early Economic Thought* (Cambridge, Mass., Harvard University Press), p. 100.

17. R. Sibthorpe (1628), *Apostollike Obedience,* E1–E2.

18. Anon., *A Way to Raise what Money shall be Necessary* . . . cn.d.: (the reference to 'our Gracious Deliverer, whom some would style Conqueror', clearly places it in the 1690s).

19. *Parliamentary History,* X, p. 944.

20. Ibid., p. 946.

21. *Some Considerations* . . . (1694), in *Works* (1823), pp. 55, 60.

22. WN, II, p. 856.

23. Ibid., p. 865.

24. Kennedy (1975), op. cit., p. 141ff. Also see pp. 121–2. A.T. Peacock provides a less critical view in 'The Treatment of the Principles of Public Finance in *The Wealth of Nations*', in *Essays on Adam Smith,* ed. A.S. Skinner and T. Wilson (Oxford, Clarendon Press), pp. 553–67.

25. The importance of financial issues is also evident in the frequent arguments on the prominence of the 'monied interest'. For more details on this and related issues, see P.G.M. Dickson (1968), *The Financial Revolution in England* (London).

26. *The Second Part of an Argument against Excises* (1733). *The Axe (once more) Laid to the Root of the Tree* (1743). As quoted by Seligman, op. cit., pp. 69 and 71.

27. R. Nugent (1749), *Considerations upon a Reduction of the Land Tax* (London), 7; Massie, op. cit., p. 5.
28. *A Letter from a Member of Parliament* (1756). As quoted by Seligman, op. cit., pp. 87–8.
29. *Proposals for Carrying on the War with Vigour* (1757). As quoted by Seligman, op. cit., p. 82.
30. Postlethwayt, op. cit., 332; *Remarks* (1764), p. 6.
31. *Essay* (1745), p. 8.
32. *Remarks* (1764), p. 4.
33. Ibid., pp. 2 and 3.
34. *Essay* (1745), p. 15.
35. Op. cit., pp. 19–20.
36. In *Predecessors of Adam Smith* (1937) (New York: Prentice-Hall). E.A.J. Johnson has provided a sympathetic account of Postlethwayt. A critical assessment of Postlethwayt's originality is to be found in E. Fraser, 'Some Sources of Postlethwayt's Dictionary', *Economic History*, February (1938), pp. 25–32. W. Darity, Jr see Postlethwayt as the most careful theorist of the slave trade in a forthcoming account in *The New Palgraves*.
37. Postlethwayt, op. cit. Massie (1757), *The Proposal Commonly Called Sir Mathew Deckers Scheme . . .* (London).
38. *Parliamentary History*, X, 953, 1063.
39. P. Langford (1975), *The Excise Crisis* (Oxford, Clarendon Press), p. 32.
40. *Essay . . . Decline of Foreign Trade* (1739), London.

2 Sir Edward Coke and Adam Smith on occupational regulation: economic efficiency, justice, and the public good

Edd S. Noell[1]

A neglected area of the study of economic thought is the development of different approaches to occupational regulation. It is the purpose of this paper to examine the works of Sir Edward Coke and Adam Smith in an attempt to begin in a small way to rectify this problem. Economic efficiency, justice and the public good are all central concerns of occupational regulation. This study argues that the common law approach of Coke is best explained in terms of the Tudor concept of the public good, while economic efficiency prevails as the central feature of the classical liberal approach of Smith.

The four sections of the paper are developed as follows. The first section seeks to analyse Coke's common law treatment of guild regulations and the proper ends of such regulations. The second section examines the writings of Smith in regards to his view of apprenticeship rules and the exclusive privileges of corporations. Section 3 makes a comparative analysis of the two approaches in regards to both the positive and normative economics of occupational regulation. In section 4 some concluding remarks are made about the implications of the common law approach associated with Coke and the classical liberal approach associated with Smith for the development of occupational regulation in the nineteenth century.

Coke on guild regulations and the Public Good
Sir Edward Coke (1552–1634) is known as the outstanding jurist and statesman of the common law in late sixteenth- and early seventeenth-century England. He was the chief expounder of the conception of the corporation in law in the sixteenth century (Davis, 1905, 2, p. 210). His decisions in the law of corporations set the mould for legal interpretation for many generations to come.

No little controversy has brewed over the nature of Coke's role in the economic thought of his time. He has been seen as the promoter, either indirectly or directly, of economic liberalism in England. Lipson (1961) is representative of the view of several economic historians who have appealed to Coke's 'aversion' to statutes regulating the terms of apprenticeship and his narrow construction of their provisions, as well as the rhetoric of 'free trade' which accompanied his denunciation of monopolies. Wagner (1935) went further and interpreted Coke's legal decisions as the work of a self-conscious economic liberal. Rejecting the claim that the common law had an inherent bias in favour of economic individualism, Wagner, instead, argued that what Coke and common lawyers of his time in fact did was reshape the common law in conscious anticipation of *laissez-faire* precepts. Wagner argued that monopolies were not inconsistent with the prevailing common law, and Coke deliberately distorted precedent in order to hold them unlawful.[2]

Malament (1967) has challenged all of these related interpretations of Coke's thought. She affirms that Coke must be understood as a man of the Tudor age, concerned to maintain stability and not to introduce *laissez-faire* notions into the legal system. Coke's opposition to monopolies was based on a notion of 'free trade' founded in the common law, but considerably different from that of economic liberalism. White (1979) finds support for this distinction in Coke's parliamentary activity from 1621 to 1628.

A brief consideration of the functions of the guild in the Tudor economy and in the law should help to shed some light on this debate. In the sixteenth century the guild and the institution of apprenticeship still remained the basis of industrial organization. Typically, craft guilds were subordinate to the particular municipal governments in whose district they operated. Municipal corporations made by-laws and ordinances for the order and government of trade in various products.[3] Craft guilds were used as a means of corporate control of quality of production and as a means of providing for the training of future generations of craftsmen and merchants. The craft guild invigilated workmanship and punished bad craftsmanship. It was enabled by government sanction to exclude foreigners, limit the number of craftsmen, and to compel members of the craft to accept common standards of quality. By controlling their own membership and conditions of apprenticeship, craft guilds regulated the supply of labour, the level of wages, and hours and standards of work.

In the medieval perspective, these regulations served to promote order and certainty in everyday life; they were the bonds of a society seen as an organic body. Society was held together by a set of mutual, though varying, obligations; the spirit of thrift, temperance and industriousness which guilds sought to engender in their members was central to this function. In this regard the role of apprenticeship was particularly significant. Nearly all craftsmen maintained one or two apprentices who offered cheap labour in return for the secrets of the craft. Guilds supplied their vocational training in an atmosphere that nurtured the cultivation of civic and moral virtues.

The major piece of labour legislation of the Tudor era, the Statute of Artificers, reinforced these values on a national scale. The statute declared that no person should exercise any trade, craft or mystery at that time exercised in England, unless he had previously served an apprenticeship of at least seven years. As Smith explained, 'what before had been the bye-law of many particular corporations, became in England the general and public law of all trades carried on in market towns' (*WN* I. x. c. 8).[4] Industry was still conceived in the light of a public service. It was an 'art' or, as we would now describe it, a 'profession', and, as in many modern professions, compulsory training was imposed to protect alike the interests of the public and the interests of the skilled worker (Lipson, 1961, 3, pp. 292–3).

The statute was said to serve the 'commonweal', a phrase in Tudor times which signified the general or public good. Promotion of the commonweal meant the insurance of social stability and full employment, for labour was seen as the central factor of production.[5] Tudor legislators sought to obtain, as Holdsworth observes, 'a reasonable supply of labour for the various callings which were necessary to secure the health and strength of the nation' (1977, 4, p. 319). A memorandum on the act stated that a seven years' apprenticeship was necessary in order that an apprentice 'should grow into greater knowledge and perfection in the art or occupation that he was brought up in' (Tawney and Power, 1962, 1, p. 356). It was declared that the provisions for apprenticeship would be a 'very good means and help to advance husbandry, to banish idleness, to reform the unadvised rashness of licentious manners of youth, . . . [so that] the commonwealth will not be in such short burdened, as it now is, with lusty beggars, rouges and vagabonds . . .'(ibid., p. 363). Because he held these same goals in mind (*Coke's Reports*, 1727, 11, p. 530), much of Coke's criticism of guilds was directed against ordinances which were either more stringent than the Statute of Artificers or which conflicted with other of the Tudor national policies (Malament, 1967, p. 1335, n. 86).

Economic historians generally recognize that guilds became very exclusive due to certain economic changes in the sixteenth and seventeenth centuries. Such factors as the integration of national life, the widening of markets, and the mobility of the population began to transform the guilds. Guild arrangements to control labour were increasingly opposed and avoided as an increasing labour supply, expanding demand for particular goods, and the growth of new industries led to developments outside guild control. The decay of the English guilds was hastened by the move of the textile industry into rural areas. This development, alongside the considerable extension of rural industry organized on the putting-out system, tended to disrupt or simply by-pass the guilds which, with a few exceptions, were unable to impose their authority on rural manufacture or new industries.

Many guilds responded with measures which attempted to maintain the control of trade that they held within their own town. Ironically, their increasingly rigorous efforts to protect this control forced trade away and undermined their prosperity. Exorbitant entrance fees forced craftsmen out of the towns into the country and neighbouring villages (Jones, 1926, p. 929). As new workers were recruited into industry to generate an increased output, the financial and territorial foundations of guilds thus came to be undermined.

Perhaps the most significant manifestation of the decline of guild authority was the fact that in the late sixteenth and early seventeenth centuries, many of the corporate towns reconstructed their guild systems and tightened up their by-laws in an effort to ensure full employment for their citizens by suppressing the enterprise of those who did not share their freedom (Fisher, 1961, p. 7). Whereas they were once regulatory bodies which concerned themselves with the quality of goods, fair dealing and high standards, the guilds increasingly became combinations in restraint of trade (Thorne, 1985, p. 231). It was in this context that Coke applied his notions of 'free trade' and 'monopoly' to various forms of guild and corporate regulations.

Coke's view of free trade is consistent with the contemporary opposition to arbitrary occupational restrictions that prevented 'free ingress' into a trade.[6] 'Freedom of trade,' Coke said, 'is the reason that the Low Countries so prosper. They are not troubled with Impositions to burden trade nor Monopolies to restrain it' (*Commons Debates*, 1621, 3, p. 66). To Coke, freedom of trade meant freedom from arbitrary restraints not recognized by the law (Holdsworth, 1977, 3, p. 350). At the same time, however, Coke contended that 'true trade and traffic cannot be maintained or increased without order or government' (*Coke's Reports*, 1727, 8, p. 125).

For Coke, monopoly meant either private acts of hoarding or exclusive trade privileges bestowed by the crown. The former type of monopoly involved acts of hoarding or price-fixing, such as the traditional economic offence of engrossing. In the common law, the 'engrossing of labour' entailed attempts by guilds artificially to restrain trade to their own advantage. Coke appealed to the tradition of common law opposition to arbitrary trade restraints by private groups for his precedents.[7]

No precise precedent existed for actions in law against royal grants of monopoly, because it was not until 1601 that royal patents became actionable at common law. Coke drew upon the common law bias against individual forms of trade intervention and applied it to exclusive privileges conferred by the Crown. He invoked the belief in open markets which was a medieval legacy, as well as the Tudor ideal of the body politic with its emphasis on public good over private gain (Malament, 1967, pp. 1345–6).

For Coke, skill in one's trade was important, as was the full employment of the labour force. The proper governance of trade required regulations to insure skilled persons would be employed in the various trades; these sort of regulations served the public good. On the other hand, 'grievances in trade' were created by guild restrictions or corporate by-laws which artificially hindered qualified persons from pursuing their lawful trade or 'calling'. Such restrictions became increasingly evident as guilds came to be challenged by new methods of production. This sort of distinction made sense in Tudor and Stuart England, as Malament observes:

> Guilds were originally meant to regulate trade whereas in their decline they resorted to restrictive practices. The distinction between regulation and restriction may seem unsound and imprecise today but it had a very real meaning in the sixteenth and seventeenth centuries. It was the difference between setting just as opposed to extortionate prices; between enforcing standards of quality as opposed to adulterating goods. And most important, it was the difference between harmonious government in a trade and acrimonious dissension caused by the exclusion of many who sought membership and training in the craft of their choice. (ibid., n. 114)

Coke applied this distinction to guild by-laws, municipal corporate ordinances, ordinances of foreign trading corporations, and royal patents for operations outside the guild system. Some examples from Coke's work as an attorney, as a judge and as a statesman in Parliament will illustrate his use of this notion.

In *Davenant* v. *Hurdis* (1599), the common law court dealt with the validity of a by-law which required members of the Merchant Taylors to employ cloth-making brethren on at least half their cloth or pay a forfeit. Coke represented the plaintiff, Davenant, who had refused to comply with the by-law. Davenant brought an action in trespass when distrained for the forfeit. Coke's basic claim was that the by-law tended to create a monopoly: 'for every subject, by the [common] law, has freedom and liberty to put his cloth to be dressed by what clothworker he pleases, and cannot be restrained to certain persons, for that would be a monopoly; . . . to exclude all others is against the law' (*Coke's Reports*, 1727, 11, p. 86). The notion of full employment was uppermost in Coke's mind, as Malament (1967) explains:

> If members could be compelled to employ cloth-making brethren on half their cloth, then eventually they might be required to employ brethren on all of it. Other members would then be put at the mercy of the cloth workers of the Company and cloth workers outside would be put out of work and compelled to subsist on relief. To deprive a skilled craftsman of the right to practise his trade, Coke said, was to deprive him of the 'liberty of the subject'. (pp. 1341–2)

The court ruled in Coke's favour, for the public good was served by the full employment of skilled craftsmen.

As Chief Justice of the King's Bench, Coke ruled on the case of *Taylors of Ipswich* v. *Shenning* (1614). The Merchant Taylors had required that their permission be obtained to exercise a trade after the prospective craftsmen had completed their apprenticeship. The defendant, a private tailor to a 'freeman of Ipswich', refused to obtain a licence from the company. Coke ruled against the Taylor's ordinance. He declared that such by-laws 'are against the freedom and liberty of the subject, and are a means of extortion in drawing money from them, either by delay or some other subtle device, or of oppression of young tradesmen by the old and rich of the same trade, not permitting them to work in their trade freely' (*Coke's Reports*, 1727 11, p. 54). He added that 'at common law no man could be prohibited from working in any lawful trade.' Coke opposed a situation in which one who was completely qualified by apprenticeship could be denied entry into a trade by some artificial pretext, for 'the law abhors idleness'.

Coke was not rejecting the apprenticeship provisions of the Statute of Artificers. Referring to this requirement, Coke supports his decision by stating that the statute 'was not enacted only to the intent that workmen should be skilfull, but also that youth should not be brought up in idleness, but . . . in lawful sciences and trades.' As Malament argues, 'What Coke objected to was not the statute but the possibility that a man qualified to work under the act might be prevented from doing so by a guild' (op. cit., pp. 1336–7). This is evident when Coke adds that 'ordinances for the good order and government of men of trades and mysteries are good, but not to restrain any one in his lawful mystery' (*Coke's Report*, 1727, 11, p. 54).

In these cases, as well as others dealing with municipal ordinances or royal patents,[8] Coke censured by-laws which were more restrictive than the provisions of the Statute of Artificers. Corporate exclusiveness hampered the Tudor's general policy of full employment (Malament, 1967, p. 1358, n. 217). This was a consistent theme in Coke's rulings, as was his acceptance of legitimate regulation. Coke reinforced the distinction between regulation and restriction by saying: 'If a corporation, for the better government of the Town, not contrary to the Law; but, if any sole Restraint, then gone [sic]' (*Journals*, 1, p. 770). Malament explains that for Coke 'the danger of "any sole Restraint" was arbitrary power and unemployment, considerations which underlay Coke's antagonism to royal patents of monopoly as well as to trade corporations' (op. cit., p. 1355).

After his time on the bench, Coke entered Parliament. many of his speeches there in the 1620s dealt with the requests of trading companies and individuals for monopoly grants, either to 'order trade' or for the purpose of introducing a new invention. Coke's responses to them made a distinction between restraints on free trade, which he believed to be illegal and inconvenient, and government of trade, which he regarded as both lawful and beneficial to the commonwealth (White, 1979, p. 89). One of Coke's most pronounced orations against restraints on free trade was made in the 1621 debates on the bill for free trade in Welsh cloth. As originally drafted, it provided that all merchants, whether native or foreign, were to be allowed to buy cloth anywhere in Wales. The purpose of the bill was to end the quasi-monopoly enjoyed by the Shrewsbury drapers over the transportation of Welsh cloth to London (ibid., p. 111). The Shrewsbury drapers tried to block this bill. They argued that it would overturn the customs of the corporate towns by enabling Welsh clothiers to sell their cloth in any English town. Coke was sceptical of this claim. Shrewsbury would suffer from this bill only because it enjoyed monopolistic privileges. Coke affirmed that monopolies that restrained trades should be done away with, for the common good was to be preferred before any particular town (*Commons Debates*, 1621, 2, pp. 317–18).

Coke apparently believed that laws, grants or customs that limited free trade or took it away were generally to be strictly construed; this principle was qualified by his claim that government of trade, like freedom of trade, promoted the public good (White, 1979, pp. 136–7). On the other hand, it is evident from this example that Coke was sceptical about claims that restraints on free trade promoted the public good, provided good order in trade, or were not really restraints on true freedom of trade (ibid., p. 138).

In sum, Coke was concerned with maintaining full employment and 'order in trade' in the face of increasing social instability in early seventeenth-century England. Certain guild stipulations appeared to him to be merely trade restraints, not promoting quality production, but hindering qualified craftsmen from pursuing their trade. In Coke's view, men should be free to pursue their lawful trades. Apprenticeship in these trades was to promote industriousness, civility and other virtues. For Coke the notion of order meant not only a society which was able to prevent poverty, idleness and unrest, but also one which advanced trade and traffic by means of good government. The goals of employment, quality of workmanship, and character formation motivated Coke's rulings and proposed legislation on the proper governance of trade for the public good.

2. Smith on exclusive privilege, efficiency and justice

In late seventeenth-century England, the perspective towards 'governance of trade' held by earlier traditions came to be increasingly questioned. Josiah Child was among the growing number of vocal advocates of the removal of constraints on industry. He proclaimed that 'to improve and advance trade' we must 'begin the right way, casting off some of our old mistaken principles in trade, which we inherit from our ancestors who were . . . unskilled in the misteries of and methods to improve trade.' Among the 'common errors' of his day, he included the notions that 'none shall use any manual occupation except he has been apprentice to the same', and that 'to suffer artificers to have as many apprentices as they will is to destroy trade' (Cited in Lipson, 1961, 3, p. 293).

Smith took up this same theme and elaborated it further. He claimed that both the Statute of Apprenticeship (that is, the Statute of Artificers) and the exclusive privileges of corporations obstructed the free circulation of labour from employment to employment and from place to place (*WN*, 1776, I. x. c. 42). Open competition would lead to an enhanced national prosperity. Smith called for the repeal of the Statute of Apprenticeship (ibid., IV. ii. 42).[9]

What lay behind Smith's opposition to the Statute of Apprentices and the exclusive privileges of corporations? In general, it was but one aspect of Smith's distrust of the 'corporation spirit', as Becker has observed: 'Smith regards all clubs, cliques, cabals, joint stock companies, and other social guilds as corporations having in common certain properties that render them positively harmful, or, at best, of dubious social utility' (1969, p. 70). In regard to apprenticeship requirements, Smith was dubious of their efficacy in most industries. For example, he doubted the need for such regulation in the weaving industry:

> It was imagined that the cause of so much bad cloth was that the weaver had not been properly educated, and that therefore they made a statute that he

should serve a seven years apprenticeship before he pretended to make any. But this is by no means a sufficient security against bad cloth [*LJ*(B), 1766, 306].

He remarked that in the common mechanical trades, 'long apprenticeships are altogether unnecessary' (*WN*, 1776, I. x. c. 16). Smith thought that if a young person started out as a journeyman, being paid in proportion to his work, that he would practise with much more diligence and attention than if he were forced to serve as an apprentice for seven years. Not only would his education be more effectual, this approach would also increase the number of competitors by making the trade more 'easily learnt', and thus: 'The trades, the crafts, the mysteries, would all be losers. But the publick would be a gainer, the work of all artificers coming in this way much cheaper to market' (ibid.). In sum, the apprenticeship system interfered with a man's right to employ his 'strength and dexterity in what manner he thinks proper without detriment to his neighbour', it gave no security against 'insufficient workmanship', and it had no tendency to 'form young people to industry' (ibid., c. 12–14).

Smith observed that the supply of labour for skilled occupations was restricted by limitations on the number of apprentices and by making the period of their training much longer than it need be:

> The exclusive privilege of an incorporated trade necessarily restrains the competition, in the town where it is established, to those who are free of the trade. To have served an apprenticeship in the town, under a master properly qualified, is commonly the necessary requisite for obtaining this freedom. The bye-laws of the corporation regulate sometimes the number of apprentices which any master is allowed to have, and almost always the number of years which each apprentice is obliged to serve. The intention of both regulations is to restrain the competition to a much smaller number than might otherwise be disposed to enter into the trade. The limitation of the number of apprentices restrains it directly. A long term of apprenticeship restrains it more indirectly, but as effectually, by increasing the expense of education. (ibid., c. 5)

Smith was confident that markets could be relied upon to generate appropriate supplies of skilled labour. Smith believed that 'to the greater part of manufacturers . . . there are other collateral manufacturers of so similar a nature, that a worker can easily transfer his industry from one of them to another' (ibid., IV. ii. 42). This process depended on freedom of entry into the different trades.

For Smith, freedom of entry was the most reliable measure of the competitiveness of an industry or trade. In his view, free competition did not imply a particular number of competitors; competition was compatible with any number of suppliers so long as entry into the industry was free (Anderson and Tollison, 1982, p. 1239). In Smith's view, the majority of corporation laws were established, in fact, to restrain such competition and thus prevent a reduction in wages and profit. The clamour and sophistry of merchants and manufacturers persuaded others, such as the landlords, farmers and labourers of the country, that 'the private interest of a part, and of a subordinate part of the society, is the general interest of the whole' (*WN*, 1776, I. x. c. 25). Smith found no merit in the argument that the corporation provided the proper ordering of a trade. The exclusive privileges of corporations led to several deleterious effects: 'the goods themselves are worse; as they know none can undersell them so they keep up the price, and as they know also that no other can sell so they care not what the quality be' [*LJ*(A), 1766, ii. 35].

Companies and associations of people in the same trade encouraged and facilitated efforts to restrict competition. Such combinations prevailed in urban areas. The putting-out system in the suburbs arose in part as a response to the higher costs of production associated with corporate towns. In observing this phenomenon, Smith made explicit his view that freedom of market activity, as against guild regulation, provides the best insurance of quality workmanship in the consumer's interest:

> The pretense that corporations are necessary for the better government of the trade, is without any foundation. The real and effectual discipline which is exercised over a workman, is not that of his corporation, but that of his customers. It is the fear of losing their employment which restraints his frauds and corrects his negligence. An exclusive corporation necessarily weakens the force of this discipline. A particular set of workmen must then be employed, let them behave well or ill. It is upon this account, that in many large incorporated towns no tolerable workmen are to be found, even in some of the most necessary trades. If you would have your work tolerably executed, it must be done in the suburbs, where the workmen, having no exclusive privilege, have nothing but their character to depend upon, and you must then smuggle it into the town as well as you can. (*WN*, 1776 I. x. c. 31)

The elimination of exclusive privileges would lead to greater consumer sovereignty; under the discipline of the market, craftsmen would be penalized for producing shoddy goods, and thus be led to a more industrious approach to their work.

Smith's attitude towards exclusive privilege and the professions is best illustrated in his letter to William Cullen as given in Rae's *Life of Adam Smith*. It was occasioned by a controversy over the laxity by which certain Scottish universities were granting medical degrees. The candidate got the degree merely by paying fees and producing a certificate of proficiency from two medical practitioners. The College of Physicians of

Edinburgh sought to prohibit the universities from granting any medical degrees to any person without first undergoing a personal examination into his proficiency and bringing a certificate of having attended for two years at a university where physic (medicine) was regularly taught. Smith opposed any suppression of competition, and he defended with great vigour the most absolute and unlimited freedom of medical education (p. 271).

Smith made an informative comparison between medical degrees and the practice of guild apprenticeships, noting some significant similarities:

> A degree which can be conferred only upon students of a certain standing is a statute of apprenticeship which is likely to contribute to the advancement of science, just as other statutes of apprenticeship have contributed to that of arts and manufacturers. Those statutes of apprenticeship, assisted by other corporation laws, have banished arts and manufactures from the greater part of towns corporate. Such degrees, assisted by some other regulations of a similar tendency, have banished almost all useful and solid education from the greater part of universities. Bad work and high price have been the effect of the monopoly introduced by the former; quackery, imposture, and exorbitant fees have been the consequences of that established by the latter. The industry of manufacturing villages has remedied in part the inconveniences which the monopolies established by towns corporate had occasioned. The private interest of some poor Professors of Physic in some poor universities inconveniently situated for the resort of students has in part remedied the inconveniences which would certainly have resulted from that sort of monopoly which the great and rich universities had attempted to establish. (pp. 277–8)

Smith noted the true reasons behind the college's opposition to the facility of obtaining degrees: there were two effects, both advantageous to the public, but which were extremely disagreeable to graduates of other universities whose degrees had cost them much time and expense. First, 'It multiplied very much the number of doctors and thereby no doubt sunk their fees, or at least hindered them from rising so very high as they otherwise would have done.' Second, it reduced a good deal the rank and dignity of a doctor, but if the physician was a man of sense and science it would not surely prevent his being respected and employed as a man of sense and science (p. 278).

Smith made individual productivity and aptitude the crucial factors in his evaluation of the regulation of professions:

> That in every profession the fortune of every individual should depend as much as possible upon his merit and as little as possible upon his privilege is certainly for the interest of the public. It is even for the interest of every particular profession, which can never so effectually support the general merit and real honour of the greater part of those who exercise it, as by

resting on such liberal principles. Those principles are even most effectual for procuring them all the employment which the country can afford. (p. 279)

The public interest was best promoted if 'the system of natural liberty' prevailed over exclusive privilege.

Smith thought that competition for the satisfaction of consumer demands should prevail over the regulations of guilds, corporations and other groups. But what are the ends that this sytem of natural liberty was to serve? Smith placed a significant emphasis on an expanding output as a criterion by which to evaluate the regulation of trades. He observed that the interest of any particular trade group always in some manner conflicted with the public interest, for it involved narrowing their competition. But the public welfare was always enhanced by a wider competition and wider markets (*WN*, 1776, I. xi. p. 10).

But focusing on greater economic output alone is misleading. The end of producing the greatest output in the most efficient manner is complemented by another goal, as Buchanan explains:

> Smith's great work, *The Wealth of Nations*, has been widely interpreted as being informed normatively by efficiency criteria. This emphasis is broadly correct, provided that the efficiency norm is not given exclusive place. Smith's purpose was to demonstrate how the removal of restrictions on free market forces and the operation of his 'system of natural liberty' would greatly increase the total product of the economy and, more importantly, how this would generate rapid economic growth, thereby improving the lot of the laboring classes. What is often missing from this standard interpretation is Smith's corollary argument, sometimes implicit, to the effect that this system of natural liberty would also promote his ideal of justice. [According to Smith] failure to allow individuals to employ 'their stock and industry in the way that they judge most advantageous to themselves, is a manifest violation of the most sacred rights of mankind'. (1978, p. 68)

One example of these rights is the 'property every man has in his own labour'. Smith declares that corporate by-laws that restrict the worker's freedom to work are a manifestation of injustice:

> to hinder him from employing this strength and dexterity in what manner he thinks proper without injury to his neighbour, is a plain violation of this most sacred property. It is a manifest encroachment upon the just liberty both of the workman, and of those who might be disposed to employ him. (*WN* I. x. c. 12)

Instead of such by-laws, the employer should have discretion as to whether or not the worker is fit to be employed. Statutory apprenticeship rules established by political authorities 'for the public good' were both impertinent and oppressive. In general, Smith's arguments for economic liberty were linked with an insistence on justice; this connection was made for reasons any reader familiar with natural law jurisprudence might readily have understood (Teichgraeber, 1986, p. 156).

Smith looked to competition and the market principle to promote such justice, by undermining politically determined sources of economic advantage and preventing the entrenchment of established industry which, he thought, always has a tendency to seek official 'protection', i.e. legal means of preservation from the possibility of competitive displacement. In Smith's view, the system of political economy which is most just is the one which allows the greatest scope for persons to labour in accordance with their capacities and aims, and which, as much as possible, enables them to gain the reward or 'produce' of their labour (Billet, 1978, p. 91).

3. A comparative analysis of the two approaches
The approaches to occupational regulation taken by Sir Edward Coke and Adam Smith have important similarities and dissimiliarities. A comparision and contrast of the salient features will help to highlight the significant ways in which each contributed towards regulatory changes in the nineteenth century. As a judge, Coke wrote essentially as a practising regulator in England, and his decisions had an important influence on the subsequent development of occupational regulation in the common law; while Smith, as a political economist, produced a grand work which had significant impact upon the theory and policy views of the classical economists. An analysis of their views of the role of self-interest, restraints on trade, the proper goals of occupational regulation, and the efficacy of existing institutions and regulations in achieving those goals should help to clarify their contributions to law and economic thought on these matters.

Both Coke and Smith were sceptical of claims that certain laws or regulations served the public interest. As a jurist, Coke recognized that guilds and other corporate groups sought to have the courts enforce and uphold exclusionary restraints on others in their own self-interest. Various groups sought to cultivate a perception of 'disorder' in their own trade, and the recognition of the need for a desired type of regulation to cope successfully with this problem; or if they already had a monopoly, they sought to convince public authorities of the disastrous consequences of opening their trade to others.[10] While guilds were originally designed to convey knowledge of the techniques of the 'mystery' to prospective craftsmen, Coke claimed that some 'arts' were not really 'mysteries' and the guilds acted by various ordinances simply to exclude others (Tawney and Power, 1962, 1, pp. 382-3).

Smith applied the principle of self-interest in a more extensive manner, in his analysis of the activity of politicians and producer groups in the economy. He saw corporate by-laws as an evidence of the spirit of monopoly at work: 'it is in the interest of the freemen of a corporation to hinder the rest of the inhabitants from employing any workmen but themselves' (*WN* IV. iii. c. 10; cf. *WN* I. x. c. 18). Where Coke found that the good government of trade *could* be a legitimate reason for regulations, for 'it breeds a corruption of manufactures . . . that men should exercise that [trade] wherein they have no skill' (*Commons Debates*, 1621, 2, pp. 124–5; 4, p. 92; 6, pp. 266, 286), Smith found no credibility in the reasons expounded by merchants for 'ordering' trade: 'I have never known much good done by those who affected to trade for the public good' (*WN* IV. ii. 9).

Coke did not equate free trade with a complete absence of governmental regulation. He regarded free trade and government of trade as complementary, and not antithetical, principles of economic policy. Coke's opposition to restraints of trade had a different basis than Smith's. Whereas Smith was confident that markets worked best without regulation and therefore urged the repeal of the apprenticeship laws, Coke upheld those laws, convinced that if ever trade were left unregulated the public would suffer from 'disorder in trade' in the form of higher prices, lower quality products, and the exclusion and impoverishment of qualified craftsmen by private restraints.

Coke never attacked guilds, trade corporations and apprenticeship regulations as Smith did. Instead, Coke objected to restrictive guild practices which stood in the way of attainment of the proper ends of occupational regulation. One must not make the mistake of assuming that since Coke censured particular guild ordinances that he disapproved of the institution itself. Coke acknowledged that corporations could make ordinances for good and government, provided that their by-laws were in agreement with the laws of the realm, and subordinate to the common law (*Coke's Reports*, 1727, 10, pp. 30–1). Faced with guilds in their period of decline, Coke's attitude towards them reflected his belief that they should not arbitrarily restrain the individual worker. But he thought their existence was necessary for the purpose of regulating their own particular art or mystery.

Coke's rulings consistently distinguished between trade regulation and trade restriction by corporate towns and guilds. Such ordinances might include stipulations of quality (such as the inspection of cloth by a municipal corporation) or fair wages or marketing time (Malament, 1967, p. 1355). Measures to advance trade and employ the maximum number of people won his support. This was consistent with the common law response to the depression and unemployment in England of the seventeenth century. Instead of entrenching local privileges and interests, the law responded by maintaining the regulatory functions of local corporations and preventing restrictive practices. As Knafla (1977) explains, 'a guild or corporation could regulate the practice of trade to prevent poverty, idleness, social dislocation, or local dissent; but it could not prescribe restrictive penalties against men who were qualified to practise their trade' (p. 150).

In terms of his normative views, Coke's approach to the regulation of guilds and other corporate bodies stressed the need for the promotion of industriousness and virtue. Guilds had long been seen as institutions which promoted character-formation. Coke's normative goals were consistent with Tudor moral precepts which stressed the public good over private gain. Regulations which served the 'good of the common-wealth' promoted the public health and welfare in a broad sense.

Smith's perspective on occupational regulation was based on a concern not with full employment *per se* but a preoccupation with output expansion and the promotion of justice. He was concerned primarily with questions of allocative efficiency. Greater output to provide consumers a wider variety of choice was the goal, the conjunction with the freedom of individuals to pursue their own desired occupations. Occupational restrictions such as corporate privileges were objectionable either because they kept labour from following the direction in which it would otherwise go, or because they attracted to a particular species of industry a greater share of the resources than would ordinarily be employed in it (Viner, 1966, p. 134).

Smith shared Coke's concern for the development of moral virtue and the formation of character as an appropriate goal of occupational regulation. However, Smith thought that the guilds did not achieve this end. Smith was aware of pride and avarice as fundamental features of human nature, and also how these features worked themselves out in institutions, as, for example, in the corporations' desire for regulation. Smith instead appealed to the market, which he saw as the fundamental institution which provides a device for channelling pride, vanity and the desire for self-approval into socially useful purposes. Open competition in the marketplace disciplined craftsmen and other 'professionals' to produce quality work, and not to be negligent or fraudulent in character.

4. Implications for occupational regulation
The views of these two men had significant impacts upon the development of occupational regulation in the eighteenth and nineteenth centuries. Their different responses to positive and normative issues shaped economic theory and policy in England and America. The

contrast in the methods to achieve economic efficiency and the public good reflects not just differences in underlying values of analysis, but in the conditions of the economy as well.

In regards to the question of legitimate regulations of trade versus unreasonable restrictions of trade, one must consider the changes in English economic conditions between the late sixteenth century and mid-eighteenth centuries. Coke lived in an era when the monopolistic control of guilds over trades was only beginning to be challenged by the putting-out system and rural industry. The great concern in his time was with the social instability, poverty and unemployment accompanying the first stages of significant commercialization. By the latter half of the eighteenth century, the advances in technology and the availability of capital turned attention away from unemployment, poverty and starvation as the dominant societal concerns. In addition, advances in road and river transport combined with improved communications to reduce drastically the monopolistic power of trade corporations. As Smith observed, 'good roads, canals, and navigable rivers, put the remotest parts of the country more nearly upon a level with those in the neighbourhood of a town. . . . They are advantageous to the town, by breaking down the monopoly of the country in its neighbourhood' (*WN* I. xi. 5). Thus Smith was understandably sceptical of regulations sponsored by various groups in the economy claiming to promote the public interest.

Moreover, by the eighteenth century there were numerous Englishmen who were pursuing profitable trades without having served a regular apprenticeship, disregarding guild regulations and statute law. Many businessmen found better and cheaper ways of producing goods and services than the craft guilds' methods. Mitchell argued that it was this pursuit of private profit, whether it ran counter to law or not, that was responsible for the change in practice that occurred a considerable time before the change in approach to occupational regulation in theory and policy. Mitchell claimed that 'the promulgation of Adam Smith's kind of thought led men to believe that the laws were wrong and ought to be changed, and what they had been doing was not only right and profitable for themselves, but advantageous to the country as a whole' (1967, pp. 118–19). Smith contended that occupational regulations which seemed reasonable when first instituted now acted as injurious restraints of trade, because freedom of individual initiative promoted the progress of society which was the original end of these regulations (*LJ* (A), 1766, ii. 40). The argument that the old regulations exercised an artificial control over occupations which obstructed progress in the nation's welfare won out when the Statute of Artificers was repealed in 1814.

In America, the common law and classical liberal approaches both shaped the debate over 'substantive due process' which went on in the state and federal courts in the latter half of the nineteenth century. State licences which restricted entry into various occupations were struck down because they deprived individuals of the right 'to be free in the employment of their faculties and to earn their livelihood by any lawful calling' based on the 'due process' clause of the 14th amendment to the constitution. More than once Coke's notion of monopoly as involving the arbitrary restraint of trade was invoked. At the same time, the defence of the exclusion of some from carrying on certain trades rested on the common law notion of the legitimate role of the police powers of the state to promote the public good. In sum, the approaches to the issues of efficiency, justice and the public good set by Coke and Smith had an enduring impact on public policy attempts to promote substantive ends in the regulation of occupations.

Notes

1. I would like to thank William Campbell and Betty Polkinghorn for their helpful comments on an earlier draft. I take responsibility for whatever shortcomings remain.
2. The legal historian Samuel E. Thorne (1985) endorsed this interpretation of Coke's rulings, at least as far as Coke's use of precedent was concerned; Coke's 'new' views on the regulation of trade were 'Elizabethan law, disguised, as legal innovations usually are, in the clothes of the past' (p. 230). Both Hill (1965) and Little (1969) built on this understanding of Coke, linking him as an ally, directly or indirectly, of the Puritan entrepreneurs who sought common law sanction for their demands for trade free from royal monopolistic intervention.
3. The right to regulate the affairs of their members by means of by-laws and resolutions had been attached to corporations in Roman law and appeared in English law at a very early period. The by-laws of a town were binding on all within its limits, and similarly the by-laws of a guild were binding on all its members (Cooke, 1951, p. 69).
4. All references to Smith's works are to the *Glasgow Edition of the Works and Correspondence*. Generally accepted abbreviations and citation codes are used.
5. See Coleman (1956) for a discussion of the significant role of labor in the Tudor and Stuart periods.
6. De Roover (1951) observed that the term 'free trade' had a particular meaning to men such as Gerard de Malynes, Edward Misselden, Thomas Mun and other contemporaries of Coke. 'Freedom of trade' was the antithesis of 'restraint of trade' and of monopoly. The accent was on the freedom of ingress into a profession or a trade (pp. 292–3).
7. In 1504 a law was passed condemning unreasonable ordinances of guilds and directing that all such ordinances should be submitted to certain judicial officers who were at the national level. All the ordinances of crafts, mysteries, guilds or fraternities were disallowed unless they were assented to by the Chancellor, Treasurer, the Chief Justices or any three of them, or by both the Judges of Assize for that county in which the ordinance had been made (Holdsworth, 1977, 3, pp. 322–3). There were several cases based on this statute brought against guilds in the king's court of law.
8. Perhaps the most famous case which Coke reported was *Darcy* v. *Allen* (1602), also

known as *The Case of Monopolies*. The King's Bench in this case for the first time tried and voided a royal patent, finding it to be a 'monopoly which is against the common law'. The court held that all trades furnishing employment to subjects were of value to the Commonwealth and an exclusive grant to exercise such a trade was against the liberty and benefit of the subject. Monopolies were not only prejudicial to the traders excluded but also to the public generally because of their three inseparable incidents: 'the price of the same commodity will be raised', 'the commodity is not so good and merchantable as it was before' and 'it tends to the impoverishment of diverse artificers and others' (*Coke's Reports*, 11, p. 86).

9. Internal regulation of industry had been undergoing a process of decay in eighteenth-century England, and it has been argued that Smith showed little awareness of this fact. Viner claims that Smith writes as though the apprenticeship requirements were part of the important activities of the government of his day (p. 154). But 'Smith's discussion of the statute makes it clear that he understood it to be interpreted in practice to apply only in market towns and to those trades established prior to 1563. It was not extended to any newer trades, such as those of Manchester, Birmingham, and Wolverhampton' (*WN* I. x. c. 9). (See Hollander, 1973, pp. 258–9.)

10. Under the pretence of maintaining food order in trade, companies like the Merchant Adventurers were using their privileges and powers to harass their competitors. About such claims to 'good government in trade', Coke observed that 'new corporations trading to foreign parts, and at home which under the pretence of order and government, in conclusion tend to the hindrance of trade and traffic and in the end produce monopolies' (*Institutes*, 2, p. 540).

References

Anderson, G.M. and Tollison, R.D. (1982), 'Adam Smith's analysis of joint-stock companies', *Journal of Political Economy*, vol. 901, pp. 1237–56.

Becker, J. (1969), 'The corporation spirit and its liberal analysis, *Journal of the History of Ideas*, vol. 30, pp. 69–84.

Billet, L. (1978), 'Justice, liberty, and economy', in F.R. Glahe (ed.), *Adam Smith and the Wealth of Nations: 1776–1976 Bicentennial Essays*, University of Colorado Press, Boulder.

Buchanan, J. (1978), 'The justice of natural liberty', in F.R. Glahe (ed.), *Adam Smith and the Wealth of Nations: 1776–1976 Bicentennial Essays*, University of Colorado Press, Boulder.

Coke, Sir Edward (1727), *Coke's Reports*, 12 vols, E. & R. Nutt & R. Gosling, London.

Coke, Sir Edward (1797), *The Institutes of the Laws of England*, 4 parts, E. & R. Brooke, London.

Coleman, D.C. (1956), 'Labour in the English Economy of the Seventeenth Century', *The Economic History Review*, vol. 8, pp. 280–95.

Commons Debates, 1621 (1935), W. Notestein, F.H. Relf and H. Simpson (eds), 7 vols, Yale University Press, New Haven, Conn.

Cooke, C.A. (1951), *Corporation Trust and Company: An Essay in Legal History*, Harvard University Press, Cambridge, Mass.

Davis, J.P. [1905] (1961), *Corporation*, 2 vols, Capricorn, New York.

De Roover, R. (1951), 'Monopoly theory prior to Adam Smith: a revision', *The Quarterly Journal of Economics*, vol. 65, pp. 273–305.

Fisher, F. J. (1961), 'Tawney's century', in F.J. Fisher (ed.), *Essays in the Economic and Social History of Tudor and Stuart England in Honour of R. H. Tawney*, Cambridge University Press, Cambridge.

Hill, C. (1965), *Intellectual Origins of the English Revolution*, Clarendon Press, Oxford.

Holdsworth, Sir William (1977), *A History of English Law*, 12 vols, Methuen, London.

Hollander, S. (1973), *The Economics of Adam Smith*, University of Toronto Press, Toronto.

Jones, F. (1926), 'Historical development of the law of business competition', *Yale Law*

Journal, vol. 35, pp. 905–38.

Journals of the House of Commons (1624), vol. 1.

Knafla, L.A. (1977), *Law and Politics in Jacobean England*, Cambridge University Press, Cambridge.

Lipson, E. (1961), *The Economic History of England* (6th edn), 3 vols, A. and C. Black, London.

Little, D. [1969] (1984), *Religion, Order, and Law: A Study in Pre-Revolutionary England*, University of Chicago Press, Chicago.

Malament, B. (1967), 'The "economic liberalism" of Sir Edward Coke', *Yale Law Journal*, vol. 76, pp. 1321–58.

Mitchell, W.C. (1967), *Types of Economic Theory: From Mercantilism to Institutionalism*, J. Dorfman (ed.), 2 vols, A.M. Kelley, New York.

Rae, J. [1895] (1965), *Life of Adam Smith*, A.M. Kelley, New York.

Smith A. [1766] (1981), *Lectures on Jurisprudence*, R.L. Meek, D.D. Raphael and P.G. Stein (eds), *Liberty Classics*, Indianapolis.

Smith, A. [1776] (1981), *An Inquiry into the Nature and Causes of the Wealth of Nations*, R.H. Campbell and A.S. Skinner (eds) *Liberty Classics*, Indianapolis.

Tawney, R.H. and Power, E. (eds) (1962), *Tudor Economic Documents*, 3 vols, Barnes & Noble, New York.

Teichgraeber, Richard F. (1986), *'Free Trade' and Moral Philosophy: Rethinking the Sources of Adam Smith's Wealth of Nations*, Duke University Press, Durham, N.C.

Thorne, Samuel (1985), *Essays in English Legal History*, Hambledon, London.

Viner, Jacob. [1928] (1966), 'Adam Smith and *laissez-faire*', in *Adam Smith, 1776–1926*, A.M. Kelley, New York.

Wagner, D. (1935), 'Coke and the rise of economic liberalism', *The Economic History Review*, vol. 6, pp. 30–44.

White, S. (1979), *Sir Edward Coke and 'The Grievances of the Commonwealth,'* *1621–1628*, University of North Carolina Press, Chapel Hill.

3 A reappraisal of Canard's *Theory of Price Determination*

Bruce D. Larson

Introduction

'Is it true, in an agricultural state, that every specie of tax ultimately falls on the landowners, and, if one decides for the affirmative, do indirect taxes fall on these same owners with excess?' This is the question proposed by the Moral and Political Sciences class of the National Institute of France for its prize of 5 January 1801. The prize-winning answer – 'Essai sur la circulation de l'impôt' – was written by Nicolas-François Canard.[1] Canard revised, corrected and enlarged the 'Essai' and it appeared a few months later as *Principes d'économie politique*.[2]

Opinions of the *Principes* have varied widely.[3] At one extreme is Cournot, who said, 'These pretended principles are so radically at fault, and the application of them is so erroneous, that the approval of a distinguished body of men was unable to preserve the work from oblivion.[4] At the other extreme is Robertson, who held, 'To Canard belongs the credit for first attempting a comprehensive treatment of the fundamental problem of price determination as a study in the equilibria of forces. To Canard likewise must be attributed the first unequivocal attempt at supply-and-demand analysis.'[5] Between these extremes are Baumol and Goldfeld, who maintained, 'There are noteworthy flashes of insight in the book as there are in Isnard's work . . . but they should not be taken to elevate the authors beyond the level of charming economic primitives.'[6]

These divergent opinions indicate that the significance of the *Principes* for the history of economic thought needs reappraisal. In order to provide this reappraisal this paper will present, in the next section, a commentary on the most significant part of the *Principes*, the theory of price determination.[7] This commentary will provide the first comprehensive examination of this aspect of the *Principes* to appear in the English language[8] and will show that Canard's analysis had substantial merits and demerits. An appraisal of these merits and demerits, as well as an explanation of the divergent opinions of the *Principes*, will be presented in the third section.

Commentary
Canard begins his theory of price determination by noting that price is the relation of the value of one good to that of another. As everything is compared to gold and silver, the price of a good is the relation of its value to a determinate quantity of gold or silver. But what assigns each good its value?[9]

Canard holds that the value of a good must be due to the labour that it cost, because everything which has a price is the result of labour. Thus if all men were limited to their absolute needs for preservation, all labour was natural (as it is when no learning is required to perform it), and all labour differed only in the amount of time, then the duration of labour would measure value. However, the different species of learned labour are too various for time to measure value.[10]

Thus Canard dismisses labour-time as a measure of value even though he holds a labour-embodied theory of value. His value theory – which leaves value undefined[11] – was undoubtedly adopted from the *Wealth of Nations*, for substantial portions of the *Principes* were taken from it.[12]

Value assignment having been dealt with Canard turns to the theory of price determination, which builds from a rationality postulate. He regards it as a fact that all individuals tend to procure for themselves the greatest enjoyment possible, and so each seller seeks to sell at the highest price possible and each buyer seeks to buy at the lowest price possible. The need of the seller makes him set a price low enough to determine the buyer to buy his good and the need of the buyer makes him offer a price high enough to determine the seller to sell his good. So it is between the need of the seller and the opposed need of the buyer that price determination begins.[13]

The sellers and buyers being brought together in a market there will necessarily be a difference between the price asked by the sellers and the price offered by the buyers; the difference between the highest price and the lowest price forms a *latitude* on which the struggles of the sellers and buyers take place. The sellers will take advantage of the need and competition of the buyers to make them pay the largest part of this latitude, while the buyers will take advantage of the need and compe-tition of the sellers to pay the smallest part of this latitude.[14]

This granted let L be the latitude, x the part of the latitude that the sellers want to add to the lowest price, and L–x the part of the latitude that the buyers want to subtract from the highest price. In addition let B represent the need and N the competition of the buyers; b represents the need and n the competition of the sellers. Canard holds that the part of the latitude added to the lowest price will grow in proportion to the need and competition of the buyers, so x:BN, and the part of the latitude subtracted from the highest price will grow in proportion to the need and competition of the sellers, so L–x:bn. When these proportions are equal to one another x:BN::L–bn, so bnx = BN(L—x). This equation is called the *equation of determinations*, because bnx represents the determination of the sellers and BN(L–x) represents the determination of the buyers.[15]

Canard interprets bn as the *force* of the buyers and BN as the *force* of the sellers, which implies that the equation of determinations expresses the equality of the moments of two opposed forces.[16] This leads him to claim that all of the theory of political economy relates to the equilibrium of the forces of buyers and sellers, just as all of the theory of statics relates to the equilibrium of the lever.[17]

It would appear, in fact, that at this level of detail the theory of political economy is formally identical to the theory of statics, an analogy which later proved fruitful in the work of Walras and Edgeworth.[18] But in so doing Canard's work has been criticized for using algebra and strict proportions, instead of calculus and general functions,[19] and employing concepts of need and competition which are indefinable.[20]

The process by which the determinations of the buyer and seller become equal may be illustrated as follows. In general each seller will weigh the determination of his buyer and compare it to his own. If the seller finds that his own determination is greater, he will diminish his price a bit, that is, diminish x. By doing this his determination will decrease and that of his buyer will increase, thereby approaching one another. In the same way the buyer will compare his determination to that of his seller. When the buyer and the seller sense that their determinations are equal, they will trade.[21]

Solving the equation of determinations for x yields x = BNL/(BN+bn), which is called the *gain of the sellers*; L–x = bnL/(BN+bn) is called the *gain of the buyers*. If the need or competition of the sellers is 0, then bn = 0, which implies that the gain of the sellers is L and the gain of the buyers is 0; if the need or competition of the buyers is 0, then BN = 0, which implies that the gain of the sellers is 0 and the gain of the buyers is L. Thus the latitude extends from the monopoly of the buyers to the monopoly of the sellers.[22]

Canard's gain concepts are of interest for two reasons. First, because they may be viewed as crude measures of consumers' and producers' surplus, concepts which have been traced to Cournot.[23] Second, because the gain of the sellers is undefined if n = N = 0. Although Canard did not make this substitution, it might be interpreted as implying that price is indeterminate under bilateral monopoly.[24]

Up to this point Canard has dealt with the division of a *given* latitude but the latitude has also to be determined. Accordingly he sets out to determine the lower and upper *limits* of the latitude, that is, the lowest and highest prices.

The lower limit of the latitude of a good is determined by the *necessary wage* of the labour applied to it; the necessary wage just enables the worker to raise his children and maintain the population of his class. As the necessary wage is also the customary price of natural labour, it is also called the *natural wage*. The natural wage cannot be precisely determined because it has a latitude of its own.[25]

The upper limit of the latitude depends upon whether or not the good is an absolute necessity and whether or not the good is purchased for resale. If it is not an absolute necessity and not purchased for resale, an increase in the price of the seller will cause the number of buyers to decrease, so while he gains by increased price, he loses by decreased sales. Thus there is a price for which he loses as much on one side as he gains from the other. This price is the upper limit of the latitude.

If the good is an absolute necessity and not purchased for resale, then it would appear that there would be no upper limit to its price. However, the upper limit is determined by the natural wage of the buyer; if the seller charged a higher price, either the wage would have to increase in proportion or natural workers (those who have undergone no training) would revolt to keep from starving.

If the good is purchased for resale, then the upper limit of the latitude would be that price which would yield the purchaser the natural wage of his labour.[26]

Canard's analysis of the upper limit of the latitude indicates an awareness of the functional dependence of demand on price,[27] a grasp of the elasticity of demand,[28] and a verbal apprehension of basic elements of the monopoly theory later developed by Cournot.[29] This last statement has been called too strong,[30] yet it is easy to imagine Cournot formalizing Canard, much as Marshall did Ricardo, and arriving at his monopoly theory.[31] This seems plausible given that Canard was the only writer of mathematical economics that Cournot had read.[32]

The discussion of the limits of the latitude indicates that the price of any good is made up of the natural wage of the labour it contains plus the gain of the sellers; the gain of the sellers represents the value of the product of the sources of rent which have been applied to it. If P is the price of the good, S the natural wage of the labour it contains, and x the gain of the sellers, it results that $P = S + x = S + BNL/(BN+bn)$.[33]

When $BN = 0$ this formula implies that price reaches its lower limit, in which case the gain of the sellers is 0 and the gain of the buyers is L; when $bn = 0$ price reaches its upper limit, in which case the gain of the sellers is L and the gain of the buyers is 0. These limits will seldom be reached for if the wage is too low in a branch of labour, a worker will quit it for another. This will tend to increase the wage in the less remunerative branch as present workers will abandon it and no new workers will join it.[34]

Such is Canard's analysis of direct exchange. This analysis was placed under two restrictions which counter some obvious objections.

The first restriction concerns need. Canard's price formula indicates that the price of a good is S when the need of a buyer is 0. It would seem that the price should be 0, for there is no reason to buy a good for which there is no need.[35]

Canard directly addresses this objection. He holds that man's desire to acquire is susceptible to an infinity of degrees, and in proportion as his desire grows he offers a higher price. If his desire for a good is so weak that he does not offer a price equal to the natural wage of the labour it contains, his desire is *ineffective* or *imaginary*, for he wants what cannot be. As Canard is only concerned with effective desires he says that a need or desire for a good of 0 corresponds to the first infinitely small degree at which desire ceases to be ineffective and becomes effective. A similar principle applies to the labour of those who buy only to sell. The first infinitely small degree at which the desire of a buyer-seller becomes effective is determined by the natural wage of their labour.[36]

The second restriction concerns labour. Labour can increase or decrease the value of an object: in the former case the labour is *real*, whereas in the latter case the labour is *mistakenly applied*. Although Canard indicates formal ways of dealing with mistakenly applied labour, he emphasizes that he is only concerned with the analysis of real labour.[37]

Thus Canard's analysis is meant to apply to cases where labour is real and need is zero or effective, that is, to the long run. The methods he used to deal with the inadequacies of his theory are open to the objection that they require knowlege of the equilibrium price. Accordingly what is to be determined can only be determined by knowledge of what is to be determined! This is a serious flaw.

Canard now goes on to consider an arbitrary number of buyer-sellers between the producer and the consumer, that is, indirect exchange. In order to keep things simple, yet include all essential points, the case of a producer, two buyer-sellers, and a consumer will be dealt with.[38]

The producer of an object is its first seller, who as the first seller has needs b and competition n. He sells to the first buyer-seller, who as the first buyer has need B and competition N. Between them they determine a latitude L and a price $S + BNL/(BN+bn)$; S is the natural wage of the labour of the producer and $BNL/(BN+bn)$ – the gain of the seller – is the payment for the product of the sources of rent.

The first buyer-seller of an object is its second seller, who as the second seller has need b' and competition n'. He sells to the second buyer-seller, who as the second buyer has need B' and competition N'. They determine a latitude L' and a price increase $S' + B'N'L'/(B'N'+b'n')$; S is the natural wage of the labour of the first buyer-seller and $B'N'L'/(B'N'+b'n')$ – the gain of the seller – is the payment for the product of the additional sources of rent.

The second buyer-seller of an object is its third seller, who as the third seller has need b'' and competition n''. He sells to the consumer, who as the third buyer has need B'' and competition N''. They determine a latitude L'' and a price increase $S'' + B''N''L''/(B''N''+b''n'')$; S'' is the natural wage of the labour of the second buyer-seller and $B''N''L''/(B''N''+b''n'')$ – the gain of the seller – is the payment for the product of the additional sources of rent. Thus the price of the object to the consumer will be:

$$P = S + BNL/(BN+bn) + S' + B'N'L'/(B'N'+b'n')$$
$$+ S'' + B''N''L''/(B''N''+b''n''),$$

the gain of the sellers will be:

$$BNL/(BN+bn) + B'N'L'/(B'N'+b'n') + B''N''L''/(B''N''+b''n'')$$

and the gain of the buyers will be:

$$bnL/(BN+bn) + b'n'L'/(B'N'+b'n') + b''n''L''/(B''N''+b''n'').$$

Each buyer repays the sum of all the labours and products of the sources of rent which have gone before him.[39]

These relations hold when each seller only considers himself relative to his immediate buyer. When the buyers and sellers consider that each object must pass through many hands, it results that the latitudes L,L',L'', are only *partial latitudes* of a *total latitude* $\wedge$, and the partial latitudes are variables rather than constants. Canard's analysis of this case follows.

First consider the consumer. If his need to buy or competition is 0, then he will pay the second buyer-seller only the natural wage of the second buyer-seller's labour, thereby reducing the need to buy of the second buyer-seller to 0. Consequently the second buyer-seller will pay the first buyer-seller only the natural wage of the first buyer-seller's labour. But the consumer – whose need or competition is 0 – could take any gain that the second buyer-seller might make. Thus each labour applied to an object will earn its natural wage and the price of the object will be $P = S + S' + S''$, which is the lower limit of the total latitude. In general, any buyer whose need or competition is 0 can reduce the price of the object he buys to the sum of the natural wages of the labours which preceded it.

Now consider the producer. If his need to sell or competition is 0, then he will make the first buyer-seller pay all of the first partial latitude, thereby reducing the need to sell of the first buyer-seller to 0. Consequently the first buyer-seller will make the second buyer-seller pay all of the second partial latitude. But the seller – whose need or competition is 0 – could take any gain that the first buyer-seller might make. Thus the producer will sell his object for $P = S + L + L' + L''$ and the consumer will pay $P = S + L + S' + L' + S'' + L''$, which is the upper limit of the total latitude. In general, any seller whose need or competition is 0 can increase the price of the object he sells by the sum of the partial latitudes which follow it.

Consequently a monopolistic buyer-seller can reduce the price of the object he buys to the sum of the natural wages of the labours which precede it and increase the price of the object he sells by the sum of the partial latitudes which follow it. Thus the partial latitudes are not absolute latitudes but only parts of a total latitude which can unite on the producer, any buyer-seller, or the consumer. In the present case price can range from $S + S' + S''$ to $S + S' + S'' + \wedge$, where $\wedge = L + L' + L''$ is the total latitude and $L, L, 'L''$ are partial latitudes. The total latitude extends from the monopoly of the consumer to the opposed monopoly of any buyer-seller or the producer.[40]

Situations where need or competition is 0 are rare. Generally, as the ability of a branch of labour to reduce the gain of other branches increases, its competition increases and its force decreases; as its ability to reduce the gain of other branches decreases, its competition decreases and its force increases. In this way the forces of the different branches tend to be put into equilibrium with one another; an *absolute equilibrium* occurs when $BN = bn = B'N' = b'n' = B''N'' = b''n''$, whereby:

$$P = S + L/2 + S' + L'/2 + S'' + L''/2 = S + S' + S'' + \wedge/2,$$

and both the sellers and buyers have a gain of $\wedge/2$. This price is a point towards which goods always tend but never stop, due to turns of events, the instability of tastes, artificial needs, the opposition of interests, and a thousand other reasons.[41]

Absolute equilibrium having been related, Canard next discusses productivity through the concept of *capacity*. Capacity was introduced to enable him to determine the values of the partial latitudes.

All other things being equal a branch which can make from a given labour twice that of another branch will absorb twice the latitude of the other – *capacity* represents this ability to produce. Accordingly let c, c', c'', be the capacities of the successive labours, $\Sigma = c + c' + c''$ be their sum and C be the capacity of the consumer. As consumption absorbs all of the successive labours, $C = \Sigma$, and as the capacities of the successive labours are in the same proportion to their partial latitudes as the sum of the capacities is to the total latitude, $\Sigma : \wedge :: c : L$, $\Sigma : \wedge :: c' : L'$, and $\Sigma : \wedge :: c'' : L''$. It follows that $L = c \wedge / \Sigma$, $L' = c' \wedge / \Sigma$, $L'' = c'' \wedge / \Sigma$.[42]

Canard's capacities, although a reasonable attempt to introduce productivity into the analysis, does not succeed in determining the partial latitudes because the total latitude depends upon the sum of the partial latitudes; once again what is to be determined can only be determined by knowledge of what is to be determined. Nevertheless he demonstrates an awareness of the importance of productivity in the determination of price and incorporates it in the last formal generalization of his model.

Each buyer-seller, whether in buying or selling, seeks the largest gain possible. This gain separates into a gain as a seller, which is produced through selling, and a gain as a consumer, which is produced through buying. The gain as a consumer is proportionate to the force of the consumer and it is this force that the buyer opposes to his seller, when there is only a producer and a consumer. In the general case, the force of the consumer must be considered in opposition to the sum of the forces of all of the sellers. Considering this case, let $\wedge$ be the total latitude, x the portion of the latitude that the consumer pays, $\wedge - x$ the portion of the latitude that the consumer does not pay, f, f', f'' the forces of the successive sellers to attract gain and F the force of the consumer. Consequently $f + f' + f'' : x :: F : \wedge - x$, whereby:

$$x = (f + f' + f'') \wedge / (f + f' + f'' + F).$$

Now the force of each seller is in direct ratio to the capacity of his labour and in inverse ratio to his need and competition, while the force of the consumer is in direct ratio to his capacity of consumption and in inverse ratio to his need and competition. Thus $f = c/bn$, $f' = c'/b'n'$, f''

$= c''/b''n''$ and $F = C/BN$. Substituting the values into x, reducing it to a common denominator, and noting that $P = S + S' + S'' + x$, yields $P = S + S' + S'' +$

$$\frac{BN \wedge (cb'n'b''n'' + c'bnb''n'' + c''bnb'n')}{BN(cb'n'b''n'' + c'bnb''n'' + c''bnb'n') + Cbnb'n'b''n''}$$

In absolute equilibrium $P = S + S' + S'' + \wedge/2$, as $C = \Sigma$, and the gain of the producer and the buyer-sellers will be equal to the gain of the consumer. Appropriate assumptions about need and competition can show that the total latitude can settle upon the producer, any buyer-seller, or the consumer.[43]

This is Canard's most general mathematical statement of his theory of price determination. It will be useful to follow him one step further as he verbally discusses the relationships of different branches of labour. This will show, contrary to the opinion of some,[44] but consistent with the opinion of others,[45] that Canard had a clear notion of general equilibrium.

Up until now only one principal branch for a good has been considered, but it is possible to consider two branches. If a seller furnishes his good to two principal branches it is evident that there must be an equilibrium between them, and that each must have a latitude proportionate to the capacity of the industrial labour and rents they contain.

Suppose, then, that an equilibrium has been established between the two branches. If the need of the consumers in one branch increases, then the gain of its buyer-sellers will increase and reach as far as the branch which connects them, causing the commodity to sell for more in that branch than in the other. Accordingly, the buyer-sellers will either not sell to the less lucrative branch or sell at the same price as to the more lucrative branch, resulting in a decreased gain which will reach as far as consumption and make it diminish. Thus whenever some cause increases the consumption – and thus the gain – in one branch of industry, it decreases the consumption – and thus the gain – of the other; whenever some cause decreases the consumption – and thus the gain – in one branch of industry, it increases the consumption – and thus the gain – of the other.[46]

The consumption of a branch can decrease or increase, but this is not true of gain. When the gains of a branch decrease, the workers who form its *extremities* quit it to join more advantageous branches, thereby returning to the level of the others; when the gains of a branch increase, workers join it, thereby diminishing its gains until it is in equilibrium with the others. Thus all branches and their ramifications communicate among themselves; human labour forms a unique system of ramifications which constantly tends to return all gains to a level, in accordance with the factors which affect them.[47]

In writing this Canard has shown an awareness of the idea of a general equilibrium and has endeavoured to show how a change in one branch affects other branches. In developing this idea he alludes to the notion of the extremities of a branch, which is nothing other than its margin; the worker who is at the extremity of a branch is one who just receives the natural wage of his labour.[48] Thus Canard apprehended and used two of the most important concepts of mathematical economics.

Canard's discussion of general equilibrium is not wholly satisfactory, for it is not given in mathematical form. This omission is all too understandable given the unwieldy formulas – sometimes covering entire pages – that Canard derived for one branch of industry.[49]

Conclusion

Canard's theory of price determination has shown to possess substantial merits and demerits. These aspects will now be summarized and reappraised.

On the merit side Canard's theory has been shown to have: employed the fundamental rationality postulate; indicated the similarity between the theory of statics and the theory of political economy; developed crude measures of producers' and consumers' surplus; developed a formula applicable to bilateral monopoly; indicated the functional dependence of demand on price and the elasticity of demand; verbally stated basic elements of Cournot's theory of monopoly; incorporated productivity into price determination; viewed the concept of general equilibrium; and employed the concept of the margin.

On the demerit side Canard's theory has been shown to have left the concept of value undefined; employed a labour-embodied theory of value; incorporated algebra and strict proportions, instead of calculus and general functions; utilized indefinable concepts like need and competition; used circular reasoning in the determination of equilibrium price and partial latitudes; and failed to develop a mathematical theory of general equilibrium. Given the substantial merits and demerits of Canard's work, it is easy to see how opinions of it could vary so widely. Emphasis on its merits – Robertson – could produce an extremely positive appraisal, whereas emphasis on its demerits – Cournot – could produce an extremely negative appraisal. But what is the proper appraisal of Canard's theory of price determination?

The present appraisal is that Canard's theory was a greatly flawed but improvable work which, in consequence of its approval by the National Institute of France, spread the idea that economics could be approached mathematically.[50] Some of this diffusion may have been injurious, for the flaws of Canard's work may have prejudiced others against applying mathematics to economics; this may have hindered the acceptance of Cournot's work which met with far less immediate success than did that of Canard.[51] However some of this diffusion may have been beneficial, for the improvable nature of Canard's work did give rise to further development. The most tantalizing possibility, but one which must remain unexplored for the present, is that Cournot's *Recherches* was developed in an attempt to improve upon Canard's *Principes*.

The present appraisal poses a question. Given the substantial merits of Canard's work, how could they have been overlooked for so long? It is suggested that few people have ever bothered to read the book, first, because it ran afoul of methodological presuppositions which prohibited the use of mathematics in economics,[52] and second, because it was uniformly castigated by the champions of mathematical economics, namely, Cournot, Jevons and Walras.[53] In France, methodological presuppositions prevented Canard's work from entering the mainstream of economic thought, as it did Cournot's. But once the methodological presuppositions had ceased to be important the view of Cournot, Jevons and Walras prevented Canard's work from being seriously considered.

Canard's theory of price determination clearly shows that the factors affecting the success of a scientific work are many. The content of the work is important, of course, but so is the approval of distinguished bodies, the disapproval of demonstrated masters, the methodological presuppositions of the time, and the talent of those who follow. Distinguished bodies and established masters – authorities – seem to have played a significant role in the success of Canard's work, and have prevented it from being seen for what it is.

Notes

1. Institut National des Sciences et Arts, *Mémoires de la classe des sciences morales and politiques*, vol 4 (Paris: Baudoin, vendemiaire an XI [September 1802]), pp. 16–17.
2. Edgard Allix, 'Un précurseur de l'école mathématique: Nicolas-François Canard', *Revue d'Histoire Économique et Sociale* 8,1 (1920): 38–67, see p.38.
3. The original work is N.F. Canard, *Principes d'économie politique* (Paris: Buisson, 1801; microform edn, New York: Pergamon Press). The *Principes* first appeared in German translation as *Grundsätze der Staatswirtschaft* (Ulm: Stettinsche Buchhandlung, 1806), as cited by Otto Weinberger, *Mathematische Volkswirtschaftslehre* (Leipzig: B.G. Teubner, 1930), p. 38, and later as *Grundsätze der Staatswirtschaft*, (Vienna: B.Ph. Bauer, 1814). The translation of 1814 has been reprinted, with the original French edition, as *Grundsätze der Staatswirtschaft*, with an Introduction by W.G. Waffenschmidt (Stuttgart: W. Kohlhammer, 1958; microform edn, Ann Arbor, Mich.: University Microfilms International).

The microform edition of University Microfilms International does not have the correct p. 200, p. 206 having been substituted for it. For the correct p. 200, see the microform edition of Pergamon Press.

4. Augustin Cournot, *Researches into the Mathematical Principles of the Theory of Wealth* (New York: Macmillan, 1927; reprint edn, New York: Augustus M. Kelley, 1971), p. 2.
5. Ross M. Robertson, 'Mathematical economics before Cournot' (PhD dissertation, University of Kansas, 1948), p. 231. These same statements were repeated in idem, 'Mathematical economics before Cournot', *Journal of Political Economy* 57 (December 1949): 523–36, see p. 535. For a thorough graphical treatment of Canard's theory of price determination in terms of supply and demand, see Waffenschmidt, Introduction to Canard, *Grundsätze*.
6. William J. Baumol and Stephen M. Goldfeld, *Precursors in Mathematical Economics* (London: London School of Economics and Political Science, 1968), p. 156.
7. The theory of price determination appears as chapter III of Canard, *Principes*, secs 11–28. Section numbers, rather than page numbers, will be used in order to facilitate the use of translations.
8. The principal treatments of Canard's theory of price are: Waffenschmidt, Introduction to Canard, *Grundsätze*; Reghinos D. Theocharis, *Early Developments in Mathematical Economics*, 2nd edn (Philadelphia: Porcupine Press, 1983), pp. 66–81, which was most responsible for demonstrating the international influence of the *Principes*; Robertson, 'Mathematical economics' (1948), pp. 49–57; and Allix, 'Un précurseur'. Of these works only Waffenschmidt can be said to be comprehensive.
9. Canard, *Principes*, sec. 11.
10. Ibid.
11. See Pierre Boven, *Les Applications mathématiques à l'économie politique* (Lausanne: F. Rouge & Cie., 1912), p. 45.
12. Canard refers to Smith in only one place, see Canard, *Principes*, sec. 74. The first work to observe that Canard employed substantial elements of the *Wealth of Nations* in the *Principes* appears to be [Francis Horner], Review of *Principes d'economie politique*, by N.F. Canard, *Edinburgh Review* 2 (January 1803): 431–50, see p. 444. The word 'appears' has been used because it has not been possible to acquire two earlier works which dealt with the *Principes*, namely, Review of *Principes d'économie politique*, by N.F. Canard, *La Décade Philosophique, Littéraire et Politique* 2 (an X [1802]): 385–99 and M. Desrenaudes, Review of *Recherches sur la nature et les causes de la richesse des nations*, by Adam Smith, *La Décade Philosophique, Littéraire et Politique* 4, 36 (an X [1802]): 518–31, both as cited and briefly discussed in Theocharis, *Early Developments*, pp. 87–8; seemingly, Desrenaudes would have discussed a relationship between Smith and Canard. Later works to relate Smith and Canard were Louis Say, *Considérations sur l'industrie et la législation* (Paris: J.-P. Aillaud, 1822), p. 112, where it is said that Canard's work is of 'the school of Adam Smith', and Allix, 'Un précurseur', p. 65, where it it noticed that Canard 'extracted from Adam Smith the theory of spontaneous economic order and translated it into equilibrium formulas.'

Other writers who were explicitly named by Canard were: the Abbé de St Pierre, see Canard, *Principes*, sec. 106; Arthur Young, see ibid., sec. 119, and the Economists, see ibid., Avant Propos. Nevertheless the influence of Malthus's *Essay on the Principle of Population,* first published in 1798, seems evident, as noted by Allix, 'Un précurseur', p. 40, and echoed by Robertson, 'Mathematical economics' (1948), p. 231. It has also been claimed – see Joseph A. Schumpeter, *History of Economic Analysis* (New York: Oxford University Press, 1954), pp. 217 and 499 – that Cantillon's influence on the *Principes* is obvious, due to its use of 'the three rents'. It seems more likely that the three rents were carried over from Smith.
13. Canard, *Principes*, sec. 12.
14. Ibid.

15. Ibid., sec. 13.
16. This interpretation of 'force' is inconsistent with later usage in section 26, where the force of the seller is defined as c/bn and the force of the buyer is defined as C/BN; c and C are 'capacities' to be discussed later. This inconsistency does not affect his results as he requires that $c = C$ and so $bnx = BN(L-x)$ implies that $(C/BN)x = (c/bn)(L-x)$. Thus the force of the buyers multiplied by x is equal to the force of the sellers multiplied by $(L-x)$.
17. Ibid., sec. 13.
18. See William Jaffé, 'A.N. Isnard, progenitor of the Walrasian general equilibrium model', *History of Political Economy* 1 (Spring 1969): 19–43, and F.Y. Edgeworth, *Mathematical Psychics* (London: C. Kegan Paul & Co., 1881; reprint edn, New York: Augustus M. Kelley, 1967).
19. The first criticism of Canard's proportionalities was J. Bertrand, Review of *Théorie mathématique de la richesse sociale*, by Léon Walras, and *Recherches sur les principes mathématiques de la théorie des richesses*, by Augustin Cournot, *Journal des Savants* (September 1883): 499–508, see especially pp. 499–500, simultaneously published as ibid., *Bulletin des Sciences Mathématiques et Astronomiques*, series 2, 7 (November 1883): 293–303, see especially pp. 293–4. Bertrand has been followed by many, see Boven, *Les Applications mathématiques*, p. 47; W. Zawadski, *Les Mathématiques appliquées à l'économie politique* (Paris: Marcel Rivière et Cie., 1914; reprint edn, New York: Burt Franklin, 1966), p. 35; Jacques Moret, *L'Emploi des mathématiques en economie politique* (Paris: M. Giard & E. Brière, 1915), pp. 70–1; Weinberger, *Mathematische Volkswirtschaftslehre*, p. 40; and Helmut Reichardt, *Augustin A. Cournot* (Tübingen: J.C.B. Mohr (Paul Siebeck), 1954), pp. 90–1.
         Canard's use of proportionalities may be better understood when it is recognized that modern functional notation – using f, F, φ, and Ψ – substantially dates from Lagrange's *Théorie des fonctions analytiques* of 1797, see Florian Cajori, *A History of Mathematical Notations* (Chicago: Open Court, 1929), vol. II, p. 269. For further discussions of the relationships between the development of mathematics and economics, see Robertson, 'Mathematical economics' (1948), pp. 248–53, and Claude Ménard, *La Formation d'une rationalité économique: A.A. Cournot* (Paris: Flammarion, 1978), pp. 154–63.
20. See Baumol and Goldfeld, *Precursors*, p. 156.
21. Canard, *Principes*, sec. 13.
22. Ibid., secs 14, 17 and 18.
23. The first work to interpret Canard's gain concepts in this way was Allix, 'Un précurseur', p. 45. For a recent survey of the consumer surplus literature, see Robert B. Ekelund, Jr, and Robert F. Hebert, 'Consumer surplus: the first hundred years', *History of Political Economy* 17,3 (Autumn 1985): 419–54.
24. For this interpretation, see Theocharis, *Early Developments*, p. 70. For the original statement of indeterminacy, see Edgeworth, *Mathematical Psychics*, pp. 28–9, and for additional discussion, see John Creedy, *Edgeworth and the Development of Neoclassical Economics* (Oxford: Basil Blackwell, 1986), pp. 53–61. This indeterminacy does not arise in Waffenschmidt, Introduction to Canard, *Grundsätze*, p. 19, because of a lack of competition for sellers and buyers was taken to be equivalent to assuming $n = 1$ and $N = 1$.
25. Canard, *Principes*, secs 15 and 21.
26. Ibid., secs 16–17.
27. Reichardt, *Augustin A. Cournot*, p. 90.
28. Robertson, 'Mathematical economics' (1948), p. 54. The elasticity concept was later developed more fully by William Whewell, on whose work see James P. Henderson, 'William Whewell's mathematical statements of price flexibility, demand elasticity, and the Giffen paradox', *Manchester School of Economic and Social Studies* 41,3 (1973): 329–42. The mathematics of Canard and Whewell have generally been viewed in a very negative light, on which see W. Stanley Jevons, *The Theory of Political Economy*, 2nd edn (London: Macmillan, 1979), p. xxiv, and Schumpeter,

History, pp. 954–5. Two recent works which create a much more positive view of Whewell's work are James Perry Henderson, 'Early British mathematical economics, 1822–1850' (PhD dissertation, Northern Illinois University, 1976), and James P. Henderson, 'The Whewell group of mathematical economists', *Manchester School of Economic and Social Studies* 52 (December 1985): 404–31.

29. This point seems to have been first made in Robertson, 'Mathematical economics', p. 54. For more forceful statements, see Reichardt, *Cournot*, pp. 89–90; Waffensch-midt, Introduction to Canard, *Grundsatze*, pp. 17 and 19; and Theocharis, *Early Developments*, p. 68.

30. Baumol and Goldfeld, *Precursors*, p. 156 in response to Theocharis, *Early Developments*, p. 68.

31. See Robertson, 'Mathematical economics' (1948), pp. 231–322, and idem, 'Mathematical economics', *Journal of Political Economy*, p. 535, for statements recognizing the improvable nature of Canard's economics.

32. See Cournot, *Researches*, p. 2, and Antoine-Augustin Cournot, *Revue sommaire des doctrines économiques* (Paris: Hachette & Cie., 1877; reprint ed., New York: Augustus M. Kelley, 1968), p. i.

33. Canard, *Principes*, secs 17 and 19.

34. Ibid., sec. 18.

35. This point was made in Zawadski, *Les Mathématiques*, p. 34, and repeated in Weinberger, *Mathematische Volkswirtschaftslehre*, p. 40.

36. Canard, *Principes*, sec. 22.

37. Ibid., sec. 21.

38. For a compressed discussion of Canard's theory of price determination in its full generality, see Theocharis, *Early Developments*, pp. 71–4.

39. Canard, *Principes*, sec. 20.

40. Ibid., sec. 23.

41. Ibid., secs 24 and 26.

42. Ibid., sec. 25.

43. Ibid., sec. 26.

44. See Boven, *Les Applications mathématiques*, pp. 47–9, and Zawadski, *Les Mathématiques*, p. 34.

45. See: Allix, 'Un précurseur', p. 40; Robertson, 'Mathematical economics', p. 231; idem, 'Mathematical economics', *Journal of Political Economy*, p. 535; Reichardt, *Augustin A. Cournot*, pp. 88–9; G.-H. Bousquet, 'N.F. Canard, précurseur du marginalisme', *Revue d'Économie Politique*, 67 (1957): 232–5; idem, 'Histoire de l'économie mathématique jusqu'à Cournot', *Metroeconomica*, 10,3 (Dicembre 1958): 121–35, especially pp. 127–8; idem, 'Le système mathématique de l'équilibre économique selon Léon Walras, et ses origines', *Revue d'Économie Politique* 73 (1963): 948–76, especially pp. 968–9, 971, and 973; Ménard, *La Formation d'une rationalité économique*, pp. 114–15; and Theocharis, *Early Developments*, p. 74.

    Neither Walras nor Schumpeter mention the general equilibrium aspects of Canard. See Leon Walras, *Elements of Pure Economics*, trans. William Jaffé (Homewood, Illinois: Richard D. Irwin, 1954; reprint edn, Fairfield, New Jersey: Augustus M. Kelley, 1977), p. 44, and Schumpeter, *History*, pp. 217, 499, and 954–5.

46. Canard, *Principes*, sec. 27.

47. Ibid., sec. 28.

48. For further discussion of the extremities of a branch, see ibid., sec. 9, which lies in Canard's chapter I, 'Of the Sources of Rent'. On Canard's marginalism, see Bousquet, 'N.F. Canard', p. 233; idem, 'Histoire', pp. 127–8; and idem, 'Le système mathématique', p. 956.

49. See Canard, *Principes*, sec. 26.

50. The improvable nature of Canard's work is emphasized in Robertson, 'Mathematical economics' (1948), pp. 231–2, and idem, 'Mathematical economics', *Journal of Political Economy*, p. 535.

51. See Theocharis, *Early Developments*, pp. 76–80 and 92–101, for a brief discussion of Canard's influence on J.C.L. Simonde de Sismondi, Lopez de Peñalver, Melchiorre Gioja, Francesco Fuoco and Karl Heinrich Rau. It is of some interest to note that Menger and Marx cited Canard, see Carl Menger, *Principles of Economics*, trans. James Dingwall and Bert F. Hoselitz (1871; reprint edn, New York: New York University Press, 1981), pp. 166 and 303, and Karl Marx, *Theories of Surplus Value* (Moscow: Progress Publishers, 1963), Part I, p. 204, and that it has been claimed that Marx took over his labour theory of value from Canard, see Roesler, 'Zur Theorie des Preises', *Jahrbücher für Nationalokonemie und Statistik* 12 (1869): 81–138, especially pp. 102–3. Finally, let it be observed that Ricardo had a copy of the *Principes* in his library – see Piero Sraffa (ed.), *The Collected Works of David Ricardo* (Cambridge University Press, 1965), vol. X, p. 399.

52. The importance of these methodological presuppositions in French economics is made clear in Yves Breton, 'Les économistes libéraux français et l'emploi des mathématiques en économie politique. 1800–1914', *Économies et Sociètès* 20,3 (March 1986): 25–63. The following French writers – generally liberal, in the sense of Breton – attacked Canard for having used mathematics: Jean-Baptiste Say, *A Treatise on Political Economy*, trans. Clement C. Biddle (Philadelphia: Claxton, Remsen & Haffelfinger, 1880; reprint edn, New York: Augustus M. Kelley, 1971), pp. xxvi–xxvii, see Allix, 'Un précurseur', p. 39 for reference to earlier editions of Say's *Treatise* and for support that Say was referring to Canard; Louis Say, *Considérations*, pp. 112–18; [Jerome Adolphe] Blanqui, *Histoire de l'économie politique en Europe* (Paris: Guillaumin et Cie., 1860), vol. II, p. 323; Joseph Garnier, *Traité d'économie politique*, 5th edn (Paris: Guillaumin et Cie., 1863), pp. 700–1, which was read by Jevons prior to writing the first edition of his *Theory*, see Jevons, *Theory*, p. xi; and Léon Say and Joseph Chailley, *Nouveau dictionnaire d'économie politique* (Paris: Guillaumin et Cie., 1891), vol. I, p. 299.

The importance of these methodological presuppositions in British economics is made clear in James P. Henderson, 'Induction, deduction and the role of mathematics: the Whewell group vs. the Ricardian economists', paper presented at the Fourteenth Annual Meeting of the History of Economics Society, Harvard School of Business, 19–22 June 1987. See [Horner], Review, pp. 438–40, for a hostile view towards the application of mathematics to economics.

53. See Cournot, *Researches*, p. 2; Jevons, *Theory*, p. xxv; and Walras, *Elements*, p. 44.

4 Some fundamental aspects of Italian eighteenth-century economic thought

Marco Bianchini

Introduction

Perhaps no one more than Schumpeter has had a better opinion of eighteenth-century Italian economic thought: 'the honours of the field of pre-Smithian system production should go to the eighteenth-century Italian. In intent, scope and plan their works were . . . systems of Political Economy in the sense of welfare economics – the old Scholastic Public Good and the specifically utilitarian Happiness meeting in their concept of welfare (*felicità pubblica*). But whereas in zeal for fact-finding and in grasp of practical problems they were not inferior to the Germans, they were superior to most of their Spanish, English and French contemporaries in analytic power and achievement.'[1]

It is true that, to the best of our knowledge, the Italians can boast of some firsts: they provided the first algebraic treatment of an economic problem (1711); one of the most complete theories of value of the century (1751, 1769); the most exhaustive studies on money, hypothesizing the commodity standard (1751); the first chairs of Political Economy (1754, 1769); the first indifference variety analysis (1764); and the first constant-outlay demand curve (1771).

The protagonists of such achievements principally come from two schools; first, the Neopolitan which includes Carlo Antonio Broggia, Ferdinando Galiani, Antonio Genovesi, Gaetano Filangieri and Giuseppe Palmieri; and second, the Milanese, which includes Gianrinaldo Carli, Cesare Beccaria, Pietro Verri and Giovambattista Vasco. We should not, however, blind ourselves to the fact that there were other interesting personalities such as Giovanni Ceva, Giammaria Ortes and Gottardo Canciani who are better identifiable within a generic Italian tradition rather than a particular group. Noteworthy also for the Milanese and Neopolitans is that they have more things in common than distinctive traits.

Since I must expound the economic thought of an entire century in very little space, it may be more useful to show the fundamental characteristics of a national tradition than to focus on the regional differences.

The roots of the Italian tradition

The social environment and the first analytical tools
Although Italian economic thought was gradually enriched with continual contributions from German, French, Spanish and English thought, a solid and clearly distinctive national tradition is evident. It goes back to the fund of economic knowledge developed by the Renaissance merchants and civil servants, starting from their practical needs and problems. The most eminent name in this field is that of Bernardo Davanzati (1529–1600). A utilitarian *ante-litteram*, he identified money with happiness, or better, considered it the second cause 'of the happy life'. He was the first to realize how the paradox of value can be solved; he supported a metallist theory of the origin and the nature of money; he supported the quantity theory; realized the importance of the speed of circulation and treated the problem of the rate of exchange with reference to the specie-points (1582–88).[2]

The first theoretical acquisitions have their roots among the lay artists, craftsmen and physicists of the seventeenth century – a group so diverse and widespread that even Galileo, in a parenthetic tract to his *Dialogue on the Great World Systems* (1629) – a work certainly without any special concerns of an economic character – considers the water-diamond paradox with admirable competence. He suggests that objects have a value in use different from their value in exchange and that 'it is scarcity and plenty that make things esteemed and despised by the vulgar, who will say that here is a most beautiful diamond, for it resembles a clear water, and yet would not part with it for ten tons of water.'[3]

The system of exchange
Given the scientific and technical environment in which the lay vision of the economy was born and developed in Italy, it is not surprising to find in a follower of Galileo – the jurist and physicist Geminiano Montanari (1633–87) – the most important landmarks of the economic thought of the *ancien régime*. They are (a) the price of an object, according to the example of the water-diamond paradox, depends on its relative scarcity and usefulness; (b) analogous to the measurement of time and space, which are expressed in terms of one another, the concept of the value of one commodity has a meaning only with reference to a given quantity of another, only if there is some relationship of substitution among the

goods; (c) the relationships of equivalence between the commodities change according to 'real wants' which, contrary to the 'imaginary needs', are translated into a money payment or into effective demand with the aim of 'attaining a good' or 'avoiding an evil'; (d) wants (i.e. money) and commodities are measurable quantities; they form a system which tends continuously to balance itself – flow with flow – like the waters of a hydraulic system because where money comes out, goods enter for an equal value; (e) economic equilibrium is determined by the competition of a myriad of small operators and cannot be influenced by the decrees of the authorities; (f) the economy is to be considered as part of natural philosophy and is studied with the same methods: calculus and fact-mindedness (1680, 1687).[4]

Primary importance of exchange, utilitarianism, quantity theory, metallism, calculus, the observation of facts and long-run equilibrium are the principal characteristics inherited from the sixteenth and seventeenth centuries. They are common, with some rare exceptions, to the entire eighteenth century.

Money

A first partial development of the scientific paradigm of Montanari is found in Giovanni Ceva (1647–1734), a highly regarded exponent of the Italian school of hydraulic engineering, who provided us with a profound insight into the nature of economic theory and the first application of mathematics to economics. Real phenomena, Ceva says, are always obscure and unmanageably complex: practice is always *minus exacta*. To understand the principles of things we must construct rational models by means of assumptions, or else we must always move in the darkest of nights; and the proper way of dealing with these models is by mathematics.[5]

His model represents a heroic attempt to show, with the help of few symbols, the effects of exogenously determined changes on a previous equilibrium state. The reality represented is an open economy with two sectors – the manufacturing and the agricultural – and with two types of money: precious metal, which also serves for international payments, and copper, destined for the consumption of subsistence and to make account money.

The variables of the model are: (a) the population or the relationship between copper money spent for subsistence and the supply of the food goods; (b) the flux of gold and silver monies spent in local manufacturing crafts; (c) the rate of exchange of the precious monies in terms of copper or account money. By applying the method of comparative statics Ceva compares the values of the variables, registered at different moments, by attributing to the rate of exchange the function of a dependent variable:

Time	Population	The gold and silver flow of money	The rate of exchange of the precious money
I	a	b	c
L	a	e	h
K	d	e	f

Since $\frac{c}{h} = \frac{e}{b}$ and $\frac{h}{f} = \frac{a}{d}$, Ceva maintains that $\frac{c}{f} = \frac{a}{d} \cdot \frac{e}{b}$. By giving all the values of equilibrium equal to 1, $\frac{c}{f} = 1$ shows a situation of equilibrium and an equal balance of payments. If $\frac{c}{f} \neq 1$, there has been an imbalance which has necessarily provoked damage to some social category. In the case of *augmentum* ($\frac{c}{f} < 1$) the agricultural producers would be hurt. They could, therefore, be helped by the public treasury with an issue of new money. The type of intervention to be effected is shown by the variation (in the flow of precious money or in the relationship between the population and the resources) which has been more responsible for determining the imbalance. The two independent variables, in fact, each represents different ranges of real phenomena: the population shows, with its growth over the unitary value, an excess of effective demand for goods of subsistence with respect to the internal supply and, therefore a debit balance of payments; the flow of gold and silver money shows a credit balance of payment if it exceeds one, and vice versa, if it is less than one, a debit or a 'concentration of wealth in few hands' or a slowing of the speed of circulation. Before, however, such once-and-for-all changes in the relative quantity of money and population result in proportional variations in the rate of exchange of gold and silver coins, a little time passes, in the real situation, as the 'public opinion' is slow to realize them (1711).[6]

Some characteristics of Italian monetary thought are clarified in Ceva, heir of seventeenth-century science: money is a commodity, that is gold and silver coins; it is a simple representation of the real sector of the economy; once-and-for-all changes in the quantity of money stand by payment imbalances. Such imbalances are produced by either prosperity or calamity. In either case the prince must intervene to re-establish the balance to ensure a static circular flow of wealth.

The systems of the second half of the eighteenth century

New protagonists
The experience of G. Ceva signals a sensitive change in the field of intellectual activity. He was a full-time 'mathematician', in the state service. For most of the preceding century the natural philosopher, an expert not only in physics but also in economics, 'acted' as temporary consultant with this or that prince, and had a social rating a little above that of the merchant or artist. At the beginning of the eighteenth century, however, he had become a permanent member of the state bureaucracy and as such collaborated with the government in public affairs and put into practice the principles of a lay pragmatic learning. Although there was undoubted progress compared with the past, the first decades of the eighteenth century were still dominated by theological and judicial learning rather than by scientific reason. In the following thirty years, around 1750, scientific learning took another step forward. After the spectacular success of Newtonian physics, some of the clerics and the aristocracy began to use natural philosophy as an intellectual tool. The former division between natural and moral philosophy now fades. The fusion took place in 1749, with the publication of a paper titled *Della pubblica felicità* by Ludovico Antonio Muratori (1672–1750). An eminent historian, a staunch Catholic he recognized almost two centuries after Davanzati, the connection between money and happiness as well as between science and welfare.[7]

These changes constituted a small revolution. Throughout Italy an intellectual class had formed, a minority in number but influential, composed of petty aristocracy, clergymen and businessmen working with the enlightened princes. For Political Economy there is a new birth, the opening of a new season. The end is the 'greater possible happiness shared with the greatest possible equality'; the means are, on the one side, the spreading of science, of the arts, of law and of enlightened self-interest; on the other side, a cautious activity of reforms and planning by the state and the conscious administration of the public finances. The ideal protagonist is a supreme moral authority – the sovereign or the scientist – who objectively judges the individual feelings and constructs the rules of the social game according to the dictates of reason. In other words the aim is to reach or regain an equilibrium in which interests, both public and private, are in a natural harmony. Such an equilibrium is based, in the last resort, upon the subjective calculus of pleasure and pain.[8]

The grafting of the refined learning of the ruling classes to the powerful conceptual tools of the scientists immediately produced, on the analytic plane, results on the highest level. The field in which the greatest successes were achieved is that belonging to exchange: money and price were studied in great depth and versatility. Almost non-existent, however, was the theoretical contribution to the subject of production, a field in which the English were making fundamental contributions at this time. The diversity of the economic fortunes of the two countries is sufficient to explain the different directions of research. But precisely because Italy understood the existing economic gap between itself and Great Britain and Holland, the nascent institutionalization of Political Economy was fostered more than elsewhere: from the dissemination of economic learning the people expect to be able to equal, one day, the wealth of the more developed countries.[9]

Value and price

All the prominent economists of the eighteenth century – Ferdinando Galiani (1728–87), Cesare Beccaria (1738–94), Pietro Verri (1728–97), Giammaria Ortes (1713–90) – shared the scientific paradigm present in Geminiano Montanari. Their analyses were, however, much more elaborate. Each of them connected price and the mechanism of pricing to what they considered to be the fundamental aim of economic activity: the satisfaction of wants. A decisive role was attributed to the significant consumer and above all to the wealthy, the significant consumers – the others live at subsistence level. Value, which has meaning only in relative terms, is explained by utility and scarcity, namely 'the relation between the existing quantity of a thing and the uses people have for it'.[10] The water-diamond paradox is resolved precisely in these terms. Giammaria Ortes, for example, discussing the value of a commodity, maintained that it is a function of demand and supply and may be represented in the form $v = \frac{r}{m}$, where v is the value, r the demand *(richiesta)* and m the quantity of the commodity *(massa)*. Water, although extremely useful, is 'incomparably greater in quantity than any other kind of commodity': its value is $\frac{r}{\infty}$, that is, 0. On the contrary, if the quantity of a particular commodity is very small or zero, when the demand is finite, $v = \frac{r}{0} = \infty$. Both r and m are expressed in rational terms, for which the relationship $\frac{2}{1}$ means that the demand is twice the supply while the point of balance in which the two variables are equal is represented by the formula $v = \frac{r}{m} = \frac{1}{1} = 1$.[11] A ratio of the two quantities different from one means a situation of imbalance or, if it exceeds certain limits, the lack of any economic meaning of one of the objects considered. The existence and the quantitative dimensions of such limits are shown by Beccaria. These extreme limits, both lower and upper, are respectively the cost of production – determined principally by the expense for the 'food' of the workers organized in the most efficient way – and the purchasing power and the need of the buyer. In the case of perfect competition between producers, the price will touch the lowest limits represented by the cost of production, in the case of a monopoly the only upper limit is represented by the capacity and the desire to buy, which the purchaser has. No sure *a prioi,* price is established, however, in the case of barter exchange.[12]

From this truth, Verri developed the argument. According to him the price depends on two factors, 'the apparent abundance' of a commodity and the need for it. The first corresponds approximately to the number of sellers and the second to the number of buyers. So, 'if the number of sellers increases, supply increases, other things being equal, and the price will continue to fall. If the number of buyers increases, demand increases, *ceteris paribus,* and price will rise proportionately.'[13] In this formulation we find expressed a hyperbolic demand law. Such a formulation will find an interesting application by the Friulian priest Gottardo Canciani (1729–92) who, in a fine example of comparative statics, will use it to demonstrate the existence of an under-employment equilibrium.

Given a constant-outlay demand for corn of the form $d = pq$, where p is the price, q the quantity and d a constant, and given a price of the national manufacturing variable in proportion to the change in the price of corn, *ceteris paribus*, a doubling of the quantity of corn produced – which is considered possible – will permit the purchase of the same quantity of national goods with a saving equal to half the figure previously spent. More generally, by increasing progressively the production of corn, the landowners will enjoy a return equal to $\frac{(b-c)\,a}{b}$, where c is the quantity of corn actually produced and equal to 1, b is the number of times c is increased, and a is the figure actually spent on the national manufacturing. Given the precision of the postulates, Canciani maintains that Friuli, by reinvesting the surplus, has the possibility of attaining a new long-run equilibrium which would be more advantageous for the landowners, for the national manufacturers, and for the foreign peoples with whom they have trading relations.[14]

Galiani, twenty years earlier, had already made use of the comparative statics method with reference to a situation in which it is possible obtain earnings – exceptional earnings in this case – and which thereafter reaches a long-run equilibrium. It is the well-known case of the Mohammedan country that suddenly embraces Christianity and thereupon develops a demand for wine: because of the small quantity available and the rising requests, its price increases. More and more wine is taken into the country until profit goes back to the 'just' level.[15]

Although they discerned the possibility of disequilibrium, the Italian authors considered that there is always a mechanism capable of restoring stability. Above all with regard to consumable goods, they think that the Supreme Hand, that is Natural Law, continuously sees to the sharing out of the resources to the population, and that, with an unchanging population and unchanging preferences (wants), prices will remain constant and proportional to *'fatica'* which means the socially necessary amount of labour.[16] It is a question of a scientifically unfounded conviction which simply reveals the existence of a true and proper faith in a harmonious natural order. Such a belief contrasts with the use of an analytic tool such as comparative statics, which was widely employed in the course of the entire century. It is the deepest and most embarrassing contradiction of eighteenth-century literature. Proceeding in the work of interpretation, we move continuously between contradictory scenarios: on the one side, the description of cycles of prosperity or misfortune, and, on the other, the idea of a general static economic balance, with the best allocative efficiency, in which the technological equivalence of the goods equals their psychological equivalence.

Money

In order to understand the theory of money it is necessary to bear in mind the type of monetary tools that were used. The means of payment were gold, silver and copper coins, and also certificates of deposit. The book-keeping and the price of goods were, however, expressed in terms of ideal money, a hypothetical unit of account. Ideal money suffered greatly from the variations in the purchasing power of copper coins. These last were a substantially fiduciary and forced currency, internally circulated, used for the purchase of goods of prime necessity, and important more for their name than for their weight. On the theoretical plane, ideal money and copper coins were considered almost equivalent and practically outside theoretical analysis. Even certificates of credit were not considered money. They were simply substitutes for gold and silver deposited. It was thought that the bankers did not create money but were intermediary lenders of what depositors temporarily did not need. In so doing, they speeded up trade and kept down the rate of interest.

With two important exceptions, namely Giovambattista Vasco (1733–96) and Ortes, money was considered to be gold or silver coins, a means of exchange for both home and international transactions.

The most interesting of the Italian monetarists was Ferdinando Galiani who, writing in 1751, had a significant influence on his successors. According to Galiani, gold and silver, because of their characteristics are 'naturally money'. Their value follows the principles of value theory (utility and rarity) because they are commodities before being used as money. Such circumstances prevent the purchasing power of money from exceeding precise upper and lower limits, namely the specie points. The exportation or importation of money, on the one hand, or the transformation of money, on the other hand, into metal, prevent exceeding such limits. The term to compare the purchasing power of a money with that of another is not its weight but rather the quantity of commodities it can buy. Such a quantity changes proportionally according to the variation in money supply and in the commodity market. The shifting from the values of equilibrium are the effect of extreme situations: famine and prosperity. In this connection the short period is distinguished from the long; the real from the monetary aspects. In the case of famine, in the short period, prices rise because 'the number of sellers decreases with respect to that of the buyers', hence 'prices increase and many people become impoverished.[17] Much of the money spent feeds a balance of payments deficit which empties the country of money and men. The long-run equilibrium, which will thereafter be re-established, will see very low prices regarding what will be a scarce demand for goods (on the agreement that the supply returns to near the original levels).[18]

With prosperity, the greater velocity of money produces an increase of 'prices and prices increase so much more because of the abundance of money'.[19] The long-run equilibrium will this time be re-established at high price levels when the quantity of money in circulation has reached dimensions such as to break the national checks and flow into neighbouring countries because of the 'force of the equilibrium which exists in everything and which is not eliminable'.[20]

Money outflows and high prices always occur at periods of either great prosperity or calamity, but the moments in which they occur, their real meaning, and the nature of the equilibrium which succeeds them are different. In both cases the exchange rate must vary so that the balance should be stable. If it does not change 'one state would absorb the money of the other'.[21]

But what happens when, in the case of persistent poverty, the state is forced to turn to a debasement of money in order to pay its own debts? Galiani's answer is that a debasement of money does not produce any change in things but only in names: nevertheless it is 'a profit that the prince and the state make from the slowness with which the multitude changes the connection of ideas about the prices of goods and money'.[22] If the adjustment between prices and monies is immediate, the only consequence would be an increase in the prices. However, since there is always an interval between the measures and their final effects, some gain in the meantime and some lose. Those who certainly gain are the debtors, who in fact obtain a discount on their debts. Among the debtors we can also count the employers, from the most modest craftsmen to the prince, who will pay the workers and the civil servant a lower real wage. On the other hand, all creditors are hurt, in particular moneylenders and landowners, whose income is reduced. Among the creditors, however, there is also the prince whose tax revenue falls. He, therefore, will have to do his accounts well and turn to a debasement only as a last resort. The only ones to gain a worthwhile advantage from the devaluation will be 'the hard-working farmer, the craftsman, the sailor and the merchant . . . since they are accustomed to hiring' and who will have to pay lighter heavy taxes. It is possible, therefore, that before the adjustment happens, the entire economy recovers.[23]

Also in the case of money, as in the case of value and price, it is assumed that a stability of equilibrium and static expectations exist. Moreover, the same contradiction between the use of comparative statics and the hypothesis of stability can be seen. Also noteworthy is the exclusive attention reserved for precious metals which are goods more than money. The monetary flows can therefore be considered as an excellent and passive reflex of the real sector of the economy. The only real effect which money can produce derive in the last instance from the imperfection of man. This contradicts another assumption which considers the individual as a good calculator of pleasure and pains, and, as such, well acquainted with surrounding reality.

The institutionalization and spread of political economy
In the course of the eighteenth century, by a process begun in Piedmont in 1715 and culminating in the period between 1750 and 1780, higher education was reformed fundamentally throughout Italy. The motivation for the reforms were: (1) the need to set up a high state bureaucracy; (2) the growing range and complexity of the new economic and social problems which needed to be kept under control; and (3) the increasing specialization of intellectual activity. The principal aims of the reformers were checking the seriousness of the studies, of centralizing in the hands of the state the feudal privileges of the religious bodies and professional colleges, and of spreading adequate knowledge and values for the economic and cultural progress of the citizens, within the framework of an enlightened despotism. The natural allies of the State were, at this time, the emerging speculating classes, the new professionals, and the enlightened nobility. The most important changes for

the Italian universities concerned the Arts Faculty. Newly erected, it was normally subdivided into two two-year periods: the first, during which natural philosophy was taught, was compulsory for anyone aspiring to attend university; the second was devoted to training technicians.

The first Italian chairs of Political Economy were found only within the Arts Faculties, namely technical schools destined for the new professionals whom the state was beginning to need in large numbers. The first Professors of Economics were Genovesi (Naples, 1754), Beccaria (Milan, 1769), Paradisi (Modena, 1772) and Sergio (Palermo, 1779). The most important of these were Genovesi and Beccaria, the former an exponent of the Neapolitan school, the latter of the Milanese. Of the two, Genovesi played a predominant role. His chair was founded on the wishes of a wealthy patron, Bartolomeo Intieri, who donated a large amount of capital to the state in order to finance the teaching. Thanks to this independent funding, the chair no longer risked being axed. The case was different in Northern Italy where teaching was paid for by the government and would be suspended and reopened according to political whims. Certainly the economic learning of Genovesi was initially stricter. He was attached to the same school as Ferdinando Galiani, namely to the discussion group of two Tuscans who had been transferred to Naples: Bartolomeo Intieri and Alessandro Rinuccini. Cultured, wealthy, very able businessmen, experts in international trade, moved by a great sense of civic pride and friends of some of the most important men of the Kingdom of Naples, such as the Prime Minister Tanucci and the Minister for Public Education Celestino Galiani, the uncle of Ferdinando. They were masters, in theory and in practice, of the problems of both economics and politics, and from their influential positions considered that the spread of science and of economic theory favoured the material and civil progress of the country.

In accordance with the wishes of the reforming authorities, the teaching should have a more technical and pragmatic orientation than theoretical. The great themes faced by the first teachers were subdivided according to the principal lines of the Genovesian example, into Political bodies, Population, Agriculture, Manufacturing, Business and Finance. The student intake was quite large. The students attending the courses at Beccaria's home numbered over one hundred in two years, coming from a broad spectrum of social classes: ecclesiastical, aristocratic and businessmen. The lectures were open to the public and given in the vernacular and not in Latin as in the other university courses.

The methodology and vision of the world which was spread from the chairs is the one we already know well: the law of self-interest regulating economic phenomena is the exact counterpart of the law of gravity; goods and money behave like fluids; economic laws like natural laws can never be violated: neither arbitrary acts nor law nor the prince can bend these principles and their effects, which is 'the constant and periodic rules set by the eternal order of the supreme providence of a regulating God'.[24]

Conclusion

The events which close the history of Italian economic thought in the eighteenth century are still clouded in mystery. One by one the protagonists of the three decades following 1750 prematurely cut short their teaching. The university chairs, with the exception of Naples, were quickly abolished or assigned to other disciplines. The generation of Galiani, Verri, Beccaria and Ortes having passed away, the achievements of the illuminist writers remained unequalled until the times of Pareto and Pantaleoni. The ancient tradition of research hingeing on problems of exchange was abandoned for almost a century in favour of themes pertaining to economic progress and to institutional problems. English economists and German language writers respectively were more advanced in these two fields.

Several circumstances might shed some light on the sharp change of course Political Economy took between the 1700s and the 1800s. First, the economists of the 1700s, pushing their analyses based on a atomistic conception of society to their logical conclusions, concluded that all people should be accorded equal dignity and asked, as a consequence, for a greater retributive, fiscal and distributive equity. Such an analysis was not welcomed by the ruling classes, who began to look at the new economic ideas with growing suspicion.[25] In the face of the early violence of the French Revolution, it was the very same intellectuals who moderated their stance and reconsidered favouring the traditional orders of power.[26] Finally, after 1796 and before 1861, a large part of Italian territory came under the control of two regimes – the French, and then, during the *Restaurazione*, the Austrian. In both cases, the political authorities were hostile to pure theory and obliged the economists to concern themselves mainly with matters of juridical and administrative nature.[27] After 1814 there was also strong hostility to illuminist theories and in particular to 'The capital errors then greatly followed of Elvezio, Rousseau, Diderot, Stewart and some of our own Italian writers, on the indefeasible rights of the individual with respect to the social order and on the impulse for progress in manufacture and trade.'[28]

Other more complex events should not be neglected. For example, there emerged the increasing group of bourgeois thinkers who were more attracted to the problems of national economic development; the decline of the aristocratic and ecclesiastical intelligentsia, who was inclined, by their very nature, to concern themselves with the problems of the commutative optimum and of that of the best allocation of resources; the actual needs of the Italian states to adjust their laws and their institutions according to the new rules of the European economic game.

While in these fields of inquiry we do not yet possess enough data, we cannot doubt the importance of the role played by the concerns of political and ideological nature in boycotting the progress of economic theories based on utilitarian and individualistic postulates.

Notes

1. J.A. Schumpeter (1954), *History of Economic Analysis,* London: Allen and Unwin, pp.176–7.
2. B. Davanzati (1588), 'Lezione delle monete', in *Scrittori classici italiani di economia politica,* ed. P. Custodi, P.te Antica: tomi 7, *P.te Moderna:* tomi 43 (Milano, Destefanis, 1803–5) (but *P.M.* XLII, Suppl. and *P.M.* XLIII, Indici: Imperiale Regia Stamperia, Milano, 1816). Rist. anast.: ed. O. Nuccio, (Bizzari, Roma, 1965–69), (hereafter *SCIEP*), P.A., T.II, p. 20 and *passim*; Idem (1582), 'Notizia de' cambi' in *SCIEP*, P.A., T.II.
3. G. Galilei (1629), 'Dialogo sopra i due massimi sistemi del mondo' (Einaudi, Torino, 1982), p. 74; H.S. Gordon 'Water-diamond Paradox' (1975), in *History of Economic Thought Newsletter*, n. 14, p. 19; S. Maital and L. Peach, 'Galileo and the Paradox of Value' (1973), in *History of Economic Thought Newsletter*, n. 11, p. 20.
4. G. Montanari (1680), 'Della moneta. Trattato mercantile' in *SCIEP*, P.A., T.III, pp. 65, 85–93, 152–3, 231, 246; Idem, 'Breve trattato del valore delle monete in tutti gli Stati' (1687) in *SCIEP*, P.A., T.III; F. Cusin (1940), 'Geminiano Montanari e la teoria del valore' in Studi Urbinati, Serie B, pp. III–38.
5. G. Ceva (1711), 'De Re Numaria' (Pazzoni, Mantova), pp. 1–2.
6. Ibid., pp. 3–10; M. Bianchini (1982), 'Alle origini della scienza economica' (Studium, Parma).
7. L.A. Muratori (1749), 'Della pubblica felicità' (Lucca); F. Venturi, 'Settecento riformatore', Tomo I (Einaudi, Torino, 1969), pp. 161–86.
8. V. Polignano (1982), 'L'etica utilitaristica di Pietro Verri', in *Gli italiani e Bentham*, ed. R. Faucci (F. Angeli, Milano), vol. I, pp. 55–62; A. Agnati (1982), 'Gli economisti italiani dall'eudaimonismo normativo de mezzo Settecento all'eudaimonismo compensatore contemporaneo', *Rivista Italiana di Scienze Economiche e Commerciali*, n. 29, pp. 252–60.
9. F. Venturi (1959), 'Alle origini dell'illuminismo napoletano: dal carteggio di Bartolomeo Intieri', *Rivista Storica Italiana*, n. 2, pp. 416–56, pp. 432, 488.
10. F. Galiani (1751), 'Della moneta', in *SCIEP*, P.M., T.III, p.72.
11. G. Ortes (1774), 'Dell'economia nazionale', in *SCIEP*, P.M., T.XXII, pp. 45–9.
12. C. Beccaria (1771), 'Elementi di Economia Pubblica', in *SCIEP*, P.M., T.XI, pp. 344–56; F. Galiani, 'Della moneta', T.III, p. 85.
13. P. Verri (1771), 'Meditazioni sulla Economia Pubblica', in *SCIEP*, P.M., T.XV, p. 47.
14. G. Canciani (1772), 'Memoria . . .' (Gallici, Udine, 1773), pp. 56–7.
15. F. Galiani, 'Della moneta', T.III, pp. 90–1.

16. G. Ortes, 'Dell'economia . . .', T.XXII, pp. 27, 91; C. Beccaria, 'Elementi . . .', T. XI, p. 353; F. Galiani, 'Della moneta', T.III, pp. 74–5, 229.
17. F. Cesarano (1976), 'Monetary Theory in Ferdinando Galiani's Della moneta', *History of Political Economy*, n. 3, pp. 380–99; F. Galiani, 'Della moneta', T.III, 179–80.
18. Ibid., T.III, pp. 179–80; T.IV, p. 191.
19. Ibid., T.III, pp. 180–1.
20. Ibid., T.IV, p. 192.
21. Ibid., T.IV, p. 85.
22. Ibid., T.IV, pp. 68–9.
23. Ibid., T.IV, p. 109.
24. C. Beccaria, 'Elementi . . .', T.XI, p. 90.
25. 'Carteggio di P. e A. Verri dal 1766 al 1797', ed. F. Novati, E. Greppi, A. Giulini (Società Storica Lombarda, Milano, 1910–42), 12 vols, vol. III, pp. 302–3.
26. G.B. Vasco (1793), 'Dedica al Sermone recitato avanti, i pari ecclesiastici e laici nella chiesa abaziale di S. Pietro in Vestminster, mercoledì 30 gennajo 1793, giorno anniversario del martirio del Re Carlo I, da Samuel, vescovo di S. David', (Milano, Galeazzi), pp. 3–5; G. Marocco, 'Giambattista Vasco' (Fondazione L. Einaudi, Torino, 1978), pp. 146–7.
27. M. Bianchini, 'Una difficile gestazione: il contrastato inserimento dell'economia politica nelle università dell'Italia nord-orientale (1769–1866). Note per un'analisi comparativa', in *Le cattedre di economia politica in Italia. La diffusione di una disciplina 'sospetta'* (1750–1900), ed. M. Augello, M. Bianchini, G. Gioli, P. Roggi (F. Angeli, Milano, 1988), pp. 17–62, 38–62.
28. Ibid., p. 62.

References

Agnati, A. (1982), 'Gli economisti italiani dall'eudaimonismo normativo di mezzo Settecento all'eudaimonismo compensatore contemporaneo', *Rivista Italiana di scienze economiche e commerciali*, no. 29, 252–60.

Beccaria, C. (1771), *Elementi di Economia Pubblica*, in P. Custodi (ed.) (1803–16), *Scrittori classici italiani di Economia Politica*, 52 vol., Milano, Destefanis and Imperiale Regia Stamperia, (hereafter SCIEP), Parte Moderna, Tomo XI.

Bianchini, M. (1982), *Alle origini della scienza economica*, Studium, Parma.

Bianchini, M. (1988), 'Una difficile gestazione: il contrastato inserimento dell'economia politica nelle università dell'Italia nord-orientale (1769–1866). Note per un'analisi comparativa', in M. Augello, M. Bianchini, G. Gioli, P. Roggi (eds) *Le cattedre di economia politica in Italia. La diffusione di una disciplina 'sospetta'*, F. Angeli, Milano.

Canciani, G. (1773), *Memoria di Gottardo Canciani udinese che ha riportato il premio della Società d'agricoltura di Udine, rispondendo al problema proposto l'Anno MDCCLXX*, Gallici, Udine.

Cesarano, F. (1976), 'Monetary theory in Ferdinando Galiani's *Della moneta*', *History of Political Economy*, no 3, 380–99.

Ceva, G. (1711), *De re numaria quoad fieri potuit geometrice tractata*, Pazzoni, Mantova.

Cusin, F. (1940), 'Geminiano Montanari e la teoria del valore', *Studi Urbinati*, Serie B: III–38.

Davanzati, B. (1582), *Notizia de' cambi*, in P. Custodi (ed.), *SCIEP*, Parte Antica, Tomo II.

Davanzati, B. (1588), *Lezione delle monete*, in P. Custodi (ed.), *SCIEP*, Parte Antica, Tomo II.

Galiani, F. (1751), *Della moneta*, in P. Custodi (ed.), *SCIEP*, Parte Moderna, Tomo III and Tomo IV.

Galilei, G. (1629), *Dialogo sopra i due massimi sistemi del mondo*, Einaudi, Torino, 1982.

Giulini, A., Greppi, E., and Novati, F. (eds), *Carteggio di P. e A. Verri dal 1766 al 1797*, 12 vol., Società Storica Lombarda, Milano, 1910–42; vol. III.

Gordon, H.S. (1975), 'Water-diamond paradox', *History of Economic Thought Newsletter*, no 14: 19.
Maital, S. and Peach, L. (1973), 'Galileo and the paradox of value', *History of Economic Thought Newsletter*, no 11, 20.
Marocco, G. (1978), *Giambattista Vasco*, Fondazione L. Einaudi, Torino.
Montanari, G. (1680), *Della moneta. Trattato mercantile*, in P. Custodi (ed.), *SCIEP*, Parte Antica, Tomo III.
Montanari, G. (1687), *Breve trattato del valore delle monete in tutti gli Stati*, in P. Custodi (ed.), *SCIEP*, Parte Antica, Tomo III.
Muratori, L.A. (1749), *Della pubblica felicità*, Lucca (Venezia).
Ortes, G. (1774), *Dell'economia nazionale*, in P. Custodi (ed.), *SCIEP*, Parte Moderna, Tomo XXII.
Polignano, V. (1982), *L'etica utilitaristica di Pietro Verri*, in Faucci, R. (ed.) *Gli italiani e Bentham*, F. Angeli, Milano, vol. I.
Schumpeter, J.A. (1967), *History of Economic Analysis*, 6th edn, Allen and Unwin, London.
Vasco, G.B. (1793), *Dedica*, in *Sermone recitato . . . nella chiesa abaziale di S. Pietro in Vestminster, mercoledì 30 gennajo 1793 . . . da Samuel, vescovo di S. David*, Galeazzi, Milano.
Venturi, F. (1959), 'Alle origini dell'illuminismo napoletano: dal carteggio di Bartolomeo Intieri', *Rivista Storica Italiana*, no 2, 416–56.
Venturi, F. (1969), *Settecento riformatore. Da Muratori a Beccaria*, Einaudi, Torino.
Verri, P. (1771), *Meditazioni sulla Economia Pubblica*, in Custodi, P. (ed.), *SCIEP*, Parte Moderna, Tomo XV.

PART II

NINETEENTH-CENTURY CLASSICAL TOPICS

5 Time concepts in the history of economic thought: the case of the stationary state

Royall Brandis

This paper explores the idea of the stationary state – an idea that appeared almost routinely in the work of economists during much of the nineteenth century. We shall note the development of the idea as well as its disappearance from the literature. This story provides a base for speculation about the way in which the economists' concept of time changed as the intellectual environment and the discipline of economics changed through the nineteenth century. Since the term 'stationary state' has been given a variety of meanings, let me make it clear that I refer to the notion of an economy whose end-point of development is one in which capital accumulation has ceased because the profit rate has fallen so low that there is no further incentive to accumulate capital. Generally, I am concerned with this idea as a predictive model, that is, one that not only had analytical uses but also was believed to have the power to predict the real-world future of an economy.

We begin with two questions: Why did leading nineteenth-century English economists like David Ricardo and John Stuart Mill conceive of the stationary state as the logical end of economic development? And why did this notion quietly disappear in the last quarter of the century with economists like Jevons and Marshall? The nineteenth-century classicals were not echoing their eighteenth-century predecessors. Adam Smith's view of the future, as we shall see, was quite ambiguous – not the only case of ambiguity in the *Wealth of Nations*. Others like David Hume or Sir James Steuart emphasized a quite different view, one of indefinite growth and change. The Malthus of the first (1798) edition of the *Essay on Population* stressed an oscillating rather than a stationary state for any human society. Yet, in the later *Principles of Political Economy* (1820) Malthus is almost casual about accepting the notion of the stationary state.[1]

The Physiocrats (Marshall cited Turgot particularly) were sensitive to the same population problem Malthus gained fame for discussing. The

Tableau Economique, although commonly taken to be a model of an already stationary economy, contains an injunction 'That less attention [should be] paid to increasing the population than to increasing the revenue . . .'[2] in order to reduce the pressure on subsistence. This suggests that the Physiocrats viewed the *Tableau* more as an attempt at static, but sequential, analysis than as a theoretical model of the real-world economy towards which France (or any other economy) would inevitably progress.

Adam Smith and the stationary state

Smith's ambiguity as to the stationary state no doubt stems in part from his tendency in other matters (most notably in his theories of value) to advance more than one treatment of a topic without coming down firmly on any one approach as the correct one. But it is also likely that in the case of the stationary state, the ambiguity results from Smith's position on the watershed between two quite different concepts of time – that of the eighteenth century and that to become dominant in the nineteenth century.

If we read Chapter IX of Book I of *The Wealth of Nations* 'On the Profits of Stock' we are told:

> In a country which had acquired that full complement of riches which the nature of its soil and climate, and its situation with respect to other countries, allowed it to acquire; which could, therefore, advance no further, and which was not going backwards, both the wages of labour and the profits of stock would be very low. In a country fully peopled in proportion to what either its territory could maintain or its stock employ, the competition for employment would necessarily be so great as to reduce the wages of labour to what was barely sufficient to keep up the number of labourers, and, the country being already fully peopled, that number could never be augmented. In a country fully stocked in proportion to all the business it had to transact, as great a quantity of stock would be employed in every particular branch as the nature and extent of the trade would admit. The competition, therefore, would everywhere be as great, and consequently the ordinary profit as low as possible.[3]

This would seem to be as clear a statement of the eventual arrival of the stationary state as one would want. Yet, if we turn to Chapter III of Book II, 'Of the Accumulation of Capital, or of Productive and Unproductive Labour', we find a quite different story. Here, Smith seems to have no notion of a stationary state as the conclusion of a period of growth. States may stagnate at any level of development; or they may decline as well as grow. There appears to be no *terminal* state to which an economy moves or even tends.[4]

Smith's discussion of the effect on the rate of interest of an increase in the quantity of stock (it lowers the rate) gives no hint of a rate being reached which discourages any further accumulation. Indeed, the effect of the lowering of the rate of profit on the use of capital as the stock of capital increases is merely to lower the rate of interest correspondingly. Furthermore, the reasons for the fall in the rate of profit are increased competition in the use of capital (with more of it) and a rise in wages (as capitalists bid in a tight labour market). This is not a path to a stationary state.

Both the history of the real world and the analytical model seem now to Smith to rule out the stationary state. After explaining how a growing capital stock is employed in both domestic and foreign markets in supplying the consumption needs of the population and 'supporting the productive labour', Smith says: 'When the capital stock of any country is increased to such a degree, that it cannot be all employed in supplying the consumption, and supporting the productive labour of that particular country, the surplus part of it naturally disgorges itself into the carrying trade, and is employed in performing the same office to other countries.'[5]

While the extent of the home trade and the foreign trade are limited, the 'possible extent . . . [of the carrying trade] is in a manner infinite in comparison of that of the other two, and is capable of absorbing the greatest capitals.'[6] The implication is clear. The likelihood of a modern (i.e. eighteenth-century) nation reaching the maximum possible capital accumulation is too remote to be considered seriously.

What about the real world? 'The course of human prosperity, indeed, seems scarce ever to have been of so long continuance as to enable any great country to acquire capital sufficient for all those three purposes [agriculture, manufacture, trade]; unless, perhaps, we give credit to the wonderful accounts of the wealth and cultivation of China, . . . Egypt, and Indostan.'[7] Smith is dubious that any of the three ever had a sufficient stock of capital to exploit fully all three of the uses to which he believes capital can be put.

Smith's ambiguity can lead respected scholars to quite different conclusions about his position on the stationary state. Thus, Hla Myint finds that Smith had pictured the economy as working under increasing returns – 'as being capable of almost unlimited expansion either by free trade or capital accumulation.'[8]

Joseph Spengler, on the other hand, commented that, 'Smith apparently believed that if geographic, technological, and other forms of progress came to an end, wages and profits would fall to a very low level and capital formation and population growth would practically come to a standstill.'[9]

David Ricardo
When David Ricardo came to write his *Principles of Political Economy* (*c*. 1815), all the ambiguity we found in Smith regarding the stationary state had disappeared. It is inevitable; furthermore, while its exact arrival date is not predicted, there is a clear implication that the date is not far off. This is emphasized by the argument that the real-world stationary state will be reached *before* the theoretical one. Thus Ricardo writes:

> The natural tendency of profits then is to fall; for, in the progress of society and wealth, the additional quantity of food required is obtained by the sacrifice of more and more labour. This tendency, this gravitation as it were of profits, is happily checked at repeated intervals by the improvements in machinery connected with the production of necessaries, as well as by discoveries in the science of agriculture . . . . The rise in the price of necessaries and in the wages of labour is, however, limited; . . . there must be an end of accumulation; for no capital can then yield any profit whatever, and no additional labour can be demanded, and consequently population will have reached its highest point.[10]

While this may be considered in some sense the *theoretical* conditions for the onset of the stationary state, Ricardo believes the *practical* conditions leading to this event would come earlier. For he adds, 'Long, indeed, before this period, the very low rate of profits will have arrested all accumulation, and almost the whole produce of the country, after paying the labourers, will be the property of the owners of land and the receivers of tithes and taxes.'[11]

But when was this terminal moment in the growth of the nation to occur? While the *principle* was a universal one, its application would vary from country to country: 'The effects then of accumulation will be different in different countries, and will depend chiefly on the fertility of the land.'[12] The less fertile the land, the earlier the nation arrived at the stationary state. What specifically was the case for Britain? Ricardo gives us no clue in the *Principles*. If the whole theoretical framework is intended to support certain governmental economic policies – and that is one way in which to read the *Principles* – then time would be a crucial element. The policy implications of the theoretical analysis in such areas as international trade, taxes and bounties had to do in one way or another with staving off the onset of the stationary state. If the stationary state were only five years away, that was one thing; if it were 500 years away that was something quite different. Certainly the latter case would not need a call for action any time soon on the part of King and Parliament.

John Stuart Mill

With Mill, we reach the apogee of the classicals' fascination with the stationary state. There is no uncertainty with Mill about the theoretical world which leads to that conclusion. Capital *will* accumulate, the profit rates *will* fall, and the stationary state *will* ensue. Furthermore, there is the 'fundamental proposition' that

> When a country has long possessed a large production, and a large net income to make savings from, and when, therefore, the means have long existed of making a great annual addition to capital (the country not having, like America, a large reserve of fertile land still unused); it is one of the characteristics of such a country, that the rate of profit is habitually within, as it were, a hand's breadth of the minimum, and the country therefore on the very verge of the stationary state. By this I do not mean that this state is likely, in any of the great countries of Europe, to be soon actually reached, or that capital does not still yield a profit considerable greater than what is barely sufficient to induce the people of those countries to save and accumulate. My meaning is, that it would require but a short time to reduce profits to the minimum, if capital continued to increase at its present rate, and no circumstances having a tendency to raise the rate of profit occurred in the meantime. The expansion of capital would soon reach its ultimate boundary, if the boundary itself did not continually open and leave more space.[13]

However, while in a country like England of the nineteenth century the stationary state could be reached 'speedily', there are 'counteracting circumstances' which currently keep postponing its arrival. They all – as the theoretical model would dictate – in one way or another prevent profits from reaching the minimum. The four Mill lists are not, upon close examination, very encouraging. One – 'commercial revulsions' in which the capital stock of the nation is reduced – is hardly likely to be cheered. Two others – 'the importation of cheap necessaries and instruments' as well as 'the emigration of capital' – are not universally available. In order to import someone else must export. Trade always requires a trading partner. So, as a generally available and attractive counteracting force to the decline of profits, we are left with 'improvements is production' as our only way out. But there is no guarantee these will continue to be made.[14]

At this point in his exposition Mill makes a curious, but understandable, shift in his argument. The social reformer and Victorian optimist finds that the stationary state as he now conceives it holds much promise: 'I am inclined to believe that it would be, on the whole, a very considerable improvement in our present condition.'[15] If only human beings will prudently control the size of their population, then a few social reforms involving income distribution – especially a strict limit on inheritance – should lead to 'a well-paid and affluent body of labourers;

no enormous fortunes, except what were earned and accumulated during a single lifetime; [and many more persons] with sufficient leisure . . . to cultivate freely the graces of life . . . '[16] This utopian society 'is not only perfectly compatible with the stationary state, but, it would seem, more naturally allied with that state than with any other.[17]

Finally, Mill is so taken with the reform prospects of the stationary state as well as with the ambience of a society no longer driven to increase its population and its capital that he urges that the stationary state be introduced 'long before necessity compels them to it'.[18] So, what had been the inevitable end of a relatively brief period of economic development and growth now becomes a socially chosen cessation of economic growth in order to enjoy 'all the advantages both of social cooperation and of social intercourse'.[19] While Mill does not explain *how* a stable population leads to the end of capital accumulation presumably the model he is using is one involving the wages-fund notion. We shall not pursue here what might be an interesting question, namely, what *would* be the result in the classical model of an end to population growth before a society reached its Malthusian limit?

Stanley Jevons

Although Jevons is certainly a revolutionary in the history of economics, he was concerned to show that his theoretical approach did not alter one important conclusion of classical economics – the coming of the stationary state. As Jevons said,

> It is one of the favourite doctrines of economists since the time of Adam Smith, that as society progresses and capital accumulates, the rate of profit, or more strictly speaking, the rate of interest, tends to fall. The rate will always ultimately sink, so low, they think, that the inducements to further accumulation will cease. This doctrine is in striking agreement with the result of the somewhat abstract analytical investigation [by Jevons] given above.[20]

Yet, Jevons reaches this conclusion without involving the Malthusian population dilemma. As he said with regard not only to his stationary state conclusion, but also with regard to his entire theoretical schema, 'The doctrine of population has been conspicuously absent, not because I doubt in the least its truth and vast importance, but because it forms no part of the direct problem of Economics.'[21]

As Schumpeter put it, 'the marginal utility system no longer depended upon a particular hypothesis on birth or death rates . . .'[22] *How* Jevons derived a stationary state for any given population size (not necessarily the Malthusian limit) is an interesting process, but not one we are here concerned with. Rather, our concern is to see that Jevons was, in this respect, a transitional, not a revolutionary, figure. However different his theoretical approach was from the classical one, he believed he could derive the classical stationary state from it.

Alfred Marshall

We so often have come to expect Marshall to provide a bridge between the classical and neo-classical schools that we are a little surprised to find that, in the *Principles*, he suggests no dynamic that would lead to a stationary state in either theoretical model or real world. Even in his discussion of population questions, we are given only the not surprising conclusion that an economy can support a certain (maximum) size population at any particular moment in time and that changes in the ability to support its population will lead in time to a corresponding change in the size of the population.

When Marshall said, in the preface to the first edition of the *Principles*, that it was 'the element of time, which is the centre of the chief difficulty of almost every economic problem . . .'[23] he was not so much giving us a motto over an entrance gate as an epitaph. For Marshall's own well-known treatment of time – his supply-defined timekeepers of 'short periods', 'long periods' and 'very long periods' – were not only independent of clock or calendar, but were also unrelated to the demand side of the market. How or why demand would accommodate itself to the time-scale set by supply was a question never raised by Marshall or his successors. Indeed, almost a century has passed, and it is doubtful that value theory or microeconomics generally has gone beyond Marshall in integrating the role of time into the theoretical analysis.

Marshall's other uses of time – like his three-generation length to the life of a business firm or the competition of trees in a forest – are more impressionistic metaphors than analytical tools. His (very slight) use of the stationary state marks a clear end to its significance in economic analysis. For Marshall, the stationary state is a 'fiction' that is a conveniently simple model with which to begin analysis. He is not concerned with how the stationary state would come about, and he clearly does not relate it to the real world. The stationary state which was so very real and not too far away in real time to John Stuart Mill was an abstract concept of limited usefulness to Marshall[24] just a half-century later. What had been the important result of a well-defined process through real time to many economists of the first century of classical economics was merely an abstract model of limited usefulness to Marshall.

Gerald Shove's conclusion regarding Marshall is a fitting one with which to close this discussion of him. According to Shove, Marshall's work was 'profoundly affected' by developments in biology in the nineteenth century. This led to 'explicit recognition that economic doctrines must to a great extent be relative to time and place.[25] 'In spite of the care lavished upon them, the long-period supply and demand curves were cast for a minor role only. . . . They cannot be used to forecast accurately and for any considerable distance into the future the direction in which outputs and values are likely to move, still less the position at which they may be expected to arrive.'[26]

The dilemma of time
At the opening of the eighteenth century there must have been few in the western world who did not accept a very simple view of that world and of time. The world had been created at a particular moment in the recent past (Archbishop Usher in the previous century had fixed the date as 4004 BC) and would be – so far at least as man was concerned – extinguished at a particular moment in the not too distant future. But when the nineteenth century opened, important changes in this view were underway. Geological investigations and fossil finds were throwing serious doubt on the generally accepted beginnings of time and the world. More and more it was becoming clear that the origin of man on earth – much less the origin of the earth itself – could not be dated so precisely and recently as 4004 BC. Both events seemed to be receding further into the mists of the past and were becoming significantly distanced in time from each other. The First Day and the Sixth Day were drawing further and further apart and were less and less connected to each other.

What the eighteenth century did to the time-scale of the past, the nineteenth century seemed destined to do to the time-scale of the future. It was not just that millenarianism was no longer a very respectable religious position. Evolution was in the air; both Erasmus Darwin and Lamarck were writing on it as the eighteenth century ended and the nineteenth began. Charles Darwin was to claim that his own version of evolution (which, of course, was to become the accepted one) was in his thought twenty years before the publication in 1859 of *The Origin of Species*. Closer to our discipline are Herbert Spencer and Stanley Jevons, both of whom had clearly accepted evolutionism well before the publication of Charles Darwin's seminal work.

Now, there are two lines of thought about the future which may be suggested by thoughts of an evolutionary process. One – and this was probably dominant in the nineteenth century – is the notion of evolution towards a predestined end. The other is the notion of a process of infinite change. The strong theological bent of much nineteenth-century scientific speculation in biology made the first notion a very agreeable one to many intellectuals. Indeed, it was comforting to view mankind as the ultimate product of the evolutionary process – truly the crowning link in the Great Chain of Being. Furthermore, one could hold such a view whether he thought it was a demonstration of how the Almighty accomplished His ends or whether he thought it a purely natural, deterministic process like the Newtonian motions of the planets.

For the social scientists, the obvious imperfections of human society suggested that the social evolutionary process still had a way to go, but a final, perfected set of social arrangements could be taken to be inevitable. In such a grand vision of the future, the economists' stationary state would comfortably find a place. True, a large segment of the population, the labouring class, would not be happily well off, but that was to be expected from the dismal science. The key matter for the more scientific minds was the completion of the historical process. It was the terminal condition of no further change, not the welfare of the worker, that was critical to this scientific investigation. After all, when had the working class *ever* been really well off? And had not any noticeable improvement in its condition always been of an evanescent nature?

The second possibility suggested by evolution is a condition of continual change going on forever. The logic of this argument is quite simple. If an evolving species is in an environment which contains other evolving organisms, then it can never become completely adapted to that environment because the organic environment itself is always changing. If, in addition, we add in the kinds of physical change which nineteenth-century geology was increasingly showing as having been underway for eons, the permanence of change is a conclusion easy to reach. Any species must, then, be either evolving in a successfully adaptive way or disappearing to make way for a new species.

However calmly biologists might choose between these two possible evolutionary paths as guides to the future of a species – even of *Homo sapiens* – for social scientists the choice was likely to be more disturbing. What were *their* options? I shall argue that they had three options, two of which I have, in effect, already discussed. One was a process of change that brought itself to an end when a stable (though not necessarily perfect) equilibrium was reached. This not only allowed the path to equilibrium to be predicted, but also led to a result which was agreeable to the desire to make social science akin to Newtonian physics. Once society reached its equilibrium state, it would be analogous in important analytical ways to the equilibrium believed to exist in the physicist's universe of Newtonian particles. For the economist, of course, the stationary state was the economy's counterpart of this universe. Marx's aberrant view came to the same thing in the end, but was more agreeable to his particular ideological viewpoint.

A second option – that of ceaseless change – seems never to have been a real competitor of the first option. The reasons why this was the case are probably two. First, if one imagines the possible future states of society as a tree on which each branch bifurcates, the two products of the bifurcation again dividing, and so on, the number of possibilities quickly becomes so large that any prediction about the future nature of human society comes to seem the wildest speculation – far removed from the constraints of scientific method. Furthermore, even explanation of the present society would be on shaky ground since that society would be one that resulted from following a particular path out of almost an infinitude of paths. For where we *are* would itself be far out in the bifurcating tree referred to earlier.

The third option would be to ignore time and concentrate one's efforts on a situation which, even if it had a past and would have a future, was unaffected by either. It was this option that was chosen in the last quarter of the nineteenth century, notably by Jevons, Menger and Walras as well as – in his usual more cautious manner – by Marshall. For marginal analysis (with or without a general equilibrium framework) had no clock nor calendar. It would be more than a half-century before the dynamics of time would again receive attention from economic theorists. But the focus now would be on the pathways of economic growth – on the trip, not the direction – and the stationary state remained buried in the brief history of the classical school. *Sic transit gloria mundi.*

Notes
1. For Malthus, see his *An Essay on the Principle of Population* [1798], Royal Economic Society reprint, London, 1926, Chapter II, and his *Principles of Political Economy* [1820], Augustus Kelley reprint of 2nd edition [1836], New York, 1974, pp. 271–80.
2. *Quesnay's Tableau Economique* [1758] edited and translated by Marguerite Kuczynski and Ronald L. Meek, London, 1972, p. 19.
3. Adam Smith, *An Inquiry into the Nature and Causes of the Wealth of Nations* [1776], Glasgow edition, Liberty Press reprint, Indianapolis, 1981, p. 111.
4. Ibid., pp. 330–49.
5. Ibid., p. 373.
6. Ibid., p. 374.
7. Ibid., p. 367.
8. Hla Myint, 'The Classical View of the Economic Problem', in Joseph J. Spengler and William R. Allen, *Essays in Economic Thought*, Chicago, 1960, p. 447.
9. Joseph J. Spengler, 'The Physiocrats and Say's Law of Markets', in Spengler and Allen, op. cit., p. 184.
10. David Ricardo, *On the Principles of Political Economy and Taxation* [1817]

Cambridge, 1951, p. 120.
11. Ibid., pp. 120–1.
12. Ibid., p. 126.
13. John Stuart Mill, *Principles of Political Economy* [1848], Toronto, 1965, p. 738.
14. Ibid., pp. 738–46.
15. Ibid., p. 754.
16. Ibid., p. 755.
17. Ibid.
18. Ibid., p. 756.
19. Ibid.
20. W. Stanley Jevons, *The Theory of Political Economy* [1871], New York, 1965, p. 254.
21. Ibid., p. 266.
22. Joseph A. Schumpeter, *History of Economic Analysis*, New York, 1954, p. 890.
23. Alfred Marshall, *Principles of Economics* [1890], London, 1961, p. vii.
24. Ibid., pp. 366–9.
25. G.F. Shove, 'The Place of Marshall's *Principles* in the Development of Economic Theory', in Spengler and Allen, op. cit., p. 723.
26. Ibid.

6 Productive and unproductive labour: Smith, Marx, and the Soviets

Fyodor I. Kushnirsky and William J. Stull

Recently there has been a resurgence of interest among economists in the theory of productive and unproductive labour. For the most part this is the result of the ongoing shift from manufacturing to services which is occurring throughout the world and causing many nations to rethink the foundations of their national income accounting systems. As pointed out by Studenski in his classic work *The Income of Nations* (1961, p. 11), there are two major systems of national income accounting in use today. The first, based on what he calls the 'comprehensive production concept', is used by all non-communist countries. It defines production to include both material and non-material output. The second, based on what he calls the 'restricted material concept', is used by the USSR and all other communist nations. It defines production to include only material goods. Both systems of accounting include certain outputs in measured national product and exclude others. Both thus distinguish, implicitly or explicitly, between productive and unproductive labour in the sense that labour which adds value to national product is productive and that which does not is unproductive. In this paper we investigate the intellectual origins of the national income accounting system used by the Soviet Union from the point of view of the distinction between productive and unproductive labour. This system is a legacy from the period of Stalinist forced industrialization during the 1930s and, as noted above, is based on the restricted material production concept. The main body of the paper is divided into four sections. In the first we examine Adam Smith's theory of productive and unproductive labour. In the second we consider Karl Marx's alternative theory. In the third we describe the Soviet theory as embodied in the USSR's system of national income accounting and compare it to its Smithian and Marxian predecessors. Finally, in the fourth we briefly speculate about the future of the Soviet accounting system.

Adam Smith

The distinction between productive and unproductive labour has a long history in economics. The mercantilists of the sixteenth and seventeenth centuries identified national wealth with money in the form of gold and silver. In countries such as England and France where these metals are not mined, they could only be acquired through foreign trade. The mercantilists, accordingly, regarded labour in the export sector as more productive than any other. The eighteenth-century Physiocrats, on the other hand, maintained that it was only labour in agriculture which deserved to be labelled productive. Labour in other sectors, while not necessarily useless, was in their view 'sterile' in the sense that it was not capable of producing value in excess of cost.

Adam Smith examines both the mercantilist and the physiocratic theories in *The Wealth of Nations*. The former he dismisses out of hand for reasons well known to all economists. The latter he treats more gently. He praises the Physiocrats for their 'great learning and ingenuity' (p. 627), but cannot accept their view that only agricultural labour is productive. Rather than reject the concept of productive labour, however, he instead expands it to encompass a broader class of workers and in so doing makes it a key element in his theory of investment and economic growth. Smith's decision to retain the distinction between the two types of labour had far-reaching consequences for the subsequent development of economic theory and policy. Smith's successors in the 'bourgeois' mainstream of the discipline struggled with the distinction for 150 years before ultimately rejecting it.[1] Marxist economists, on the other hand, embraced the distinction and eventually incorporated it into the national income accounting procedures of communist countries.

Useful labour

The opening sentence of Smith's Introduction provides a point of departure for the analysis of his theory of productive and unproductive labour:

> The annual labour of every nation is the fund which originally supplies it with all the necessaries and conveniences of life which it annually consumes, and which consist always either in the immediate produce of that labour, or in what is purchased with that labour from other nations. (p. lvii)

This statement is noteworthy on several accounts. First, it tells us that the focus of the volume is on the nation's annual flow of production (what Cannan calls 'income wealth') rather than on its stock of assets ('capital wealth').[2] Second, it suggests that labour might be classified as productive or unproductive in accordance with whether or not it helps to provide the 'necessaries and conveniences of life'. Further down on the same page Smith takes a step in the direction of such a classification by distinguishing between 'those who are employed in useful labour, and . . . those who are not so employed'. He then tells us that useful labourers are those who 'endeavour to provide the necessaries and conveniences of life' and hints at the possibility that productive labour and useful labour are the same thing (p. lviii).[3] Had he chosen to continue this line of argument by explicitly defining productive labour to be equivalent to useful labour, much controversy in the nineteenth century would have been avoided. In addition, he might have reached the conclusion that virtually all labour is productive since there is little human effort which is not directed towards producing either necessaries or conveniences. Instead, as we shall see below, he defines productive and unproductive labour in such a way that both are 'useful'.

Productive labour: The vendible commodity definition

Smith's formal theory of productive and unproductive labour appears in Chapter iii of Book II.[4] In this chapter he uses two somewhat different definitions of productive (and hence unproductive) labour. The first definition, and the one he is best known for, is given at the beginning of the chapter. Here labour is defined to be productive if it adds value to a physical good which is to be sold on a market. Smith refers to such a good as a 'vendible commodity'. This definition has a number of implications. First, in order for labour to be productive it must 'fix and realize itself' in some 'subject' which lasts for some time at least after that labour is past'. Its final product, therefore, must be a good not a service. Second, the good which it produces must be ultimately destined for market sale. In other words, the value which productive labour adds is, in Smithian terms, 'value in exchange' rather than 'value in use'. Although Smith does not mention it, this means that the unpaid labour of household members producing goods for their own consumption is unproductive. Third, value can be added to a vendible commodity either directly or indirectly. Therefore all persons who work for a firm producing or distributing such a commodity are productive regardless of their occupations. In addition, all persons who work for the firm's suppliers are also productive, even when what is supplied is a service not a good.

The archetypal productive worker for Smith is a 'manufacturer' – i.e. a factory or workhouse operative (p. 314). A manufacturer obviously adds value directly to the commodity produced by the firm for which he works. In addition, however, the owner of the firm is also classified as productive (p. 343). It follows, though Smith does not make this point explicitly, that all non-operative employees of manufacturing firms – including, for example, the 'principal clerk' whose labour consists of 'inspection and direction' (p. 49) – are productive. Note that both the owner and non-operative employees add value to the firm's output only indirectly since they are usually not in physical contact with it. Farmers and their 'labouring servants' are also productive workers (pp. 50, 344) and so presumably are mine and fishery operators and their employees, though these are not mentioned. Finally, retail and wholesale merchants are productive workers, as are the sailors and carriers hired by the latter (pp. 342–4). The logic of the definition requires that retail employees should also be counted as productive, but Smith tacitly assumes that all stores are single proprietorships. Those who work in the retail and wholesale sectors are classified as productive not because they physically transform commodities, but because they add value indirectly by moving them from one place to another.

The preceding indicates that capitalists in the extractive, manufacturing and trade sectors are considered by Smith to be productive workers under the vendible commodity definition. Overall, he sees the capitalist as someone who contributes valuable time and effort to the firm in addition to financial resources:

> The persons whose capitals are employed in [extraction, manufacturing, or trade] are themselves productive labourers. Their labour . . . fixes and realizes itself in the subject or vendible commodity upon which it is bestowed and generally adds to its price . . . (p. 343)

As long as such non-financial contributions occur in sufficient quantities alongside the financial ones, there is no problem classifying the individuals involved as productive. It should be noted, however, that elsewhere Smith observes that 'In many great works . . . the owner of the capital is discharged of almost all labour' (p. 49). Such individuals are outside the labour force altogether (along with landlords who 'reap where they never sowed') and therefore by definition they cannot be productive workers. The inconsistency between these two passages can perhaps be explained by the fact that absentee owners of large firms represented only a small portion of the capitalist class in 1776.

All labour which is not productive is necessarily unproductive (p. 315). An unproductive worker under the present definition is therefore one whose labour does not add value to a vendible commodity. Unproductive workers are found either in the household sector or the service sector. In the former case the output may or may not be material, but it is never sold on a market. In the latter case the output may or may not be sold on a market, but if it is, it is never material. The service sector itself consists of two parts: private and public. Private services are sold to consumers; public services, except in certain cases, are provided free and are paid out of tax revenues.

The archetypal unproductive worker in the private portion of the service sector is the menial (i.e. personal) servant.

> The labour of the menial servant . . . does not fix or realize itself in any particular subject or vendible commodity. [It] . . . adds to the value of nothing. His services generally perish in the very instant of their performance and seldom leave any trace or value behind them for which an equal quantity of service could afterwards be procured. (p. 315)

A menial servant could be classified as unproductive either because his output is usually non-material or because it is not destined to be sold on a market. Smith emphasizes both elements in the preceding quotation. In spite of this, he was criticized by his bourgeois successors (but not by Marx) for ignoring the fact that menial servants often produce physical output equivalent to that produced by their counterparts working for business firms.[5] For example, a seamstress employed by a dress shop and one employed as a personal servant both produce garments. Smith does not address this criticism directly. Had he done so his rejoinder would probably have been, first, that most menial servants produce services rather than goods and, second, that the goods they do produce are almost always destined for immediate consumption rather than sale.

Professionals make up the second group of unproductive workers in the private sphere identified by Smith.

> In the same class [i.e. unproductive workers] must be ranked, some both of the gravest and most important, and some of the most frivolous professions: churchmen, lawyers, physicians, men of letters of all kinds; players, buffoons, musicians, opera-singers, opera-dancers, etc. . . . Like the declamation of the actor, the harangue of the orator, or the tune of the musician, the work of all of them perishes in the very instant of its production. (p. 315)

Unlike menial servants, these individuals produce output which is sold on the market. Smith classifies them as unproductive under the vendible commodity definition because their output is non-material. Throughout his discussion he implicitly assumes that all members of these occupations sell their services either directly to consumers or indirectly to them through for-profit or not-for-profit service firms. He never considers the possibility that a professional might sell his services to a firm which produces or distributes commodities. A lawyer, for example, might work for a manufacturing company either as an employee or as a member of a law firm retained by that company. Such a lawyer is in essentially the same position as the principal clerk mentioned above in that his labour indirectly adds value to a physical product destined for sale. He would thus be a productive worker according to Smith's vendible commodity definition.

The only remaining unproductive workers explicitly named by Smith are public servants. In Book V he argues that government has three principal duties: national defence, administration of justice, and erection and maintenance of certain public works and institutions. The latter include domestic transportation projects such as roads, bridges, canals and harbours; the coinage; forts and ambassadors in foreign countries when required by trade; and (more ambiguously) elementary and religious schools. Obviously the performance of each of these duties requires the hiring of public employees. In his discussion of unproductive labour, however, Smith mentions only the sovereign and those employees engaged in the provision of justice and national defence.

> The sovereign . . . with all the officers both of justice and war who serve under him, the whole army and navy, are unproductive workers. They are the servants of the public, and are maintained by a part of the annual produce of the industry of other people. Their service . . . produces nothing for which an equal quantity of service can afterwards be procured. The protection, security, and defence of the commonwealth, the effect of their labour this year, will not purchase its protection, security, and defence for the year to come. (p. 315)

Public employees engaged in the erection and maintenance of public works and institutions are not considered in this passage. This is a convenient oversight because some of these do in fact add value to vendible commodities. Consider, for example, a manufacturing firm that conducts its business through the mail and ships its product by wagon along a government toll road. The cost of both postage and tolls must be included in the price of the final product in order for the firm to make a profit. It follows from Smith's definition that the postal workers and toll collectors involved must be productive because their service adds value to something 'for which an equal quantity of service can afterwards be procured'. Such cases are the exception, however, so it is perhaps understandable that Smith ignores them and simply assumes that all public servants are unproductive.

Finally, it must be noted that Smith does not believe that the services rendered by unproductive labour as defined in this subsection are valueless to society. The labour of unproductive workers who sell their services to consumers 'has its value' and this value is 'regulated by the very same principles which regulate that of every other sort of labour'. Moreover, this labour 'deserves its reward'. Similarly, the labour of public servants is 'honourable', 'useful' and 'necessary'. Smith's vendible commodity definition thus clearly distinguishes between productive and useful labour.

Productive labour: The hired-for-profit definition

Smith's second definition of productive labour partially overlaps his first but is conceptually distinct. He never formally acknowledges its presence but uses it extensively in the chapter, particularly after the first few pages. According to this definition, workers who are hired to earn a profit for their employers are productive and all other workers are unproductive. In the former case the workers are maintained by 'capital' (i.e. the input expenditures of business firms); in the latter (except in the case of household production) they are maintained by the 'expense of revenue' (i.e. the consumption expenditures of households).

Many types of labour are classified the same way under both definitions. A manufacturer, for example, is a productive worker under both because he adds value to a vendible commodity and is hired for profit.

> . . . [T]he labour of a manufacturer adds, generally, to the value of the materials which he works upon, that of his own maintenance [i.e. his wages] and of his master's profit. . . . Though the manufacturer has his wages advanced to him by his master, he, in reality, costs him no expence, the value of those wages being generally restored, together with profit, in the improved value of the subject upon which his labour is bestowed. (p. 314)

Indeed, by extension, all workers who are productive under the vendible commodity definition must also be productive under the hired-for-profit definition because the whole purpose of vending a commodity is profit.

Menial and public servants, on the other hand, are unproductive under both definitions. In the case of menials Smith comments as follows:

> The labour of menial servants does not continue the existence of the fund which maintains and employs them. Their maintenance and employment is altogether at the expence of their masters and the work which they perform is not of a nature to repay that expence (p. 639). . . . A man grows rich by employing a multitude of manufacturers: he grows poor by maintaining a multitude of menial servants. (p. 314)

In the case of public servants he implicitly assumes that government produces services only for households and that all taxes are personal. He thus ignores the fact that much government output consists of intermediate goods. It follows from these assumptions that public servants are just like menial servants except that they are hired by the collectivity rather than by individuals. Both represent consumption expenditures and both are maintained by revenue rather than capital.

> Thus, not only the great landlord or the rich merchant, but even the common workman, if his wages are considerable, may maintain a play or puppet-show, and so contribute his share towards maintaining one set of unproductive workers; or he may pay some taxes, and thus maintain another set, more honourable and useful, indeed, but equally unproductive. (p. 317)

It is interesting to consider how an alternative system of taxation might have changed Smith's argument here. If he had considered a system in which the business sector paid significant taxes, he might have been led to the conclusion that at least some government workers were the indirect employees of private firms 'hired' through the public sector to enhance profits. Such a conclusion would have greatly complicated the enumeration of productive and unproductive workers but would have been more consistent with the numerous passages elsewhere in the volume which stress the dependence of the private sector on the public.

In spite of these similarities the two definitions are not identical. The hired-for-profit definition is the broader of the two because it, unlike the vendible commodity definition, includes the employees of private, for-profit firms producing services for consumers (as well as the employees of service firms selling to such firms). Such individuals do not add value to a vendible commodity, but they do add to the profit of their employer. Consider, for example, the last quotation in the previous paragraph. Therein Smith asserts that the patrons of a theatre or puppet show maintain only unproductive workers. If we ignore, as Smith does, the possibility that the play or puppet show uses material inputs purchased in the market (such as props or costumes), this assertion is unambiguously true under the vendible commodity definition.[6] Under the hired-for-profit definition, however, the issue is more complicated. Here it is necessary to distinguish between plays and puppet shows put on for profit and those put on for other purposes (amateur and public service productions, for example). All workers involved in the latter, even if paid, are unproductive and all those involved in the former, even though their output is non-material, are productive. An actor working for, in Marx's phrase, an 'entrepreneur of theatres' earns profits for his master just as a manufacturer earns profits for his. In both cases the employees are maintained by capital and in both cases their labour 'continues the existence of the fund which maintains and employs them'. Even in the case where the theatre entrepreneur employs no helpers (a one-man mime show for example), he himself is still a productive worker under this definition. Smith makes it quite clear elsewhere that the return to an individual proprietor includes both a wage and a profit component (pp. 53, 111–12). Smith thus views such individuals as hiring their own labour to earn a profit for themselves.

Reconciliation of the two definitions
The presence of two different definitions of productive labour in *The Wealth of Nations* causes an obvious problem of interpretation for Smith scholars – namely, which of the two definitions is the 'correct' one? Smith's bourgeois successors avoided having to answer this question only because they were unaware of the need to do so. They saw only one definition, the vendible commodity, and focused their attention almost exclusively on the logic of its materiality requirement. Marx, on the other hand, faced the problem squarely. He was the first writer to note that Smith in fact used two different definitions and his opinion as to their relative merits from the point of view of the analysis of capitalist dynamics is clear: the hired-for-profit definition is correct and the vendible commodity definition is incorrect because it is profitability (i.e. the ability to create surplus value), not materiality, which is the hallmark of capitalist production (*Theories of Surplus Value*, pp. 163–4).

Our conclusion is the opposite. We evaluate the correctness of the two concepts from the point of view of the author's ultimate intention. On this basis, we conclude that it is the vendible commodity definition that represents 'the' Smithian definition of productive labour. We take this position for three reasons: first, the vendible commodity definition appears at the very beginning of the chapter on productive and unproductive labour while its hired-for-profit counterpart appears only later; second, it is the more clearly articulated of the two; and third, it provides the conceptual foundation for Smith's aggregate production concept, the annual produce.[7] We then interpret the appearance of the hired-for-profit definition in various passages in the chapter as the result of oversights on Smith's part. In his eagerness in these passages to emphasize the profits that productive workers earn for their employers by producing marketable output, he forgets to remind the reader that his earlier definition requires that this output be material. Smith's carelessness in this regard can perhaps be justified by the fact that the number of workers employed by firms selling services to consumers for profit at the time he was writing was small.

Karl Marx
Although Adam Smith was the father of the classical theory of productive and unproductive labour, most of the attention in the

modern literature on the subject has focused on Marx's version of the theory. As was true for Smith, there are many controversial points in Marx's analysis and these have been the source of a prolonged debate over its internal consistency.[8] In the present paper we are not concerned with this debate, however. Instead, we look at Marx's definition of productive labour from the standpoint of its usefulness in building national income accounts.

Industry

For Marx, labour is productive if it creates surplus value and unproductive if it does not, a conception which is similar to Smith's hired for profit definition. In Marxian economics, surplus value is created only when value is created and this occurs only under capitalist production. In general, the labour of the working class in the industrial sector is productive. There are, however, exceptions to this rule because not all of the labour of the proletariat is directly transformed into capital (i.e. employed by a capitalist). If, for example, a proletarian takes a second job working for an individual, his labour on this job appears outside of the capitalist system of production and is therefore unproductive.

> Where the direct exchange of money for labour takes place without the latter producing capital – that is, when it is not productive labour – it is bought as a service; which in general is nothing but an expression for the particular use value which labour, like any commodity, provides. (*Theories of Surplus Value*, pp. 188–9)

To make clearer the distinction between the productive and unproductive labour of such a worker, Marx provides the following illustration:

> For example, the worker employed by a piano maker is a productive worker. His labour replaces not only the wage which he consumes; but in the product, the piano, the commodity which the piano maker sells, is contained a surplus value over and above the value of the wage. If on the other hand I buy all the materials required for the piano (or for all it matters the worker himself may possess them) and, instead of buying the piano in a shop, have it made in my home – then the worker who makes the piano is an unproductive worker, because his labour is exchanged directly against my revenue. (ibid., p. 157)

Why does Marx draw a distinction between the two pianos if they would, assuming equal quality, be of the same value to the customer? To answer this question one must realize that the idea of a commodity manufactured outside the system of capitalist production is unacceptable to him. To put it differently, accepting the idea that value can be attributed to all products implies that surplus value is created not only inside but also outside of capitalist production. In the example above it would mean that the worker making the piano in Marx's house, after reimbursement for materials and tools, would receive the same wage as he did in the capitalist's factory. Marx as a customer would then acquire value greater than he paid for, the difference being exactly equal to the surplus value earned by the capitalist in the case of a factory-made piano. Only if Marx paid the market price for the piano would surplus value, accruing now to the worker, disappear as a category of exploitation. There are, of course, a variety of intermediate possibilities lying between these two extremes, each associated with a greater or lesser degree of exploitation. From the worker's point of view, of course, exploitation exists whenever there is underpayment, whether by a private employer, a customer or a state enterprise. From Marx's point of view, however, exploitation, and the surplus value which results from it, can only occur when the worker is hired by a capitalist. Within this relationship, exploitation disappears only with the elimination of surplus value, which is essentially equivalent to the elimination of profit.[9]

From the national income accounting standpoint, as noted earlier, productive labour results in output which contributes to national product and unproductive labour does not. Hence, in a 'Marxian' accounting system the piano manufactured in the factory would be included in the national production aggregate and the one manufactured in the home would not. It should be noted that although Smith's hired-for-profit approach is similar to Marx's, he would not discriminate between the two pianos because to him both are produced by productive workers under either of his definitions. Both pianos are vendible commodities, and both produce a profit for a 'capitalist'. The piano manufactured in the factory earns a profit for the factory owner and the piano produced at home earns a profit for the piano factory worker in his capacity as an independent craftsman. Smith's approach is much more useful than Marx's from the point of view of national income accounting because a nation can build a rational system of accounts only if every commodity passing through the market is entirely included in or excluded from them.

Agriculture
Marx also comments on productive and unproductive labour in the non-industrial sectors of the economy – briefly in the case of agriculture and more extensively in the case of distribution and trade ('circulation of capital'). For agriculture, Marx distinguishes between the labour of waged workers and that of independent farmers. The farm employee is productive, like his industrial counterpart, because he creates a surplus

value for his employer. The independent farmer, on the other hand, is given a special status by Marx.

> What is then the position of the independent handicraftsmen or peasants who employ no workers and therefore do not produce as capitalists? . . . They belong neither to the category of productive nor to that of unproductive workers, although they are producers of commodities. But their production does not fall under the capitalist mode of production. (ibid., pp. 191–2)

As this quotation indicates, independent farmers are in the same position in Marx's system as independent handicraftsmen. Neither fits into his formal analysis of capitalist production, so both are excluded from it. As a result, a third category of labour appears, that which is neither productive nor unproductive. It follows that two identical agricultural products may be produced by two different types of labour – one by labour which is productive and one by labour which is neither productive nor unproductive.

There are even more options in the case of a handicraftsmen. First, he can either produce independently or become a factory operative working for a capitalist. Second, in the latter case he can either work exclusively for the capitalist or also work part-time on his own after hours. It then follows from Marx's reasoning that an industrial commodity (like the piano in the previous example) can be produced by any one of three different types of labour. If it is manufactured in a factory, it is the result of productive labour; if it is produced by a moonlighting factory operative working independently for a consumer, it is the result of unproductive labour; and if it is produced by an independent handicraftsman, it is the result of labour which is neither productive nor unproductive. It may be mentioned in passing that Smith does not use this confusing third category. For him, as noted earlier, labour which is not productive is necessarily unproductive.

Anyone trying to build a system of national income and product accounts on the basis of Marxian principles would find the work greatly complicated by these various distinctions. Marx perhaps needed to distinguish between a moonlighting operative and an independent handicraftsman because he did not want to equate the work of a proletarian, even when done in his free time, with that of a petty bourgeois. None the less, conceptually they are in exactly the same situation. Furthermore, there is an asymmetry in Marx's treatment of the industrial and agricultural sectors. In the former there are three types of labour, while in the latter there are only two since he does not consider the possibility that an agricultural worker might be unproductive (a case of considerable potential importance to the Soviet Union, as we shall see below).

Circulation

In addition to production in the industrial and agricultural sectors, Marx pays considerable attention to what he calls the circulation of capital – i.e. the process by which capital in the form of commodities is exchanged for money that, in turn, is exchanged for the inputs needed to continue production in the next period. In general, Marx believes that commodity values do not increase in the process of circulation because the process and the labour engaged in it are intrinsically unproductive.

> Costs of circulation, which originate in a mere change of form of value in circulation, ideally considered do not enter into the value of commodities. The parts of capital expended as such costs are mere deductions from the productively expended capital so far as the capitalist is concerned. (*Capital*, p. 136)

However, he realizes that, in part, the process of circulation may be a continuation of production.

> The costs of circulation which we shall consider now are of a different nature. They may arise from processes of production which are only continued in circulation, the productive character of which is hence merely concealed by the circulation form. (ibid., p. 136)

None the less, he refuses to classify most of the functions of the circulation process (and hence the labour employed in them) as productive in the sense of creating value and surplus value.

> It is not necessary to go here into all the details of the cost of circulation, such as packing, sorting, etc. The general law is that all costs of circulation which arise only from changes in the forms of commodities do not add to their values. They are merely expenses incurred in the realization of the value or in its conversion from one form into another. (ibid., p. 149)

He makes an exception for the transportation of commodities, however. He argues that transportation is a continuation of the production process within the process of circulation (as suggested in the penultimate quotation) and, therefore, that the labour engaged in it is productive and creates value.

> Quantities of products are not increased by transportation. Nor, with a few exceptions, is the possible alteration of their natural qualities, brought about by transportation, an intentionally useful effect; it is rather an unavoidable evil. But the use value of things is materialized only in their consumption, and their consumption may necessitate a change of location of these things, and hence may require an additional process of production, in the transport industry. (ibid., pp. 149–50)

It is, of course, true that the process of consumption often necessitates the transportation of goods from one location to another. It is equally true, however, that this process also requires other closely-related activities, such as sorting and packing. None the less, Marx declares all of these other activities to be unproductive. Why does he do so? The reason perhaps is that freight transportation had become an advanced industry with a clear-cut class division at the time he was writing. The activities of sorting and packing, on the other hand, had not yet been 'conquered by capital' so that only petty bourgeois employment was involved.[10]

Labour employed at other stages of the circulation of capital, such as finance and trade, is unambiguously unproductive since in Marx's system these stages do not continue the production process into circulation as does transportation. A salesman, for example, is an unproductive worker even if he works for wages and is underpaid, because in Marx's scheme he does not create value. Put differently, such a salesman provides his employer with 'surplus labour' but not with surplus value.

> Whatever his pay, as a wage labourer [a salesman] works part of his time for nothing. He may receive daily the value of the product of eight working hours, yet functions ten. But the two hours of surplus labour he performs do not produce value any more than his eight hours of necessary labour, although by means of the latter a part of the social product is transferred to him. (p. 132)

Marx also provides other examples of unproductive labour in the process of circulation. Thus, the labour of a rent collector or bank messenger is unproductive because it 'does not add one iota or tittle to the value of either the rent or the gold pieces carried to another bank by the bagful' (p. 130). Book-keepers are similarly regarded. Book-keeping is necessary, but it too is an 'unproductive expenditure of labour time' (p. 134).

Marx versus Smith

The preceding examples demonstrate that there is no close equivalence between Marx's definition of productive labour and Smith's hired-for-profit definition, even though the underlying idea is similar for both. The packers, sorters, salesmen, rent collectors, bank messengers and book-keepers labelled unproductive by Marx are all hired for profit by their employers and therefore are productive under Smith's hired-for-profit definition.

When we compare Marx's definition with Smith's vendible commodity definition, we see that Marx, unlike Smith, distinguishes clearly between service workers hired for profit and those hired for other reasons. Thus, for example, he writes that 'an actor . . . is a productive worker, if he works in the employ of a capitalist . . . while a jobbing tailor who comes to the capitalist's house to patch his trousers for him . . . is an unproductive worker' (*Theories of Surplus Value*, pp. 153–4). Marx thus does not see a difference between goods and services as long as they are produced by a capitalist:

> The same labour can be productive, when I buy it as a capitalist, as a producer, in order to make a profit out of it, and unproductive, when I buy it as a consumer, a spender of revenue, in order to consume its use value, no matter whether this use value perishes with the activity of this labour power itself, or realizes, fixes itself in an object. (ibid., p. 162)

It follows that the labour of actors, musicians, prostitutes, etc. is productive if it is bought by an entrepreneur of theatres, concerts, brothels, etc. and unproductive if bought by anyone else.

Summing up, Marx's classification of labour as productive or unproductive depends on whether or not that labour produces surplus value for a capitalist, no matter what the form of the final product. Since not all workers who work for profit, as Smith uses the term, produce surplus value for a capitalist as Marx uses these terms, Marx's definition is less inclusive than Smith's hired-for-profit definition. The comparison between Marx's definition and Smith's vendible commodity definition is more complex. On the one hand, Marx's definition is broader because, as we have just seen, it includes the employees of for-profit firms selling services to consumers and Smith's does not. On the other, it is narrower because it omits most of the workers engaged in wholesale and retail trade whom Smith includes. Either of Smith's definitions of productive labour could provide the basis for a rational, internally consistent system of national income accounting. Marx's definition, on the other hand, cannot without great difficulty provide such a basis because he did not organize his arguments in terms of sectors of the economy or types of activities that could be either completely included in or completely excluded from the account.

Soviet national accounting

Marx's general idea of the primacy of material production is the philosophical foundation of Soviet national income accounting. Yet, as we have seen, when he gets down to specifics and defines the realms of productive and unproductive labour, they do not correspond very closely to the spheres of material and non-material output. In light of this incongruence, one way of institutionalizing Marx's labour categories would be to classify each sector of the economy as productive or unproductive on the basis of the activities which, in his classification scheme, predominate there. Thus, since factory production prevails in manufacturing, it would be logical to regard the whole sector as productive even though some of its output is produced outside of factories. The same principle could be applied to agriculture. When wage labour prevails there, the agricultural sector would be viewed as productive.

Although the Soviets did not follow this line of reasoning, they did end up placing the manufacturing and agricultural sectors in the productive sphere. They did this because they chose to operationalize the ideas of productive and unproductive labour on the basis of the type of product rather than the type of labour *per se*. They thus defined the composition of their national product first and then denoted all the labour used in the production of the included items as productive. For reasons we shall discuss in more detail below, the Soviets chose to include only material output in their national production aggregate. Thus, for them the productive and material spheres are the same. Overall, the material sphere is made up of the sectors that create tangible goods (manufacturing, mining, electric power, agriculture, forestry and construction) and the sectors that increase the value of these goods by delivering them to the households, producers or government agencies which use them (freight transportation, business communications, trade, catering and material supply). The non-material sphere is made up of all other sectors. Obviously, this division of the economy is very close to the one implicitly proposed by Smith with his vendible commodity definition.

According to the methodology of Soviet national accounting, all of the labour in the material sphere is considered to be productive regardless of where it is employed. Thus, for example, the total product of the industrial sector (manufacturing, mining and electric power generation) is the sum of the values of the goods produced by all of the organizations in this sector – i.e. state enterprises, collective farms and cooperatives. Until May 1987, private manufacturing was illegal and so the output of individual proprietorships (what the Soviets call 'individual labour') was not included in the official totals, even though the volume of this output has probably been of some significance in recent years given the growth of the Soviet underground economy. Since that date, many industrial activities in this second economy have been legalized so the procedures for national accounting will have to be adjusted accordingly. Similar adjustments will have to be made for the freight transportation sector since private activity is now allowed here also.

Unlike industry and freight transportation, agriculture is a sector of the economy in which a substantial amount of output has always been produced by individual labour. Most of this output, as is well known, comes from the private plots cultivated by collective farm workers and their families. Recent data suggest, in fact, that almost one-third of official Soviet agricultural production comes from these plots. The construction industry is in a similar situation because in rural areas many people build their own houses, often with the aid of moonlighting or independent contractors. If the Soviets had followed Marx's ideas, they would have had to exclude the private output in these two sectors from the national accounts because, as we saw in the previous section, he classifies the labour which produces it as either unproductive or neither productive nor unproductive. The Soviets chose not to do so because it would have led to too great an understatement of national production in these sectors.

The Soviets' treatment of trade is especially interesting because it involves a similar conflict between theoretical and pragmatic considerations. Following Marx, they regard the wholesale and retail operations of packing, sorting, etc. as a continuation of the production process into circulation. But, unlike Marx, they classify these operations, and hence the labour involved in them, as productive. On the other hand, they unofficially regard salespeople and cashiers as unproductive just as Marx did. Conceivably, it would have been possible to partition the trade sector into productive and unproductive subsectors, but it would have been cumbersome and costly to do so, particularly when the trade workers are both salespersons and packers or sorters. Such considerations dictated that the entire trade sector had to be either included in or excluded from the national accounts – i.e. classified as either entirely productive or entirely unproductive. Faced with this dilemma, the Soviets chose to include trade in the productive sphere, a decision consistent with Smith's vendible commodity definition of productive labour, but not Marx's.

Table 6.1 sums up the preceding discussion by comparing Smith's Marx's and Soviet classifications of productive and unproductive labour by sector of the economy. The sectors identified in the table are those customarily used by Soviet planners. The notation is as follows: P = productive, U = unproductive and M = mixed. The term 'mixed' here refers to those sectors of the Soviet economy in which some labour would be classified by Marx as productive and the rest as either

Table 6.1
*Alternative classifications of productive and unproductive labour, by sector**

Sector of the Economy	Soviet	Smith	Marx
Industry	P	P	P
Agriculture	P	P	M
Forestry	P	P	P
Construction	P	P	M
Freight transportation	P	P	P
Business communication	P	P	P
Trade	P	P	U
Catering	P	P	M
Material supply	P	P	U
Passenger transportation	U	U	P
Residential communication	U	U	P
Education	U	U	P
Science	U	U	P
Medicine	U	U	P
Recreation	U	U	P
Housing	U	U	M
Personal services	U	U	P
Municipal services	U	U	P
Government	U	U	U

Source: See text.
* P = productive, U = unproductive, M = mixed.

unproductive or neither productive nor unproductive. In the official Soviet classification, the first nine sectors in the table constitute the productive (i.e. material) sphere and the remaining ten the unproductive (i.e. immaterial) sphere. The classifications for Smith and Marx are taken directly from their writings whenever possible. For Smith, the classification is based on his vendible commodity definition. In those cases where a sector is not explicitly mentioned by these writers, its classification is inferred from their general definitions.

Note first that Smith's classification corresponds exactly to that of the Soviets. This is because both are based on the underlying idea that a productive labourer is one who adds value to a vendible commodity. Marx's classification, on the other hand, only partially overlaps with the Soviet even though the latter is allegedly based on his theory of productive and unproductive labour. There are three major reasons for this discrepancy. First, the output of individual labour is included in the total product of such Soviet sectors as agriculture and construction. In Marx's view such labour is not productive. Second, the Soviets regard labour in the trade and material supply sectors as productive and Marx does not. And, third, the Soviets regard all labour in the non-government service sector as unproductive, while to Marx it is productive as long as it is performed as an employee. We are left then with the conclusion that the Soviet accounting system follows the precepts of Adam Smith, the patron saint of capitalism, more closely than it follows those of Karl Marx, the patron saint of socialism.

There are no doubt a variety of reasons for this rather ironic result. One possible explanation is that many Soviet planners simply misinterpreted Marx or chose, for whatever reason, to follow what they believed to be the 'spirit' of Marx rather than what he actually said. A second, more pragmatic explanation is rooted in the historical origins of the Soviet system. When the victorious proletariat took power in 1917, its leaders immediately began showing a harsh official animosity towards all white-collar occupations because they were perceived as representing a bourgeois threat to the new society. Recognizing anyone in those occupations as a productive member of society was, under the circumstances, out of the question. Everyone had to be identified with one of two social groups: factory workers and peasants, on the one hand, and office workers and professionals, on the other. Those in the latter group were severely penalized. Working in this political environment, it was both logical and expedient for Soviet planners to divide the economy into productive and unproductive spheres based on which of the above two types of labour predominated there. This led naturally to the identification of the productive sphere with the material and the unproductive sphere with the non-material.

Concluding comments
The official standing of the service sector has gradually improved in the USSR since Stalin's death. Since the 1960s articles have regularly appeared in Soviet economics journals, arguing that particular services and occupations are really 'productive' from the point of view of the Soviet economy, and, therefore, should be treated differently in the national accounts. Some authors have argued, for example, that medical and educational personnel should be classified as productive because they enhance the nation's human capital. With the appearance of the

Gorbachev economic reforms, the foundations of Soviet political economy are now being questioned more openly than ever before and some economists are beginning to challenge the wisdom of the whole productive labour concept.

In a recent article in a leading Soviet publication, Shatalin (1987) explicitly criticizes the restricted material approach to national income accounting because it excludes the service sector whose relative importance in all advanced economies is increasing over time. He argues further that this approach is a legacy from Marx.

> Such an approach follows from the principles and the concepts of productive and unproductive labour suggested by Marx for the capitalist economy at its outset when the service sector was not yet developed and did not have an industrial base. (p. 11)

He ends by asserting that a transition to a more comprehensive national product concept similar to those used in the West is necessary. Such a change would, in his view, improve Soviet economic analysis and planning and in the long run lead to increased productivity and social welfare.

We conclude this paper with several comments on this interesting article. First, we agree with Shatalin that there is no conceptual justification for the Soviet practice of treating some occupations and sectors as productive and others as unproductive. Second, in spite of this we do not share his view that a switch to a 'better' accounting system would revitalize the Soviet economy. Based on other research, the details of which are beyond the scope of this paper, we believe that the productive or unproductive status of a Soviet sector has had little to do with its ability to command resources from the central authorities and hence to grow. It follows that eliminating the distinction between the two types of labour is not likely to have a significant resource allocational effect. Third, his attempt to justify Marx's support for the restricted material production concept is misguided. As we have shown in this paper, it was Smith, not Marx, who with his vendible commodity definition excluded services from the productive sphere and it was Marx who criticized him for this omission!

Notes
1. George Stigler (1976) classifies Smith's theory of productive and unproductive labour as an 'improper success'. It was a success because it influenced the work of later generations of (mainstream) economists; it was an improper success because it was ultimately deemed scientifically invalid.
2. Edwin Cannan (1924, pp. 14–18). It should be noted, however, that Smith does not consistently maintain this emphasis throughout the volume. He is always concerned about the 'wealth' of a nation, but sometimes the wealth in question is a stock rather

than a flow. On occasion both usages appear in the same paragraph (*Wealth of Nations*, p. 241).

3. Cannan's footnote to the relevant passage in Smith's Introduction is instructive: 'The word [productive] slips in here as an apparently unimportant synonym of "useful", but subsequently ousts "useful" altogether, and is explained in such a way that unproductive labour may be useful' (ibid., p. lviii).

4. Many of the same ideas are repeated in Chapter ix of Book IV.

5. John McCulloch (1925) for example, argues that '[t]o produce a fire, it is just as necessary that coals should be carried from the celler to the grate as that they should be carried from the bottom of the mine to the surface of the earth; and if it is said that the miner is a productive labourer, must we not also say the same of the servant who is employed to make and tend the fire? (pp. 406–7). Marx, on the other hand, asserts that 'Adam Smith knows quite well' that some menial servants produce material output and, further, that this output could under some circumstances end up being sold on a market. (Homemade articles might, for example, have to be pawned or sold at auction.) Marx's (1952) interpretation is that servants in this position are 'a very small category among unproductive workers' and therefore that it is appropriate for Smith to ignore them (pp. 161–2).

6. Since such props and costumes would be vendible commodities, all workers involved in their production and distribution would be productive.

7. The annual produce is the aggregate of all material output produced for market sale in a given year. Since Smith asserts that 'the whole annual produce' is 'the effect of productive labour' (*Wealth of Nations*, p. 315), the productive labour that he has in mind must be that which produces vendible commodities. For further discussion of these matters, see Cannan (1924, p. 24).

8. See, for example, David Leadbeater's article in which he concludes that 'Marx's categories of productive and unproductive labour do not have inconsistent and ineffective character . . .' (1985, p. 617).

9. This is why Soviet political economists have had a difficult time providing a plausible justification for profit as an accounting category in the workers' state. They use Marx's definition when analysing or describing capitalist economies. But in their own economy there is by definition no exploitation and hence no surplus value. They are therefore forced to define profit to be the result of productivity growth, technological change, and other factors.

10. The fact that Marx regards labour engaged in freight transportation as productive and that engaged in the other operations that continue the production process into circulation as unproductive has occasionally been overlooked in the literature. The following passage from Karl Kuehne is an example: 'Marx explicitly recognizes that a large part of marketing activity (for instance, packing, forwarding, and transport) is part of the production process and therefore productive in the capitalist sense' (1979, p. 134).

References

Cannan, Edwin (1924), *A History of the Theories of Production and Distribution*, 3rd edn London: P.S. King and Son.

Kuehne, Karl (1979), *Economics and Marxism*, Vol. I, New York: St Martin's Press.

Leadbeater, David (1985), 'The Consistency of Marx's Categories of Productive and Unproductive Labor', *History of Political Economy*, 17, p. 4.

Marx, Karl (1970), *Capital: A Critique of Political Economy*, Vol. III, New York: Independent Publishers.

Marx, Karl (1952), *Theories of Surplus Value*, New York: Independent Publishers.

McCulloch, John (1925), *Principles of Political Economy*, Edinburgh: Tait.

Shatalin, Sergei (1987), 'Kak izmerit' ekonomicheskii rost', *Ekonomicheskaia Gazeta*, 31, p. 7.

Smith, Adam (1937), *The Wealth of Nations*, ed. Edwin Cannan, New York: Random House.
Stigler, George (1976), 'The Successes and Failures of Professor Smith', *Journal of Political Economy* 84, p. 6.
Studenski, Paul (1961), *The Income of Nations*, New York: New York University Press.

7 On the question of continuity in classical economic thought

Giovanni Caravale

Introduction

The thesis of substantial continuity in classical economic thought from Ricardo to Sraffa (and after), rests, I believe, on a firm basis – the central role attributed to the concept of natural prices reflecting the dominant conditions under which commodities are made available for the economic system's needs.

The same thesis is however often maintained in terms of other arguments which appear of a more controversial nature: on the one hand the determination of the profit rate in 'physical' terms; and on the other the complete irrelevance of demand conditions in the determination of prices.

My purpose here is to offer a general evaluation of these latter arguments with reference to Ricardo's analysis and to Sraffa's theoretical contribution. In particular I shall attempt to shed some light on the following points:

1. To what extent Sraffa's Standard Commodity can be said to fit in the reconstruction of a line of continuity that goes back to Ricardo's corn model and to his search for invariable measure of value.[1]
2. In what sense natural equilibrium positions, i.e. situations characterized by the presence of a uniform rate of profit in all productive sectors – a family to which both Ricardian and Sraffian equilibria strictly belong – can be said to be totally independent of demand conditions.

**Ricardo's invariable measure of value and
Sraffa's Standard Commodity**

The basic problem Ricardo had in mind – in political and historical terms before analytical terms – was that of the relation between decreasing returns in agriculture and the growth prospects of the economy.

All his theoretical research tends to clarify that relation in as general terms as possible, and thus to offer an unambiguous point of reference to a policy choice capable of modifying the foreseeable course of historical events and of guaranteeing a continuous and sustained process of growth.

In his first relevant essay[2] Ricardo based his argument[3] on the 'rational foundation' of a hypothetical economic system in which corn is produced by means of corn. Here an increase in the quantity of labour needed to produce a unit of corn immediately determines a reduction in the rate of profit and, given the behaviour assumptions of the social classes, in the accumulation rate.

The corn model was a good example, but obviously not a full-fledged theory. To escape its restrictions (wages consisting only of corn; no fixed capital) Ricardo devised it with other, more general models, in mind, a common feature of these being the validity of the labour theory of value,[4] i.e. a rule of exchange between commodities relating *only* to their labour contents. Here again the 'general proposition that the productivity of labour on land which pays no rent is fundamental in determining' the general rate of profit and thus the pace of the system's expansion remains rigorously valid. No interference can occur from the side of distribution to spoil this neat picture.

These 'models', although less restricted than the corn model, were however not *general* in the sense that they could not allow for the 'different proportions of fixed capital' in the various sectors. When this phenomenon was taken into account, confusing effects emerged from movements in relative prices due to changes in distribution. The 'invariable standard of value' was designed to play the role of eliminating these 'confusing effects' thus restoring the straightforward connection between diminishing returns and the rate of profit which was found with the labour theory of value. The indication of the requisites of the 'standard value' – that it should at all times require the same amount of labour for its production, and it should be such as to make the prices of the other commodities invariant to changes in distribution – accompanies however Ricardo's awareness that 'neither gold . . . nor any other commodity, can ever be a perfect meaure of value for all things' (*Principles*, p. 45), because each commodity 'would be a perfect measure of value for all things produced under the same circumstances precisely as itself, but for no others' (ibid.).

In other words, the perfect measure of value could be identified only with reference to a situation in which it would be of no use whatsoever. Ricardo was thus obliged to base his general conclusions (or intuitions) about the long-run prospects of the rate of profit on his previous analytical models considered as an acceptable approximation to the in vain searched for general theory.

Ricardo's objective, we now know,[5] could have been reached and his theoretical efforts can now be fully reconstructed within an analytical schema in which all the various questions that engaged his mind (value, prices, distribution, accumulation) appear as parts of a single *mosaic work* and not as separate pictures. They appear as parts of a schema – let it be said in passing – founded on the concept of *natural equilibrium* (strictly linked to the idea of an exogenously given real wage rate) and on the connection between changes in 'technology' and changes in distribution. We also know that Ricardo's ingenious efforts – notwithstanding the fact that all the elements for the *general* solution he was aiming at were there to be used – were not successful simply because he did not have at his disposal the analytical tools (in substance Sraffa's price system) on the basis of which his target could have been reached.[6] Ricardo was therefore obliged to 'settle on an approximate solution', at the end of a long theoretical journey of which the 'corn model' and the invariable standard of value were two significant phases. Although not strictly in a chronological sense, they were the starting and finishing times.

Piero Sraffa in his *Production of Commodities*, presents the Standard Commodity as a 'development' of Ricardo's idea of the invariable measure. Some have saluted it as the fulfilment of Ricardo's dream of the perfect standard of value.[7] In order to clarify the relation between Ricardo's theory and Sraffa's construction it is useful to recall the most relevant characteristics of the Standard Commodity, distinguishing between its intrinsic properties and the properties it possessed when it is chosen as *numéraire* of the system.[8]

The intrinsic properties of the Standard Commodity – those that do not depend on its choice as *numéraire* of the system – are the following.

(i)   Being the rate of physical surplus for each of the commodities produced in the standard system and uniform by construction, these rates represent 'also the rate by which the total product . . . exceeds its means of production'. The ratio between the *value* of the net standard product and the *value* of its means of production is thus independent of prices and of distribution.

(ii)   The standard system implies the existence of a linear relation between the rate of profit and wages as a proportion of the standard net product.

(iii) The Standard Commodity presents a 'regularity of layers' both from the point of view of the quantity of (dated) labour and from the value of its means of production.

These characteristics, however, have no implication whatsoever for the notion, often accepted, or implicit, in the literature, of what can be called the 'invariance *per se*' of the Standard Commodity. Sraffa's discussion of what he calls 'the critical proportion' between labour and means of production, and his construction of the standard *qua* balanced commodity seems to imply that such a commodity is invariant *per se* with respect to distribution. The argument rests on the idea that it is possible to define the notion of 'deficit' and 'surplus' industries *without the prior definition of the relation between wages and the rate of profit.*

It must be emphasized instead that the definition of deficit and surplus industries requires the prior knowledge of the inverse relation between w and r, which in turn requires the choice of a *numéraire*. For the commodity chosen as unit of measure, changes in the wage rate are, by definition, exactly compensated by changes in the opposite direction in the rate of profit. This fact is totally independent of the 'circumstance of production' of the commodity chosen as standard – it may be Ricardo's shrimps or the most technologically advanced type of robot – and is not in the least associated with the idea that it may represent 'a social average'. In effect this is precisely what Sraffa does in passing from his Chapter 2 to his chapter 3. Although the choice is somehow concealed in this passage, he makes the assumption that both total labour and net national income are taken as equal to one; with this hypothesis the price model is complete and Sraffa's reasoning in Chapter 3 is based on a fully specified w and r relation.

On the other hand, when the Standard Commodity is chosen as *numéraire*, we have the following.

(a)   The linear relation between the two distributive variables holds true also for actual systems. This fact, however appealing it may appear, does not justify the claim – advanced for instance by Pasinetti[9] and Eatwell[10] – of a difference in the *quality* of the results obtained when a different *numéraire* is chosen. The w–r inverse relation is no longer linear. The alleged presence of 'disturbances' is an aesthetic and not an analytically relevant fact.

(b)   As with the corn model, with the construction of a 'physical analogue' it is seen that the general rate of profit can be determined prior to, and independently of, prices. Prices would then be determined on the basis of the equations in which both the wage rate and the profit rate would be given. It will be remembered however that this is only one way of solving the model, the alternative being represented by the simultaneous solution of the price equations, given the technology and the level of the wage rate.[11]

(c)   When the Standard Commodity is chosen as *numéraire* it is possible to trace the origin of price movements to the 'peculiarities of production' of the commodities which are being compared with the Standard Commodity.[12] As a whole this specific characteristic of Sraffa's *numéraire* could not have been of particular interest for Ricardo, who knew very well what the *origin* was of the price movements that played such a relevant role in his theoretical research: the continuous change in the 'peculiarities of production' of agricultural commodities.

In the light of the foregoing points we can now briefly examine the relation between the Standard Commodity and Ricardo's corn model on the one hand, and that between Sraffa's *numéraire* and Ricardo's invariable measure of value on the other.

(i) As to the former aspect it is evident that the first of the intrinsic properties of the Standard Commodity listed above makes this latter legitimately appear as a generalization of the corn models to the case of plurality of goods. This fact however does not in the least imply that the analytical role of the two models is the same.

The corn model, as I have pointed out above, was designed to establish a straightforward connection between *changes* in technology and the rate of profit *given the real wage*. Sraffa's problem – in relation to which the Standard Commodity is defined – is represented by the study of the effects of changes in real wages on the rate of profit and prices *given the state of technology*.

The generalization of the corn model obtained with the Standard Commodity does not therefore represent a progress from Ricardo's point of view. Although the question of the existence of the Standard Commodity in a Ricardian general model has a positive answer,[13] the Standard Commodity *qua* generalized version of the corn model, is, in other words, structurally unable to perform the role that Ricardo attributed to the corn model, although in its very limited sphere of validity.

(ii) The second aspect relates to the possibility of assigning to the Standard Commodity the role Ricardo had envisaged for his invariable standard of value.

The use of the Standard Commodity *qua* invariable standard in a

Ricardian contexts would meet the following insurmountable difficulties. As the Standard Commodity reflects the production conditions of the commodities produced in the system, including of course agricultural goods, we would have a continuous change in the technology of the standard system and therefore the existence of an infinite set of standard commodities. It is clear that a 'Ricardian' Standard Commodity would not fulfil Ricardo's first requirement for the invariable measure of value.

In Ricardo's natural equilibrium context changes in distribution can only arise as consequence of changes in the conditions of production of agricultural commodities. It is, therefore, conceptually difficult even to envisage the use of a composite commodity as a unit of measurement which is defined with reference to a given technology for the study of the effect of changes in this technology.[14]

The attempt to use the Standard Commodity in the Ricardian framework does not appear, therefore, to be fruitful. Sraffa's *numéraire* does not seem to represent, in other words, an analytical tool capable of resolving the issues from which Ricardo's search for the invariable measure had originated. The difficulties can be substantially traced back to the circumstance that the Standard Commodity and the invariable measure of value move on different logical planes – the study of distribution and prices for a given technology and the analysis of changes in distribution caused by change in technology respectively.[15]

In conclusion, great caution seems to be necessary in making reference to the Standard Commodity as evidence of a continuous line of development that goes back to Ricardo's corn model and to his 'invariant standard of value.'[16] In Joan Robinson's words,[17]

> The definition of the Standard Commodity takes up a great deal of Sraffa's argument but personally I have never found it worth the candle. Each technical system has its own standard commodity so that one quantity cannot be compared with another. This is not the unit of value like a unit of length or of weight that Ricardo was looking for.

The role of demand conditions
I now come briefly to the second question – that relating to the sense in which Ricardian and Sraffian long period positions – as centres of gravity for the system – in their respective contexts, can be said to be independent of demand conditions. A warning is perhaps necessary at the outset. What follows has nothing to do with the neoclassical-type positions that view the classical theory of prices as 'incomplete' (needing a demand side to be added to it), nor with the neoclassical-type reinterpretations of Ricardo founded on the notion of market prices.[18]

It moves instead within the natural equilibrium approach which is characteristic of the classics and of Sraffa.

In spite of unqualified affirmations as to the irrelevance of demand in the determination of *natural equilibria*, serious analyses in the classical tradition of thought, for example by Meek,[19] emphasize that classical price analysis does not ignore demand. Demand is in fact recognized to be a prerequisite for exchange value, to play an important role in the determination of market prices (whose movements are essential for the gravitation process to take place), and to be a determinant of monopoly prices and of the level and proportion of the labour force allocated to each productive sector of the economy. It seems important to emphasize in particular the relation between demand conditions and the notion of uniformity of profit rates in the various sectors – a central concept, as is well known, for Smith, for Ricardo, for Marx, and for Sraffa.[20] These conditions, in other words, must be given in order that competition may work itself out producing the result of the equalization of profit rate, through appropriate movements of capital.

In fact, if during the process of 'mobility and change' – a process which implies the assumption that economic agents have 'static expectations'[21] – demand conditions were to vary, the natural equilibrium condition would not be reached. And it would not be reached until demand conditions took a definite pattern.[22] Now this very obvious fact certainly underlies both Ricardo's and Sraffra's natural equilibria and makes demand conditions relevant in both schemes from this point of view. But there is, I believe, a relevant difference which confers on Ricardo's theory very 'modern' features. The whole dynamic process in Ricardo is in point of fact 'activated' by population growth. It is the necessity to feed a growing number of mouths that compels the system to either import corn from abroad or to cultivate progressively poorer lands. With the assumption of diminishing returns in agriculture, which is central for Ricardo, technology will continuously change and natural prices will accordingly change. Demand conditions, through the definition of the level (and the structure) of the physical output that has to be realized, thus determine the technology of the system and this in turn, determines the set of natural prices. This role of demand conditions is not to be found in Sraffa's analysis where technology is given once and for all.[23]

From this point of view, a striking similarity emerges instead between Ricardo's analysis and a recent contribution to growth theory, Pasinetti's multisector dynamic model,[24] in which both technology and demand conditions have a role to play:

> In the dynamic scheme representing the evolution of both technology and
> demand . . . natural prices at a certain point in time and through time

depend exclusively on technical factors: labour and means of production required in the production of each unit of output. In other words . . . in the long run, the cost of production determines prices. . . . But on the other hand the quantities to be produced depend on demand factors, namely on the per capita evolution of consumers' preferences and on population. In other words, in the long run, demand determines the quantity of each commodity which has to be produced. . . . Both technology and demand are thus relevant . . . but they determine two different things. Costs of production, i.e. technology, determine *relative prices*; consumers' decisions determine the evolution over time of the structure of production. (Pasinetti, 1981, p. 141)

With technical progress proceeding at different exogenous rates in the various sectors and with a given rate of population growth, long-run increases in per capita incomes determine a continuous change in *structure* of demand, and a non-proportional growth in the quantities produced by the various sectors. In a certain sense, this fact continuously *pushes* the system on to a different level in which technology is different and natural prices are accordingly different. As in Ricardo's theory, demand determines the level and structure of production to be realized in each period, to which there corresponds an ever-changing technology, and an ever-changing structure of prices of production.

It does not seem true, as Pasinetti says, that 'Ricardo . . . implied . . . that demand has no role to play in the long run' (Pasinetti, ibid.). On the contrary, Ricardo's picture of the role of demand in the long run is even clearer than in Pasinetti's multisector growth model. Ricardo's analysis depends, of course, on the extremely simplified assumptions he makes as to technology (diminishing returns in agriculture, constant returns elsewhere). These make it possible to predict both the evolution of the general rate of profit through time and the direction of change of the various prices in the face of the continuous increases in the money wage rate, given the natural real wage.[25] If, instead, productivity growth rates in the various sectors do not behave in a predictable way, the picture is more complicated. But the greater complication does not detract from the basic similarity between the two schemes. They are built upon the same basic logical structure of relations among the different elements of a dynamic economic system.

Notes

1. Marx's 'average industry' has also been included in this 'line' for example by R. Meek (see his 'Sraffa and the Rehabilitation of Classical Economics', *Scottish Journal of Political Economy*, June 1961; and *Smith, Marx and After*, Chapman and Hall, London, 1977, esp. pp. 149–64). This circumstance has obviously emphasized the ideological implications of the thesis.
2. *An Essay on the Influence of a Low Price of Corn on the Profits of Stock* in 'Works

and Correspondence' (ed. P. Sraffa with the collaboration of M. H. Dobb), Cambridge University Press, vol. 4, pp. 1–41.

3. This is a controversial issue. See for example Hollander's and Garegnani's paper in G. Caravale (ed.), *The Legacy of Ricardo*, Basil Blackwell, Oxford, 1985.

4. G. Caravale and D. Tosato, *Ricardo and the Theory of Value, Distribution and Growth*, Routledge & Kegan Paul, London, 1980, Ch. 2.

5. See G. Caravale, 'Diminishing Returns and Accumulation in Ricardo', in *The Legacy of Ricardo*.

6. Ibid.

7. See, for example, L. Pasinetti, *Lectures in the Theory of Production*, Macmillan, 1977, p. 120: 'After a century and a half, Sraffa's standard commodity has . . . fulfilled Ricardo's dream of an "invariable measure of value".' Pasinetti however appends to this sentence the following footnote: 'This, at least, with reference to the property of being invariable with respect to changes in income distribution.'

8. These points are discussed at length in G. Caravale and D. Tosato, 1980, ch. 3.

9. L. Pasinetti, *Lectures on the Theory of Production*, London, Macmillan, 1977, pp. 118–20.

10. J. Eatwell, 'Mr. Sraffa's Standard Commodity and the Rate of Exploitation', *Quarterly Journal of Economics*, December 1975.

11. The only warning here is that relating to the role to be assigned to the 'institutional rules' of price determination, i.e. the necessarily prior definition of the rules according to which the payment of the productive resources, labour and produced means of production, is to be made. See on this point G. Caravale and D. Tosato, 1980, pp. 70–2.

12. See Caravale and Tosato, 1980, pp. 72–6. See also P. Sraffa, *Production of Commodities by Means of Commodities*, Cambridge University Press, Cambridge, 1960, p. 18.

13. Caravale and Tosato, 1980, pp. 80–2.

14. On this point see also E. Burmeister, 'The Irrelevance of Sraffa's Analysis without Constant Returns to Scale', *Journal of Economic Literature*, 1977, vol. 15.

15. See also G.C. Harcourt, 'The Sraffian Contribution: An Evaluation', in *Classical and Marxian Political Economy*, ed. I. Bradley and M. Howard, Macmillan, London, 1982, pp. 255–75.

16. Pasinetti's 'dynamic Standard Commodity', though presented as a 'sort of physical dynamic counterpart of Ricardo's "invariable standard of value",' and in spite of certain family resemblance with the latter, does not meet the requirements of Ricardo's perfect measure of value and cannot play the role Ricardo attributed to it; it concentrates in fact only on the first of Ricardo's requisites (reinterpreted in dynamic terms) and is defined in a logical context opposite to that of Ricardo (productivity and real wages growing precisely at the same rate, the weighted average of all rates of productivity changes, with a constant rate of profit). See L. Pasinetti, *Structural Change and Economic Growth*, Cambridge, Cambridge University Press, 1981, pp. 104–6.

17. Joan Robinson, 'The Theory of Normal Prices and the Reconstruction of Economic Theory', in G. Feinwell (ed.), *Issues in Contemporary Macroeconomics and Distribution*, Macmillan, London, 1985, p. 163.

18. S. Hollander, *The Economics of David Ricardo*, Heinemann, Toronto, 1979.

19. Ronald L. Meek, *Studies in the Labour Theory of Value*, second edition, Lawrence and Wishart, London, 1973, pp. 178ff.

20. See for instance J. Eatwell, 'Competition', in *Classical and Marxian Political Economy*, pp. 203–38.

21. That is the idea that economic agents believe the existing level of the profit rates will not be affected by their decision to move capital from one sector to the other, or at least that they will be able to benefit from the change even in the presence of a certain degree of variation in profitability conditions.

22. P. Garegani, 'The Classical Theory of Wages and the Role of Demand Schedules in

the Determination of Relative Prices', in *American Economic Review, Papers and Proceedings*, May 1983, has lucidly pointed out the difference between the classical concept of 'effectual demand' and the neoclassical notion of 'demand curve'. It is the level of 'effectual demand' and its structure that must be given in order that the 'competitive' processes may work out its gravitational effects.

23. As Hicks has recently pointed out, Sraffa's theoretical system is compatible with a situation of stationarity, or if the assumption were added of constant returns to scale, semi-stationarity. It could be said, it is compatible with a situation of non proportional growth not affecting the technological conditions under which commodities are produced. See J. Hicks, 'Sraffa and Ricardo, A Critical View', in G. Caravale (ed.), *The Legacy of Ricardo*.

24. Pasinetti, *Structural Changes*.

25. Caravale and Tosato, 1980, ch. 2 and Appendix.

26. M. Baranzini and R. Scazzieri, 'Knowledge in Economics', in *Foundations of Economic Theory*, ed. M. Baranzini and R. Scazzieri, Oxford, Basil Blackwell, 1986.

8 The role of demand in the classical theory of price

Gary Mongiovi[1]

Introduction

From a neoclassical perspective Ricardian value theory appears to be a tool that is imperfectly suited to its task. The standard criticism, put forth by the early marginalists, is that under conditions of variable costs, prices of production cannot be determined independently of outputs, while outputs are themselves functions of prices. By ignoring the demand side of the market, Ricardo and his followers obscured the fact that prices and outputs must, in general, be determined simultaneously by the interaction of the forces of supply and demand. Their model, then, either refers to the special case in which production costs are constant in all sectors; or it is indeterminate. (See Walras, 1926, pp. 425–6; Jevons, 1879, pp. 256–9; Wicksell, 1934, I, pp. 20–6; and Shove, 1942, p. 297.) A modern elaboration of this critique asserts that the possibility of determining relative prices through the classical price equations, independently of demand, requires that the conditions of a special non-substitution theorem be met (Bliss, 1975).

In so far as this critique attributes, implicitly or explicitly, to Ricardian analysis the position that demand is irrelevant to the determination of relative prices, it is unfounded. While demand considerations do not form part of the classical core, the proposition that demand, properly understood, can exert some (perhaps considerable) influence on natural prices is fully compatible with the surplus approach. The data of the core, it will be recalled, are the size and composition of output, the technical conditions of production, and the real wage (or, in Sraffa's case, the profit rate); these data are used to determine, at a primary analytical stage, necessary quantitative relationships between the distribution variables and relative prices. Relationships of a less quantitatively exact nature – among which are the relationships linking incomes, relative prices and outputs – must be examined outside the core at a second analytical stage. *Interrelationships between relative prices, distribution and demand are acknowledged to exist, as are their possible feedback effects on cost of production.* But because these relations and effects are conditioned by a complex set of social and psychological factors, they cannot be given precise analytical expression, and so must be excluded from the core (Garegnani, 1984). Demand does indeed matter; but it matters in such an indefinite, subtle and intricate way that it cannot enter the story on an equal footing with cost of production. Reference to the classical literature, we shall see, supports this interpretation.

Classical equilibrium and the law of demand

Reading the classicals one is struck by the imprecision with which they used the term demand. At various places throughout their work they take demand to mean: the quantity demanded at a particular price (usually the natural price); quantity demanded irrespective of price; total expenditure on a given product; the price that consumers are willing to pay for a certain quantity; and occasionally a *bona fide* demand schedule. Malthus (1820, pp. 65–6) draws a confusing distinction between the extent and intensity of demand, but he fails to differentiate between movements along a demand function and shifts of the function itself; Ricardo appears in one instance (1821, p. 382) to have used the concept of demand to denote the amount of a good actually taken from the market, rather than the amounts that buyers might choose to purchase at alternative prices (V. Smith, 1951, 1956). In the writings of Smith, James Mill and Ricardo this lack of clarity is perhaps understandable in light of the secondary role accorded by them to demand; similar fuzziness in the work of Malthus, Say and others for whom demand occupied a more central role can possibly be explained by the fact that a clearly specified conception of demand as a functional relationship among variables was not yet available.

What any of these writers meant by the term 'demand' is less important, though, than the fact that they all accepted as a fundamental behavioural principle the idea that the quantity demanded of a good is inversely related to its price. The Law of Demand is a commonplace empirical regularity, and its acceptance by the classicals is not in any way remarkable. But the use to which Adam Smith put the Law, in his explanation of how a commodity's price is pushed towards its natural level, was a pathbreaking theoretical innovation: When market price exceeds natural price in a particular market, higher than normal profits attract resources to the industry and output increases; if the larger output is to be sold – if the profits which it represents are to be realized – firms must lower the commodity's price. Similarly, where accidental overproduction drives a good's price below its natural level, the resulting cutback in industry output causes market price to be bid up until all buyers who are not willing to pay the natural price are excluded from the market.

The mechanism described by Smith ensures that, in markets where outputs can be adjusted, there will be a gravitation towards a position in which (a) market price coincides with natural price; and (b) quantity demanded is equal to quantity produced. A vital component of that mechanism is the supposition that price and quantity demanded vary inversely: If demand were entirely inelastic with respect to price, supernormal profits *would* cause industry output to expand, but initially there would be no reason for price to fall towards its natural level since all of the additional output could be sold without any reduction in price. Because of the abnormally high profits, capital will continue to be drawn into the industry, even after the level of output is brought up to the fixed amount demanded; once this threshold is breached firms will find that they are producing goods which cannot be sold. As firms compete for custom, market price will indeed begin to drop. (Though total market demand is fixed, households will of course prefer to buy from the seller with the lowest price.) When firms' profit rates, under pressure from falling prices and unsold goods, start to drop below the normal rate, output will be reduced. But since market demand is fixed there will be no competition among buyers acting to raise price so long as output is greater than market demand. As soon as output falls below the amount demanded, competition among buyers kicks in, causing price to jump sharply until it exceeds the natural price; capital will again be drawn into the industry, output will expand and the adjustment sequence described above will recur. Market price moves in the right direction when it deviates from natural price; but if demand is absolutely unresponsive to price changes, market price adjustments will tend systematically to shoot past the natural price, so that there is no real convergence toward it. Smith did not, of course, develop his argument in these terms; but the gravitational mechanism he described can operate effectively only if quantity demanded is at least somewhat responsive to market price changes.

Thus the Law of Demand enters the classical system as a (weak) condition for the stability of long-period equilibrium. Both Ricardo (e.g. 1821, p. 382) and Marx (1894, pp. 179–99) followed Smith in assigning this equilibrating function to the Law of Demand. (See also, oddly enough, Malthus, 1820, p. 69.) The relevance of demand is confined, at least in the first instance, to the disequilibrium dynamics of value theory, leaving the classical core, as outlined by Garegnani, intact.

It is an altogether different matter, however, to claim that demand plays a critical part, co-equal with cost of production, in the determination of the equilibrium position itself. Ricardo was adamant in his opposition to the crude but deeply-rooted supply-and demand explanation of value which ran through much of the economic thought of the early nineteenth century. The most important of Ricardo's contemporaries to embrace this theory were, of course, Malthus (1820) and Say (1821); but the list of noteworthy adherents includes also Lauderdale (1819), Bailey (1825) and Buchanan (1822).[2]

Ricardo and Malthus on the role of demand
In retrospect the celebrated Ricardo–Malthus dispute on value appears to have been less a real debate than a tedious sequence of repetitions. Ricardo's position is well known: fluctuations in demand and supply, he realized, could lead to variations in market prices; he also knew that day-to-day price movements must be understood in terms of such fluctuations. But where competition prevails, production must eventually respond to any divergence between market price and natural price, ensuring that the former gravitates toward the latter. Hence it is cost of production which ultimately regulates value. Demand and fluctuations in demand are relevant mainly to the movements of the (transitory) market price; to the extent that they exert any influence on the natural price, they do so – as we shall see – in a secondary and indirect fashion. Ricardo never wavered on this matter, and his many statements against the supply-and-demand argument vary only in their wording:

> I do not dispute either the influence of demand on the price of corn and on the price of all other things, but supply follows close at its heels, and soon takes the power of regulating price in his own hands, and in regulating it he [sic] is determined by cost of production. (Ricardo to Malthus, 24 November 1820; in Ricardo, 1951–59, Vol. VII, p. 302)

> . . . however great the demand for a commodity may be, its price will be finally regulated by the competition of the sellers, – it will settle at or about its natural price. . . . The market price of a commodity may from an unusual demand, or from a deficiency of supply, rise above its natural price, but this does not overturn the doctrine that the great regulator of price is cost of production. (Ricardo, 1820, pp. 38–9)

> It is the cost of production which must ultimately regulate the price of commodities, and not, as has been often said, the proportion between the supply and demand: the proportion between supply and demand may, indeed, for a time, affect the market value of a commodity, until it is supplied in greater or less abundance, according as the demand may have increased or diminished; but this effect will be only of temporary duration. (Ricardo, 1821, p. 382)

(See also, e.g., Ricardo, 1951–59, Vol. VII, pp. 276–7, 279; 1820, pp. 24–5; and 1821, pp. 119–20.)[3]

Just what Malthus meant when he wrote (1820, p. 65) that commodity prices depend upon 'the mutual relation of supply and demand' is not altogether apparent. The main difficulty is that while he clearly wished to maintain that supply and demand interact to determine both market *and* natural prices (Malthus, 1820, pp. 71–6, 83–4), his reasoning in the end always leads back to Ricardo's conclusion. Malthus's inability to see this suggests that the differences between the two men were caused by semantic difficulties for which Malthus was mainly responsible. These difficulties arise at the start of the latter's discussion of the distinction between the extent and intensity of demand: The extent of demand refers simply to the amount of a commodity which is bought, and, as this amount will in general tend to coincide with the amount made available by sellers – i.e. since 'in this sense demand and supply always bear the same relation to each other'– it cannot enter into an explanation of price (Malthus, 1827, pp. 244–5). By intensity of demand Malthus meant nothing other than what would today be called the demand price of a good – the price which would cause a given quantity to be purchased. (To my knowledge this has not hitherto been noticed, though V. Smith (1956) comes close. An objection might be raised that Malthus is explicit in referring to market price as only the 'expression' of intensity of demand and not as the intensity itself. Against this it may be argued that since Malthus clearly understood market price to be an *index* of intensity of demand (pp. 66, 68), and since, in the absence of a measureable concept of utility, the word 'intensity' can be given no formal analytic meaning with respect to psychological phenomena, the only plausible interpretation is that Malthus meant by 'intensity of demand' what modern economists call 'demand price'.)

According to V. Smith (1956, p. 213), 'The concept of intensity of demand made demand and supply a useful explanation of prices and strengthened Malthus's case regarding people's wants and tastes . . . as the active force in the determination of the level of business activity.' In fact the concept does no such thing. On the contrary, by treating demand as a price which is, so to speak, activated by market supply, Malthus *weakened* his claim that natural prices are determined by the interaction of supply and demand; for demand, in this sense, is not independent of market supply: it is a determined, rather than a determining, magnitude. Malthus's own examples work against him, and he was forced by his definition of demand to resort to verbal contortions: Considering the effect of a permanent increase in produc-

tion costs, in a market where quantity demanded is perfectly inelastic
with respect to price, Malthus (1820, p. 68) writes that

> there would be the same quantity supplied and the same quantity demanded;
> but there would be a much greater intensity of demand called forth; and *this
> may be fairly said to be a most important change in the relation between the
> supply and demand of [this] commodity*; because, without the increased
> intensity of demand [i.e. the increased market price] . . . the commodity
> would cease to be produced. (Emphasis added.)

Beyond bearing out my interpretation of the intensity of demand, this
passage, in the awkward and peculiar meaning it assigns to 'the relation
between the supply and demand', suggests that Malthus may himself
have been uncertain about how to extend the supply-and-demand
argument to the long period.

Indeed, Malthus (1820, pp. 69–71) proceeds almost immediately to
sketch out a conventional scenario in which demand influences the path
of gravitation toward the natural price, but plays no role in the
determination of the latter:

> If . . . the cost of producing any particular commodity were greatly
> diminished, the fall of price would . . . be occasioned by an increased
> abundance of supply. . . . In almost all practical cases it would be a
> permanent increase, because the competition of sellers would lower the
> price; and it very rarely happens that a fall of price does not occasion an
> increased consumption. On the supposition . . . that a definite quantity only
> of the commodity was required, whatever might be its price, it is obvious that
> from the competition of the producers a greater quantity would be brought to
> market than could be consumed, til the price was reduced in proportion to
> the increased facility of production; and this excess supply would be always
> contingent on the circumstances of the price being at any time higher than the
> price which returns average profits.

Referring again to his curious definition of demand, Malthus observes
that

> [though] the actual quantity of the commodity supplied and consumed may
> . . . be the same as before[,] . . . it cannot be said that the demand is the
> same . . . [For] such has been the alteration in the means of supply compared
> with the demand that . . . the same intensity of demand [is] no longer
> necessary to effect the supply required; and not being necessary, it is of
> course not called forth, and the price falls.

After presenting this argument, which except for its quirky terminology
is identical to that put forth by Smith and Ricardo, Malthus, astonish-
ingly, sums up as follows:

> If the terms demand and supply be understood in the way here described,
> there is no case of price, *whether temporary or permanent*, which they will not
> determine, and in every instance of bargain and sale it will be perfectly

correct to say that the price will depend upon the relation of the demand to the supply. (Emphasis added.)

In the light of the discussion leading up to this statement, Malthus's insistence that supply and demand *determine* natural price must be taken as evidence of either profound confusion or a Humpty-Dumpty approach to words – or both.

The interpretational ambiguity is compounded by Malthus's apparently casual observation (p. 73) that the supply-and-demand mechanism 'is found to operate not only permanently upon the class of commodities which may be considered as monopolies, but temporarily and immediately upon all commodities, and strikingly and pre-eminently so upon all sorts of raw produce.' By singling out monopolized commodities as the class of goods for which demand exerts a *permanent* influence upon price – Ricardo, of course, never denied this – Malthus comes close to implying that under normal (i.e. competitive) conditions demand has only a temporary influence upon price.

Moreover, Malthus devotes an entire section of his *Principles* (1820, pp. 72–85) to an ineffectual critique of the cost-of-production theory which, in the end, only draws attention to the fragility of his own position. A good part of the argument amounts to a restatement of the undisputed and irrelevant fact that where output is fixed, price depends upon the relation of demand to supply. While Malthus makes the correct observation that the forces of supply and demand govern the path taken by market prices in their gravitation towards the natural price, the conclusion he draws from it – 'that the relation of the supply to the demand . . . is the dominant principle in the determination of prices whether market or natural' – is a *non sequitur* (pp. 75–6).

Perhaps sensing the vulnerability of his position, Malthus plays one last card: Demand, he argues, influences a commodity's price through the pressure it exerts upon input prices (pp. 78–80). If labour, capital and land are to be drawn into the production of a commodity the demand for which has increased, *their* prices must rise; in cases where these inputs have special characteristics and are scarce, the increase in their prices will be permanent, so that the price of the final product must also be permanently higher. (The reasoning applied by Malthus anticipates the neoclassical principle of imputation, illustrating in a uniquely clear and simple way Garegnani's point (1983) that demand is relevant to price determination in a neoclassical model only to the extent that it influences the distribution of income.)[4] But as Ricardo (1820, pp. 52–3) pointed out, this argument ultimately reduces to the proposition that a commodity's price is determined by its cost of production, with supply and demand entering the story through the back-door as determinants of factor prices. The question then becomes whether wages and profits are market-determined, and this Ricardo denies; see, for example, Ricardo (1820, pp. 226–8) for his view on the determination of wages.

The foregoing discussion points to the conclusion that Malthus did not truly comprehend either his own argument or that of Ricardo. This conclusion is reinforced by the failure of Malthus to raise the one issue that could have put Ricardo on the defensive – the problem of price determination under conditions of non-constant returns. Rankin (1980) notes, rightly, that Ricardo's repudiation of the supply-and-demand argument constitutes an interpretational problem when viewed against his theory of rent, which was itself based upon the assumption of diminishing returns in agricultural production. There can be no doubt that Ricardo was aware of the modifications imposed upon his argument by the presence of variable returns; for in his chapter on Profits (1821, pp. 119–20) he wrote that:

> prices vary in the market, and in the first instance, through the comparative state of demand and supply. [The price of cloth may rise above its natural price] from . . . any . . . cause which should suddenly and unexpectedly increase the demand, or diminish the supply of it. The makers of cloth will for a time have unusual profits, but capital will naturally flow to that manufacture, till the supply and the demand are again at their fair level, when the price of cloth will again sink to its natural or necessary price. In the same manner, with every increased demand for corn, it may rise so high as to afford more than the general profits to the farmer. If there be plenty of fertile land, the price of corn will again fall to its former standard, after the requisite quantity of capital has been employed in producing it, and profits will be as before, but if there be not plenty of fertile land, if, to produce this additional quantity, more than the usual quantity of capital and labour be required corn will not fall to its former level. Its natural price will be raised, and the farmer . . . will find himself obliged to be satisfied with the diminished rate [of profit] which is the inevitable consequence of the rise of wages, produced by the rise of necessaries.

Here Ricardo appears to be inconsistent. If he realized that demand could exert some influence over natural price, how can his opposition to the supply-and-demand argument make any sense?

According to Rankin (1980, pp. 250–1), Ricardo's objections to supply and demand as determinants of natural price rest upon a narrow and somewhat peculiar understanding of the supply and demand mechanism: What Ricardo criticizes is the idea of a price-elastic demand schedule interacting with a perfectly inelastic supply of output to determine price, without reference to cost of production and without recognition of the fact that where market price diverges from cost of production an adjustment in supply must occur in the long run. Ricardo was indeed aware of the role played by demand in determining price, particularly in primary resource industries where diminishing returns prevail. However, Rankin argues, he understood the term 'supply-and-demand' to refer *only* to the short-period situation in which output is fixed. It was this restricted conception of supply-and-demand theory which Ricardo rejected; but his own model of price determination is in essence nothing more than a broader formulation – i.e. one in which output can respond to profit rate differentials across sectors – *of that same theory*. Thus Ricardo's story differs from that of the neoclassicals only in its nomenclature.

Rankin's interpretation, which is shared by Hollander (1979, pp. 273–93), is attractive because it seems to clear up an apparent ambiguity in the Ricardian system. In fact the interpretation is not well founded, and the ambiguity it aims to resolve is illusory. We have already seen that Malthus attempted in at least one instance (1820, pp. 68–70) to develop the supply-and-demand argument in terms of *price-elas 'c* output adjustments. To this Ricardo (1820, pp. 40–1) responded: 'Mr Malthus here substantially admits, that it is not the relation of demand to supply, which finally and permanently regulates the price of commodities, but the cost of their production.' Thus Ricardo rejects the supply-and-demand theory even when it explicitly allows for changes in output. To be sure, Malthus employs an example characterized by constant returns – rendering demand irrelevant and playing into his opponents hands – precisely where it would have made the most sense for him to deploy the variable return critique. This suggests, first, that his understanding of the supply-and-demand mechanism was imperfect, i.e. that it did not coincide with or anticipate the neoclassical conception; and, second, that he also did not understand Ricardo's argument against it. And if, as Rankin and Hollander claim, Ricardo was using a supply-and-demand model, he certainly would not have passed up the opportunity, presented to him by Malthus, to correct his friend's argument by pointing out that demand becomes relevant only under conditions of non-constant returns; that he did not do so indicates that Rankin and Hollander have misread him.

Ricardo does admit that when returns to scale are not constant there *is* a role for demand in the price determination process. But the passage in which he makes this point (1821, pp. 119–20, quoted above) contains no trace of the idea that the forces of supply and demand – represented by two independent functional relationships – interact *simultaneously* to determine both prices and outputs. Rankin's attribution to Ricardo of a neoclassical treatment of price rests upon an incorrect reading of this reference to an 'increased demand for corn'; Rankin interprets Ricardo to mean a rightward shift of a price-elastic demand *schedule*. There is however no textual evidence to suggest that Ricardo was thinking in these terms; given the state of demand theory at the time, and his own scepticism about the possibility of isolating a definite relation between price and quantity demanded (1951–59, Vol. IV, pp. 219–20), it is unlikely that Ricardo could have had such a notion in mind. Moreover, the context of the passage – Ricardo was considering the effects of changes in the *output* of corn on the profit rate – leaves little doubt that what he meant by 'increased demand' was in fact an increase in the amount of corn demanded at the natural price. Once this is recognized, the Rankin– Hollander interpretation appears contrived and, indeed, untenable.

Ricardo was not aiming at the simultaneous determination of price and output; he was instead engaged in a comparative static exercise in which the real wage (in terms of corn) *and* the gross output of corn appear as data, while the variables to be determined or explained are the price of corn and the profit rate. This exercise is an uncommonly clear illustration of the analytical approach which Garegnani (1984) attributes to the classical economists: Ricardo is concerned with the consequences of an increase in the effectual demand for corn, i.e. in the amount of it demanded at the natural price (Smith, 1776, Book I, p. 49). As output expands in response to increased demand, diminishing returns cause the natural price to rise. The prices at the two levels of demand are determined by cost of production in the usual way, while any residual impact of the price rise on quantity demanded is left for consideration at a separate analytical stage. In discussing the implications of diminishing returns for the profit rate and the price of corn, Ricardo was merely crossing over from the core of classical analysis, where price is determined by cost of production, to a secondary analytical stage in which the feedback effects of output variations on unit costs are taken into account.

The role of demand in the marginalist theory of price
Garegnani (1983) has made the point that what enabled the classicals to explain prices without reference to demand functions was their treatment of distribution. Following the classicals, the early marginalists held that price would gravitate towards long-period unit cost, including normal profits; but unlike their classical predecessors the first neoclassicals were unable to do without demand functions because, in the marginalist system, consumer preferences are crucial to the determination of factor prices and hence of long-run unit costs. This can easily be seen. Let us suppose at the outset that production is everywhere characterized by constant returns to scale. (This assumption is indispensable since without it there is no way to be certain that factor payments, which in a neoclassical equilibrium must be equal to the value

of each factor's marginal product multiplied by the volume of production, will add up to the value of total net product.) Now, it is clear that demand can make a difference to normal price only if the long-run average cost curve (the supply curve) is not horizontal – that is, only if unit costs vary with output. If returns to scale are constant, output changes can generate changes in costs only by influencing the prices of inputs: according to the typical marginalist story, any change in the structure of final demand will alter the demand for factors used in different production processes; and the resulting adjustments in factor prices are what determine (a) the characteristics of the supply function for each good, and (b) the price variations that result from changes in demand. Because orthodox theory attempts to determine outputs, distribution and commodity prices all at once, household preferences, embodied in demand functions, are essential to the derivation of a solution; for these preferences are what ultimately regulate the prices of the scarce resources with which the economy is endowed.

Thus demand functions are in neoclassical analysis relevant to the determination of prices only in so far as they enter into the formation of factor rewards. By contrast, a distinctive feature of classical political economy is the separation of the theory of distribution from the process by which commodity prices are established. The wage (or profit) rate is determined prior to and independently of, relative prices by forces that are as much social, historical and political as they are economic; causality runs sequentially from a *given* distribution variable to price, so that there is no need to incorporate demand into the analysis. Preferences are of secondary importance for the classical explanation of prices because the classical approach to distribution does not explain factor rewards in terms of the relative scarcity of inputs (Garegnani, 1983 p. 310).

Hollander's Ricardian imputation mechanism
An alternative and increasingly influential view of Ricardian value theory has been put forth by Hollander (1979), who sees no fundamental discontinuity between classical and neo-classical analysis. According to Hollander, Ricardo's separation of the determination of factor rewards from the price formation process rests upon an unstated assumption that the machine labour ratio is uniform across sectors. This assumption, in combination with Say's Law of Markets, prevents a change in the composition of demand from influencing factor returns: The equality of machine labour ratios ensures that the wages fund remains undiminished relative to the stock of machine capital, while the Law of Markets guarantees that any resources released by a change in

the pattern of demand will be fully absorbed by increased outputs in other sectors; hence no pressure is exerted upon either the wage or the profit rate.

Hollander argues that constancy of the wage and profit rates in the face of shifting consumer preferences is not an essential feature of Ricardo's system but a 'simplifying device' adopted to facilitate his critique of Smith's theory of profit. Ricardo was able to take the wage rate as a datum because an implicit assumption about the equality of sectoral factor proportions eliminates the possibility that a change in the structure of demand will have feedback effects on the distribution variables. Hollander (1979, pp. 299–300) argues that:

> [w]hen a characteristic of this kind flows logically from a specific assumption of the model it is difficult to argue that what is involved is a *matter of principle*. There seems no reason to expect that if Ricardo had been obliged to face the issue of an exogenous change in the pattern of demand, assuming differential factor proportions, he would have refused to recognize that the (aggregate) demand-supply relations in the labour market must be influenced.

The key to seeing how Ricardo might have handled the problem lies, Hollander believes, in the well-known chapter on Machinery, which appeared for the first time in the third edition of the *Principles*. In that chapter Ricardo considers the consequences of an increase in mechanization by examining the effects of labour-saving technical change on the composition of the economy's capital stock. If a particular innovation substitutes machine-capital for labour-capital, the reorganization of the capital stock required by the implementation of the new technique may entail an absolute reduction of the fund out of which wages are paid (Ricardo, 1820, p. 388).

It is Hollander's contention that where factor proportions differ across sectors, this same argument may be extended to demonstrate that changes in the composition of demand can influence the wage and profit rates. For example, an autonomous shift in preferences away from, let us say, a labour-intensive good in favour of a machine-intensive good will lead to a reduction in the wage component of the economy's total capital stock as the machine component expands. Hollander concludes from this that, given the size of the labour force, the wage rate must fall, while the profit rate rises (1979, pp. 299–300). Thus distribution is not independent of the structure of preferences and, consequently, natural prices also cannot be independent of demand. While the mechanism by which this result is achieved involves changes in the economy's capital structure rather than technical substitution in the usual sense, the conclusion appears – superficially at least – to support the idea of a continuous tradition leading from Smith and Ricardo through Mill to the first marginalists.

Hollander is careful to point out that Ricardo himself never extended the discussion of the Machinery chapter to investigate the impact of changes in demand on distribution and normal prices. But what matters, Hollander (1979, p. 680) insists, is that the extension

> is fully consistent with the existing corpus of Ricardian theory. There are, accordingly, no 'paradigmatic' differences between Ricardian and neo-classical theory in so far as concerns the effects upon distribution of a change in the pattern of final demand. Again the notion of a sharp divorce between distribution and pricing encountered in secondary accounts of Ricardo's system does not stand up to close examination.

In fact, it is Hollander's interpretation that will not bear scrutiny.

First, a crucial element of Hollander's argument is the idea that insensitivity of factor rewards to changes in the structure of demand rests upon the implicit assumption of equal factor proportions across sectors. But, while Ricardo was certainly aware that such an assumption would permit commodities to exchange at their labour values (1823, passim), nowhere in his writings can evidence be found that he adopted it as a working hypothesis. Hollander infers that the assumption must be *implicitly* present, else Ricardo would have had no basis for treating the real wage as a datum. But the fact that Ricardo was, in general, highly conscientious about stating his assumptions substantially weakens this view. Furthermore, the precise function of the 'simplifying device' is not at all evident: Ricardo does not require it since his case against Smith's profit rate theory is made once Say's Law is granted; the technical conditions of production are irrelevant to that critique. What Hollander has overlooked is the possibility that Ricardo's parametric treatment of the wage rate might be grounded not in some phantom assumption about technical coefficients, but in a specifically classical understanding of distribution which has nothing to do with the feedback effects of preferences on rewards to inputs.

Secondly, with reference to the chapter on Machinery, it is clear that the introduction of a new cost-reducing technique (whether labour-saving or machine-saving) can alter the wage-profit rate frontier, so that given the value of one distribution variable, the value of the other will change. A change in preferences can produce a similar result under conditions of variable returns to scale – witness the effect on the profit rate of diminishing returns in agriculture. Under these circumstances it may be legitimate to refer to the feedback effects of preferences on distribution. But there is nothing un-Ricardian or unclassical about such phenomena: a striking feature of the mechanism considered here is that it has nothing in common with the neoclassical process by which the value of output is imputed to individual factors of production. Had Hollander made this argument he would have remained on defensible ground; in moving beyond it to claim that there are no significant incompatibilities between classical analysis and modern general equilibrium theory, he has left himself open to criticism.

For, thirdly, Hollander has failed to recognize that Ricardo's approach to distribution was altogether different from that of modern theory in that he – as well as Smith and Marx – did not explain factor rewards in terms of the market-clearing interaction of the forces of supply and demand. It is of course true that a change in the composition of demand will alter the ratio of machine-capital to labour-capital in the economy; thus exogenous changes can lead to a reduction (or increase) in the fund available for the support of labour. But in his chapter on machinery the main practical result Ricardo anticipates from this, insofar as the labour market is concerned, is a reduction in *employment*. Writing specifically about the effects of increased mechanization, Ricardo (1821, pp. 388, 390) observes that

> the . . . fund, from which landlords and capitalists derive their revenue, may increase, while the . . . [fund] upon which the labouring class mainly depend, may diminish, and therefore it follows . . . that the same cause which may increase the net revenue of the country, may at the same time render the population *redundant*, and deteriorate the condition of the labourer. (Emphasis added.)
> . . . [A]s the power of supporting a population, and employing labour, depends always on the gross produce of a nation, and not on its net produce, there will necessarily be a diminution in the demand for labour [by which Ricardo clearly means a diminution in the *quantity* of labour demanded], *population will become redundant*, and the situation of the labouring classes will be that of distress and poverty. . . . [T]he discovery and use of machinery may be . . . injurious to the labouring class, *as some of their number will be thrown out of employment, and population will become redundant, compared with the funds which are to employ it.* (Emphasis added.)

These remarks clearly convey the idea that – for Ricardo at any rate – the primary effect of a contraction of the wages-fund will be reduced employment, while the wage rate is only incidentally affected – if it is affected at all. (With respect to the consequences of technological labour displacement, there is no reason to suppose, as Hollander does, that *real* wages must decline even if *money* wages do fall. If commodity prices fall as a result of mechanization real wages may remain constant or even rise, regardless of what happens to money wages or employment.)[5]

It is precisely the non-market nature of wage determination in the

Ricardian model which differentiates it from modern analysis. Hollander supposes that in equilibrium the labour market must clear, and that the wage rate will typically adjust to eliminate any excess supply of labour. This amounts to the imposition of marginalist rules on a classical model. In the latter, however, it is employment – not the wage – which feels the pinch when the wages-fund contracts. There is evidently more than a trace of question-begging in Hollander's interpretational approach: neoclassical general equilibrium theory is taken as the standard for analytical completeness and economic coherence; an embryonic understanding of that theory is inappropriately attributed to – or, more correctly, imposed upon – Ricardo; and the conclusion that there is no essential break between classical and modern economic theory becomes inevitable.

None of this means that persistent high unemployment will not or cannot exert some downward pressure on the wage rate. But there is no reason to believe, within the context of a classical model, that a reduction in the wages-fund must be associated with a decrease in the natural wage rate, or that a fall in the wage will do anything to maintain or increase the level of employment. Hollander seems to suppose that a wage reduction will move the economy in the direction of full employment; but in as much as he does not demonstrate the presence of a modern technical substitution mechanism in Ricardo's system, the supposition is unwarranted. And if wage flexibility cannot guarantee full employment, there is no reason to expect that the *natural* wage must respond systematically to excess labour supply.

Conclusion
The preceding discussion has established that Ricardo did not ignore the impact of demand upon price; rather, he recognized that the subjective nature of demand prevents its role from being assessed with real analytical precision. Thus the investigation of outputs must be relegated to a secondary stage of analysis external to the classical core.

The surplus approach still lacks a well-articulated theory of output – a deficiency which has led to much confusion regarding the need for a constant returns assumption in modern formulations of the model (Mongiovi, 1987). But recent attempts by some historians of thought to fit the classical model into a marginalist straitjacket do not offer a solution: Not only do they lack textual support; they also rob the classical theory of one of its enduring strengths – its flexibility and openness with respect to the incorporation of historical and institutional considerations into the analysis of distribution, outputs and accumulation.

Notes

1. I am indebted to Pierangelo Garegnani, Edward Nell and Pier Luigi Porta for advice and encouragement on an earlier draft of this paper.
2. Marx's views on the role of demand were in all essential respects identical to those of Ricardo. See Marx (1894, pp. 179–99).
3. This argument did not originate with Ricardo. As early as 1804 Francis Horner had refuted Malthus's supply and demand theory by pointing out that in the long run supply would accommodate itself to any change in demand, leaving price unaltered (V. Smith 1956, p. 210n). Horner almost got it right. His argument is correct under constant returns; but where returns are variable, a change in demand will result in a change in the natural price.
4. Malthus (1820, p. 82) goes so far as to say that profits 'are only a fair remuneration for that part of the product contributed by the capitalist, estimated exactly in the same way as the contribution of the labourer', and he makes a similar argument with respect to rent.
5. Discussing the economic consequences of a long tax-financed war, Ricardo (1821, p. 394) does make explicit reference to the impact of increased unemployment on wages. Here, though, Ricardo is speaking of a *short-period* response by the economy to an exogenous disturbance, in this case the termination of international hostilities.

References

Bailey, S. (1825), *A Critical Dissertation on the Nature, Measure and Causes of Value*, R. Hunter, London.
Bliss, C. (1975), *Capital Theory and the Distribution of Income*, North-Holland, Amsterdam.
Buchanan, D. (1822), 'Observations on Mr Ricardo's doctrine of the principles which regulate prices', *Caledonian Mercury* (May).
Garegnani, P. (1983), 'The classical theory of wages and the role of demand schedules in the determination of relative prices', *American Economic Review*, vol. 73, no. 2 (May), pp. 309–13.
Garegnani, P. (1984), 'On the theory of distribution and value in Marx and the classical economists', *Oxford Economic Papers*, vol. 36, no. 2 (July), pp. 291–325.
Jevons, W.S. (1879), *Theory of Political Economy*, 2nd edn, A.M. Kelley, New York.
Lauderdale, J.M. (1819), *An Inquiry into the Nature and Origin of Public Wealth*, 2nd edn, A.M. Kelley, New York.
Malthus, T.R. (1820), *Principles of Political Economy*, reprinted as vol. 2 of Ricardo (1951–59); references are to Malthus's pagination.
Malthus, T.R. (1827), *Definitions in Political Economy*, John Murray, London.
Marx, K. (1894), *Capital*, vol. 3, International Publishers, Moscow.
Mongiovi, G. (1987), 'Returns to scale, the standard commodity, and Sraffa's *Production of Commodities by Means of Commodities*: a note', *Studi Economici*, vol. 42, no. 1, pp. 35–50.
Rankin, S.C. (1980), 'Supply and demand in Ricardian price theory: a re-interpretation', *Oxford Economic Papers*, vol. 32, no. 2 (July), pp. 241–62.
Ricardo, D. (1820), *Notes on Malthus*, vol. 2 of Ricardo (1951–59).
Ricardo, D. (1821), *Principles of Political Economy and Taxation*, 3rd edn, vol. 1 of Ricardo (1951–59).
Ricardo, D. (1823), 'Absolute value and exchangeable value', in vol. 4 of Ricardo (1951–59), pp. 358–412.
Ricardo, D. (1951–59), *The Works and Correspondence of David Ricardo* (P. Sraffa, ed.), vols 1–10, Cambridge University Press, Cambridge.
Say, J. B. (1821), *Treatise on Political Economy* (4th edn; trans. C.R. Prinsep), Wells and Lilly, Boston.

Shove, G. (1942), 'The place of Marshall's *Principles* in the development of economic theory', *Economic Journal*, vol. 52 (December), pp. 294–329.

Smith, A. (1776), *An Inquiry into the Nature and Causes of the Wealth of Nations*, University of Chicago Press, Chicago.

Smith, V.E. (1951), 'The classicists' use of "demand" ', *Journal of Political Economy*, vol. 59, no. 3 (June), pp. 242–57.

Smith, V.E. (1956), 'Malthus's theory of demand and its influence on value theory', *Scottish Journal of Political Economy*, vol. 3, no. 3 (October), pp. 205–20.

Walras, L. (1926), *Elements of Pure Economics* (definitive edn; trans W. Jaffe), A.M. Kelley, New York.

Wicksell, K. (1934), *Lectures on Political Economy* (trans. E. Classen), vols 1–2, George Routledge and Sons, London.

PART III

NEOCLASSICAL TOPICS

9 On the role of general equilibrium theory in Walras's theory of a just society

Peter de Gijsel

Introduction

This paper eliminates an ambiguity which arises from a recent controversy on the roles of general equilibrium theory (GE-theory) in Walras's system of political economy. The question under consideration is whether Walras used his GE-theory as a normative or as a positive theory in his system of political economy. It is argued in this paper that GE-theory forms a systematic part of Walras's normative theory of a just society formulated in his *Etudes d'économie sociale*. Walras's theory of a just society consists in fact of several sub-theories. The role of GE-theory in these sub-theories is analysed leading to the conclusion that Walras used GE-theory as a positive theory.

By thus using GE-theory Walras gives an interesting example of a 'scientific socialism', the task of which should be to prove in a scientific way the viability of a socialistic society.

Up to the 1970s it was generally thought that Walras's GE-theory could be regarded as an analytical framework which allowed the consistent and thorough analysis of a system of competitive markets being in equilibrium (Friedman, 1955). Within this framework empirical meaningful hypotheses on the working of real existing market economies could be derived by modifying the assumptions on which general equilibrium theory is based. It was argued that this was also intended by Walras himself, though he did not succeed in developing an acceptable theory of a growing capitalistic economy (Morishima, 1977, 1980).

This view has severely criticized in recent years by Jaffé (1977, 1980), widely acknowledged as one of the most competent interpreters of Walras's scientific work. According to Jaffé, Walras never intended to develop a model of a capitalistic society. Instead, his objective was 'to portray how an imaginary system *might* work in conformity with principles of "justice" rooted in traditional natural law philosophy. . . . The *Elements* was intended to be and is, in all but the

133

name, a realistic utopia' (Jaffé, 1980, p. 530). As Jaffé admits himself, this view of the *Elements* is diametrically opposed to that of 'all twentieth-century commentators on Walras's economics' (ibid.) (see for example Hicks, 1934; Friedman, 1955; Morishima, 1977, 1980; Walker, 1984).

Jaffé's interpretation of Walras gives rise to some confusion. Does his view imply that GE-theory should be regarded as a normative scheme (Walker, 1984)? Or did Jaffé simply want to say that GE-theory should be considered as a *systematic* part of Walras's normative theory of a just society? From a methodological point of view the latter interpretation would leave open the question concerning the normativeness or positiveness of GE-theory, because as a sub-theory of a normative theory GE-theory could be both. So how did Walras use GE-theory in his theory of a just society?

When speaking of a 'realistic utopia' Jaffé could have meant that Walras intended to describe a structure of a free-market economy which would not exist in reality but could be realized by economic policy. But does this imply that Walras used GE-theory as a normative theory? Clearly not: whether a theory is positive or normative does not depend on the question whether objects of a theory's domain exist in reality or not. To speak of a 'realistic utopia' being described by GE-theory therefore does not imply that GE-theory should be regarded as a normative theory. Yet that is what Jaffé seems to suggest and how he has been understood by Walker (1984).

In his paper Walker comes to the conclusion that on

> the basis of the evidence it must be concluded that Walras's economic theory does not carry within it a particular conception of social justice and that his objective was to analyze the workings of the economic system. . . . The basic idea expressed by Walras's general-equilibrium theory is that markets are interrelated, which is not a normative concept. Walras's desire to analyze their interrelatedness was the reason for the character of his theory of general equilibrium, not a desire to use simultaneous equations and the ideas of interrelated markets as a vehicle and veil for his moral convictions. (Walker, 1984, pp. 466–7)

Walker does not deal explicitly in his critique on Jaffé with the role of GE-theory in Walras's theory of a just society. When discussing passages in the *Etudes d'économie sociale* in order to refute Jaffé's thesis that GE-theory should be regarded as a normative scheme, Walker makes the important distinction between the formulation of a positive theorem and the normative conclusions which could be drawn from it. To him, Walras formulated positive theorems in the *Elements d'économie politique pure* and drew normative conclusions from these theorems in both his *Etudes d'économie politique appliquée (1898)* and *Etudes d'économie sociale (1896)*:

> Instead of mixing together science and his moral views, Walras first expressed that theorem, which he believed was an expression of a scientific truth, and then he made a normative judgment on it. . . . For the positive theorem of maximum satisfaction, Walras referred to the *Elements*, lesson 20, 21 and 22. . . . For the normative conclusion he referred . . . to his 'Théorie de la propriété', which appears in his volume on social economics. (Walker, 1984, p. 459 and 459n)

Though it may be that Walras drew normative conclusions from his GE-theory in his social and applied economics, the role of GE-theory in Walras's theory of a just society is not exhausted by this interpretation. Why does GE-theory play such an important role, as Walras himself maintains when stressing that GE-theory (or mathematical economics) plays an 'indispensable' role in his applied and social economics (Walras, 1936b, p. 469; see also Walras, 1936a, p. 207, Jaffé, 1965, Vol. I, p. 148, and Vol. II, pp. 453, 464)? The clue, I think, has to be found in Walras's belief that the just society which he envisaged could be realized by way of economic reforms. GE-theory is the basis of his 'scientific socialism', the task of which should be to prove in a scientific way how a socialistic society could work (Walras, 1936a, p. 233).

This interpretation of Walras will become clear in the following sections. It will be argued that Walras used his GE-theory as a positive sub-theory in his overall normative theory of a just society. Thus the following analysis can be understood as an extension of Walker's analysis (1984) by investigating the role of GE-theory in Walras's 'realistic utopia'. The paper is organized as follows. In the next section a short outline of Walras's theory of a just society is given. Then the role of GE-theory in that theory will be analysed. The paper ends with a summary.

Walras's theory of a just society
Though Walras never presented his theory of a just society in a closed form the elements of such a theory can be found in his general theory of society (théorie générale de la société), theory of property (théorie de la propriété), and his theory of the price of land and the nationalization of land (théorie mathématique du prix des terres et de leur rachat par l'état), all published in the *Etudes d'économie sociale (1896)*.

From these sub-theories it follows that Walras's just society can best be characterized as one of liberal socialism or – which amounts to the same thing – as one of social liberalism (Gram and Walsh, 1980; Cirillo, 1979, 1984; de Gijsel, 1985). It is a society in which land is nationalized, all income taxes are abolished, and in which the state finances its expenditures solely out of rents or capital income being earned by selling capital services to the private sector. The nationalization of land and the abolishment of taxes determine a just distribution of initial resources between the state and individuals, guaranteeing equal opportunities for every individual:

> the land belongs to everyone in common, because all rational and free persons have the same right and the same duty to pursue their objective themselves and to achieve it themselves, and to achieve themselves their own destiny, and are, in virtue of those considerations, responsible for that pursuit and those achievements. Here applies the principle of the equality of conditions aimed at enabling us all to benefit equally from the resources that nature offers us to undertake our efforts. (Walras, 1936a, p. 218)

Besides a just distribution of property a just society is characterized by competitive markets leading to an efficient production and distribution of scarce resources and to a just distribution of income and wealth. According to Walras, this society could be realized by a peaceful nationalization of land and by an economic policy which ensures the competitiveness of markets by discarding private monopolies. Such a nationalization of land by the state could be carried out by buying land at prevailing prices. To be able to do this it is necessary that the state incur debts which can be amortized in a growing economy because of rising rents.

GE-theory as a positive sub-theory in Walras's theory of a just society
It can be concluded from this short outline of Walras's theory of a just society that Walras believed this society to be attainable. He believed that an economy, given the right conditions of collective ownership of land and state intervention to ensure the workability of free competition, could function quite closely to the theoretical model of free competition. It should be clear that Walras's theory of a just society consists in fact of several sub-theories, GE-theory plays a role in Walras's theory of property and in his theories of the price of land and of the nationalization of land.

In the theory of property GE-theory solves two problems. First, how can the value of initial resources, being owned by individuals and the state, be explained? Second, how can it be ensured that the distribution of income and wealth being produced in a competitive market economy will be just, given that the distribution of initial resources is just? The first question was posed by Walras's father and teacher, Auguste Walras, to whom the understanding of property was impossible without a theory of value, because nothing is appropriated unless it has value (Jaffé, 1984, p. 12).

> As Auguste Walras saw it, the source of value is *rareté*, literally scarcity, by which he meant the relative limitation in quantity of anything humanity deems useful. Only things characterized by *rareté* constitute wealth; only such things are exchangeable in trade; and hence only such things are appropriated. . . . So Auguste Walras established the link between value and property. Indeed, he argued, the theory of value is logically anterior to the theory of property. (Jaffé, 1984, pp. 12–13)

Léon Walras posed the problem of value in his theory of property by stating that the owner of a good would also be the owner of the value of that good, which he could receive when selling the good in the market. But how can the value of this good be explained? Walras attached great importance to a scientific answer to this question, because without such an answer it could not be explained why a just initial distribution of scarce resources, with which the state and individuals are endowed, will not result in an unjust distribution of income and wealth, when these resources are exchanged on competitive markets. Once a just initial distribution of scarce resources is given a competitive market system would produce a just distribution of income and wealth if it could be shown that equivalents are exchanged. By changing goods with the same market value money gains from trading are excluded.

Walras stated quite explicitly that the exchange of equivalents in a free market system has to be considered as a genuine problem of any scientific theory of property. According to him this problem could be solved by mathematical economics.

> It is therefore necessary here to demonstrate that free competition does not favour the buyers to the detriment of the sellers, or the reverse. Some readers will perhaps think that proposition is self-evident. I am not of that opinion. I consider the proposition as one of the most ticklish ones that mathematically economics is able to prove. Moreover, I see it as the knotty part of the scientific theory of property. (Walras, 1936a, p. 207)

In fact Walras solves this problem by explaining exchanges at equilibrium prices under a regime of free competition. His point may perhaps become clearer when it is illustrated in an Edgeworth box as is shown in Figure 9.1.

In Figure 9.1 point x^1 denotes the initial endowments of individuals A and B. The equilibrium allocation x^* lies on the budget constraint of A and B which goes through the initial endowment point x^1. Because both x^1 and x^* lie on the same budget line, it can be concluded that the value of the initial endowment must be the same as the value of the equilibrium allocation, i.e., $px^* = px^1$.

Figure 9.1   Exchange of equivalents

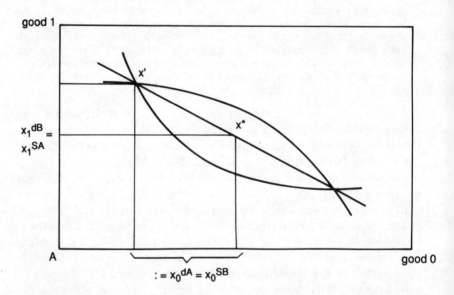

If individuals start from point x^1 and are confronted with the assumed equilibrium prices, they will choose the equilibrium allocation x^*. To realize x^{*A} will demand an amount of $x_o^{dA} = x_o^{*A} - x_o^{1A}$ of good O and supply $x_1^{SA} = x_1^{1A} - x_1^{*A}$ of good 1. Because $px^{*A} = px^{1A}$ and x^* is an equilibrium it follows that:

(1) $P_o x_o^{dA} = p_1 \times_1^{SA} = p_1 x_1^{dB} = p_o x_o^{SB}$

From (1) it can be concluded that A (B) will get the same value when changing x^{SA} units of good 1 for x_o^{SB} units of good O. This means that A and B are changing equivalents. Because the values of the initial allocation x^1 and the equilibrium allocation x^* are the same it can be said that the value of the distribution of initial resources is preserved when only exchanges at equilibrium prices are allowed. This is what Walras means when he speaks of 'commutative justice', being realized in a general equilibrium under a regime of free competition.

From the discussion it should be clear that once equilibrium prices in an economy with free competition are explained, both questions being asked at the beginning of this section can be answered: first, the value of the just distribution of initial resources is determined; second, it can be demonstrated that the value of this distribution will be preserved by exchange, excluding gains in terms of the *numéraire* good by trading.

That Walras in fact adopts his GE-theory in this way can now easily be demonstrated by inspecting the three conditions which must be fulfilled for equivalents to be exchanged and commutative justice to prevail in the market sphere. These conditions will in fact rule out transactions at disequilibrium prices.

The first condition is 'that there be only a single price ruling on the market' (Walras, 1936a, p. 212). If more than one price for a good would exist, gains by arbitrage could be realized which, in a competitive market, would lead ultimately to one price, the equilibrium price. It is the equilibrium price which Walras thinks to be just:

> If there were, at a given moment, several prices of a given commodity, the sellers would have the right to move from the place where the price is lower to the place where it is higher, and the buyers, inversely, from the latter place to the former; and these operations would have the effect of equalizing the different prices. It is perfectly just to quote the unique price immediately. At that price, when it has become the ruling value, it is perfectly just that, if a trader gives two units of a commodity and receives four of another for them, the one who gives five units should receive ten, and similarly for different quantities (ibid.).

The second condition for commutative justice is that money does not change its exchange value between the dates of its receipt and its expense. If money would change its exchange value, then there would be a gain or a loss to the money-holder. 'The intervention of money does not at all derange the conditions of justice in exchange, provided that the value of money does not change between the moment at which it is received and the moment at which it is paid out (ibid.).' This will, of course, be the case when exchange takes place at equilibrium prices.

The third and last condition for commutative justice is that firms produce at minimal costs (ibid.). If this would not be the case then free competition would lead to price reductions by more efficient firms. Again losses and gains by trades and a change of the value of the initial distribution of wealth could not be prevented and commutative justice could not be maintained. Again it must be concluded that Walras's condition of commutative justice rules out transactions at disequilibrium prices.

The three conditions to be fulfilled in order to realize commutative justice can therefore only hold in a general equilibrium.

It should be clear that Walras did not draw any normative conclusion from his GE-theory in order to argue that exchanges at equilibrium prices can be characterized as being just. In fact his line of argument can be summarized as follows. First, it follows from natural law that there exists a just distribution of initial resources, prices of which are to be determined. Once these are determined, the just initial distribution of wealth is determined too. This distribution of wealth will be preserved in market economies if equivalents are exchanged. Then the resulting distribution of income and wealth will be by definition also just.

What is needed is a positive theory of value which determines the prices of the initial distribution of resources and which formulates the conditions under which a just initial distribution of wealth will be preserved when exchange takes place. The answer is given by GE-theory. In a general equilibrium, equilibrium prices determine simultaneously the value of the initial distribution of resources and the value of goods traded in the market. A just initial distribution of wealth will be preserved in a general equilibrium because of the existence of the budget constraint which leads to the exchange of equivalents. Thus Walras uses GE-theory in his theory of property as a positive sub-theory giving answers to questions which he derived solely from normative considerations!

Of course, to argue that in a general equilibrium commutative justice will prevail is only one half of the route to prove the viability of a just society. Since in reality such a society would hardly ever be in a general equilibrium, a proof of the stability of such an equilibrium remains the second task to be fulfilled. Walras has never given such a proof. But there can be no doubt that he believed in the viability of a just society. This becomes clear in his critique of the Marxian theory being formulated in his theory of property.

According to Walras the Marxian theory is completely unsuited to form the scientific basis of socialism, because it does not answer the question how a socialist society can work. Yet that is what a scientific socialism should be able to demonstrate:

> socialism . . . ought to explain why and how such and such a principle will lead to and maintain the equilibrium of supply and demand of services and of products; in that way socialism will emerge from the literary phase and enter into the scientific phase. That is what Marx's collectivism has not done: more unfortunate even than 'economism,' which claims that a system is operating well when in fact it operates badly, Marxism claims that a socialist system must operate well when in fact it cannot operate at all. (Walras, 1936a, p. 233)

The reason why the Marxian theory fails must be found in the labour theory of value. The labour theory of value is not able to determine planning-prices in a socialist economy, because it does not allow the systematic incorporation of demand factors in the pricing process. This will inevitably make a socialist society inefficient because of the misallocation of resources. The main problem with the Marxian theory is therefore its failure as a theory of resource allocation.

Such a theory is however provided by the theory of marginal utility: 'This problem of the distribution of products is extremely complicated. Only the consideration of *the intensity of the last want that is satisfied*, of the *Final Degree of Utility*, of *Grenznutzen*, furnishes the solution of the problem; and one cannot complain of either the socialists or the economists who have preceded us for not having solved it' (Walras, 1936a, p. 236). The conclusion which Walras draws from his GE-theory is that a socialistic society will solve its distribution problem if it relies on competitive markets. Again this conclusion cannot be characterized as a normative one. When defining a socialist economy by a special distribution of initial resources, as Walras does, the proof of his assertion consists simply in stressing that equilibrium prices exist in such an economy. From his theory of property Walras concludes that it is not the socialization of the means of production that will solve the social problem as Marxian theorists believe but only the nationalization of land and the suppression of artificial monopolies. In such a rational society the state and the individuals can become owner of means of productions, i.e. capitalists, which are financed either out of individual savings or out of rents. That is what Walras did call his 'synthetic socialism' (socialisme, synthétique, Walras, 1936a, p. 239).

GE-theory plays not only a role in Walras's theory of property, but it contributes also to the solution of a problem arising from the question how the state can succeed in a peaceful nationalization of land without violating commutative justice. Preserving commutative justice in the market sphere implies that the state should buy land at equilibrium prices. In order to buy land the state must however incur debts. This gives rise to a feasibility problem. According to Walras the state is only allowed to incur debts in a period of transition. In a just society where the state is the sole owner of the land all expenditures have to be financed out of rents. Since the state has to pay interest on its debts the question arises whether the rent, which the state can earn on land by leasing it to the private sector can ever cover repayments and interest payments. Walras believed that with some qualifications this could be the case in a progressive economy where land becomes scarcer and scarcer.

To understand his analysis it is convenient to introduce the following notation. Let A be the present price of land, and 'a' the rent which the state can earn on land today. Let i denote the prevailing interest rate in the capital market. Both a and i are determined in general equilibrium. From them the equilibrium landprice, A^*, can be derived by

(2) $A^* = a^*/i^*$,

where a^* and i^* denote equilibrium values of a and i. A progressive economy is characterized by a growing stock of capital and by a growing population. Because capital becomes more affluent, the interest rate i can be expected to fall. As land will become scarcer the rent on land, a, can be expected to rise. From (2) it follows that in a progressive society the price of land will rise.

Assuming that the growth rate of a, z, is constant, Walras shows that the equilibrium price, A^*, equals infinity if $z>i$ and is determined by

(3) $A^* = a^*/(i^*-z) <=> a^*/A^* = i^*-z$ for $z<i$

In the case of (3) both the land and capital markets are in equilibrium. If, for instance, $a/A>i-z$ would hold, it would be gainful to lend money on the capital market and to buy land. This will lead to a rising price of land and to a fall in a/A until equality is reestablished.

If the state would like to finance land purchases via rising rents the following inequality must hold if $z<i$:

(4) $a/A > i-z$

(3) and (4) show that a self-financing nationalization of land is incompatible with a simultaneous equilibrium in the land and in the capital market. Hence a self-financing nationalization of land does not seem to be feasible, if the position is held, that the state should buy land at equilibrium prices thus preserving commutative justice. Walras, however, finds a solution to this problem by a trick. He assumes that the growth rate of a, z, will not be constant in the long run. Instead, he assumes that z is rising in a progressive economy and that a change of z can be manipulated by the state (Walras, 1936a, p. 345). Further he makes the crucial assumption that the private sector will not anticipate a rising z through a rising landprice A^*. Assume for example that in the future $z'> z$ and individuals are expecting z. Then equilibrium in the land and capital market can hold because competition in these markets will lead to $a^*/A^* = i^*-z$. Because $z'>z$ it follows immediately that $a^*/A^* > i^*-z'$ and the condition for a self-financing nationalization of land will be fulfilled in the future. This means that as long as the private sector forms no rational expectations with respect to the development of z the state can be sure to finance the nationalization of land out of rising rents.

Because the state buys land by paying the equilibrium price A^* commutative justice will be preserved. The extra rent because of a rising z in the future cannot be claimed by landowners because they do not anticipate a rising z:

At each increase of the rate of this added value, the price of land . . . increases because of the appearance of a new added value. This profit, over which the landlords have no rights of ownership because it has not been either looked forward to or forecast and because they have not paid it when buying the lands, must be reserved for the State, which will permit it to amortize the purchase price of the lands by means of charging rent. (Walras, 1936a, pp. 341–2)

Again it should be noted that Walras does not draw any normative conclusions from his GE-theory when analysing the feasibility of a self-financing nationalization of land. Instead he applies GE-theory as a positive theory. Walras himself explicity refers in his analysis to his *Elements d'économie politique pure,* where he explained the equilibrium price of land. He admits that his analysis in the *Elements* is insufficient with regard to a progressive economy, calling therefore for a further elaboration (Walras, 1936a, p. 279). Walras has given this elaboration in his analysis of the feasibility of a self-financing nationalization of land in his *Etudes d'économie sociale* which can therefore be seen as a straightforward continuation of his positive analysis of the price of land in the *Elements* (ibid.).

Conclusions

Walras formulated a normative theory of a just society, which he thought to be realizable. GE-theory used as a positive sub-theory gives a solution to two intricate problems of a theory of a just society as a 'realistic utopia': First, can a just society be viable? Second, can a just society be realized by a peaceful nationalization of land? By referring to GE-theory Walras shows that commutative justice, being defined in a proper sense, will be realized in a general equilibrium. Though Walras did not prove the stability of a general equilibrium he thought a just society to be stable. By applying his GE-theory to the problem of a peaceful nationalization of land, Walras comes to the conclusion that such a plan would be feasible in a progressive economy, if one assumes that individuals will not form rational expectations with regard to the development of rents and the price of land. Though Walras did integrate his GE-theory in his theory of a just society, this by no means implies that he restricted the domain of his GE-theory solely to the proof of the viability of a 'realistic' utopia (see his *Etudes d'économie politique appliquée*).

It must be recognized that the development of a theory of a just society belongs to one of the intriguing problems with which Léon Walras concerned himself during his life. It is this theory and not only his GE-theory which formed the basis of a proposal for awarding Léon

144   *Classical and neoclassical economic thought*

Walras the Nobel Prize in 1906, though without success (see Jaffé, 1965, Vol. III: 270ff.).

v. Bortkewitsch, L. (1898), 'Etudes d'economie sociale', *Schmollers Jahrbuch für Gesetzgebung*, vol. 22, no. 3, p. 1075ff.

Cirillo, R. (1979), 'The "socialism" of Léon Walras and his economic thinking', *American Journal of Economics and Sociology*, vol. 39, no. 3, p. 294 ff.

Cirillo, R. (1984), 'Léon Walras and social justice', *American Journal of Economics and Sociology*, vol. 43, no. 1, p. 53ff.

Friedman, M. (1955), 'Léon Walras and his economic system', *American Economic Review*, vol. 45, no. 5, p. 900ff.

de Gijsel, P. (1985), *Von Léon Walras (1834–1910) zur Neoklassik oder: die Verkürzung der Walrasschen Politischen ökonomie durch die Neoklassik und das Walrassche Gerechtigkeitsproblem*, Regensburger Diskussionsbeiträge zur Wirtschaftswissenschaft, no. 181, University of Regensburg.

Gram, H. and Walsh, V. (1980), *Classical and Neoclassical Theories of General Equilibrium*, Oxford University Press, New York/Oxford.

Hicks, J.R. (1934), 'Léon Walras', *Econometrica*, vol. 2, p. 338ff.

Jaffé, W. (ed.) (1965), *Correspondence of Léon Walras and Related Papers*, vols. I–III, North-Holland, Amsterdam.

Jaffé, W. (1977), 'The normative bias of the Walrasian model. Walras versus Gossen', *Quarterly Journal of Economics*, vol. 91, no. 363, p. 371ff.

Jaffé, W. (1980), 'Walras's economics as others see it', *Journal of Economic Literature*, vol. XVIII, no. 2, p. 528ff.

Jaffé, W. (1984), 'The antecedents and early life of Léon Walras'. ed. D.A. Walker, *History of Political Economy*, vol. 16, no. 1, p. 1ff.

Morishima, M. (1977), *Walras' Economics: A pure theory of capital and money*, Cambridge University Press, Cambridge.

Morishima, M. (1980), 'W. Jaffé on Léon Walras. A comment', *Journal of Economic Literature*, vol. XVIII, no. 2, pp. 550ff.

Walker, D.A. (1970), 'Léon Walras in the light of his correspondence and related papers', *Journal of Political Economy*, vol. 78 (July–August), p. 685ff.

Walker, D.A. (ed.) (1983), *William Jaffé's Essays on Walras*, Cambridge University Press, Cambridge.

Walker, D.A. (1984), 'Is Walras's theory of general equilibrium a normative scheme?', *History of Political Economy*, vol. 16, no. 3, p. 445ff.

Walras, L. (1954), *Elements of Pure Economics or the Theory of Social Wealth*, trans. W. Jaffé, Irwin, Homewood, Ill.

Walras, L. (1936a), *Etudes d'économie sociale*, ed. G. Leduc, 2nd edition, Rouge, Lausanne.

Walras, L. (1936b), *Etudes d'économie politique appliquée*, ed. G. Leduc, 2nd edition, Rouge, Lausanne.

10 The founding fathers of the Swedish school: Wicksell and Cassel

Hans Brems[1]

Knut Wicksell (1851–1926)

The long run: fixed and circulating capital
Capital is necessary in production, and its necessity has something to do
with time. In the capitalist production process, what precisely is it that
takes time? Two different types of capital have been distinguished by
economists: fixed and circulating capital. In the case of fixed capital,
what takes time is the utilization of durable plant and equipment. In the
case of circulating capital what takes time is the maturing of output in
slow organic growth in agriculture, cattle-raising, forestry, and winery
or in time-consuming construction.

The pioneer of circulating-capital theory was Eugen von Böhm-
Bawerk (1889, 1923). Using simple interest, Böhm-Bawerk had built a
verbal aggregate model of capital and labour in which all available
labour inputs were invested in the same period of production. Given
available labour force and available real capital stock, Böhm-Bawerk
determined the equilibrium interest and real wage rates. Still using
simple interest, Knut Wicksell (1893, 1954) restated Böhm-Bawerk
mathematically and summarized his main result in one sentence – the
Wicksell Effect: 'In the case of a relative increase of the national capital
the wage [rate] increases and the level of interest decreases.'

Eight years later Wicksell (1901, 1934) adopted compound interest
with continuous compounding, dropped the assumption that all available labor inputs were invested in the same period of production, and
drew his famous triangles. Their base showed how a year's available
labour inputs were allocated between current and future uses, and their
height showed in *how* distant a future they would mature. As a result,
the area of his triangles would show the size of existing capital stock
broken down into vintages.

Under given technology, thrift would increase the area of a triangle
by increasing its base as well as its height, thus leaving less current

Figure 10.1

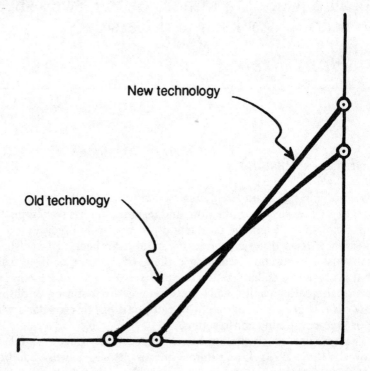

New technology

Old technology

Distance of future in which labour will mature

Allocation of available labour inputs

labour unabsorbed, hence raising the marginal productivity of current labour. Wicksell (1901, 1934, p. 164) concluded that 'the capitalist saver is thus, fundamentally, the friend of labour'.

Under given thrift, 'so long as no further capital is saved', technological progress might be labour-saving. In that case the area of the triangle would stay the same but with a narrower base and a taller height, thus leaving more current labour unabsorbed, hence reducing the marginal productivity of current labour. Wicksell (1901, 1934, p. 164) concluded that 'the technical inventor is not infrequently [labour's] enemy'.

On fixed capital Böhm-Bawerk had been silent and so was Wicksell in (1893, 1954) and (1901, 1934). But three years before his death, Wicksell (1923, 1934) was inspired by Åkerman (1923) to take up the theory of fixed capital. In an elegant mathematical restatement of Åkerman he built a model of an economy whose capital stock consisted of axes and whose equilibrating variable was the optimal useful life of such axes. Here, Wicksell found an elasticity of optimal useful life with respect to the rate of interest equaling *minus* one or, in Wicksell's (1923, 1934, p. 278) words: 'it follows that the product of the rate of interest (with continuously compound interest) and the optimal lifetime of the axe is a *constant* . . .'

The short run: the cumulative process

Having restated Böhm-Bawerk, Wicksell (1893, 1954) began to wonder how a 'natural' rate of interest thus determined was related to the rate of interest observed in markets where the supply of money met the demand for it. If commercial banks could create money in the form of drawing rights upon themselves, disposed of by checks, such a supply of money would be quite flexible. Would the 'money' rate of interest determined by such supply coincide with the 'natural' rate? If it didn't, would some equilibrating variable be set in motion and keep moving until the two rates coincided? Wicksell's answer was the following.

The money rate of interest would not have to coincide with a Böhm-Bawerk 'natural' rate of interest at all times. If it did not, Böhm-Bawerk's physical output and real wage rate would still prevail – determined as they were by available labour force and available real capital stock. But nominal values would be changing. If the natural rate of interest were higher than the money rate of interest, entrepreneurs would be induced – and the money supply correspondingly expanded – to pay a higher money wage rate. Physically speaking, nothing would come of this, for when labour spent the higher money wage rate, prices would rise correspondingly and unexpectedly leave the real wage rate unchanged. There would be a cumulative process of inflation expected by nobody. Eventually, such inflation would drain the banks for cash, so the money rate of interest would have to be raised to equality with the natural rate – thus stopping the expansion of credit.

If the natural rate of interest were lower than the money rate of interest, entrepreneurs would be induced – and the money supply correspondingly contracted – to pay a lower money wage rate. Again, physically speaking, nothing would come of this, for when labour spent the lower money wage rate, prices would fall correspondingly and unexpectedly leave the real wage rate unchanged. There would be a cumulative process of deflation expected by nobody. Eventually, such deflation would leave the banks with so much cash that the money rate of interest would have to be lowered to equality with the natural rate – thus stopping the contraction of credit.

Wicksell's (1898, 1936) answer was made possible by a method fundamentally new in three respects. First, Wicksell's method was explicitly macroeconomic, second, it was explicitly dynamic and, third, it was an explicit disequilibrium method based upon adaptive expectations whose disappointment constituted the motive force of the system.

Such a short-run, macroeconomic, dynamic, disequilibrium method was just what was needed in the thirties. All that remained to be done was to add physical output as an additional variable. Ohlin (1934) was inspired by Wicksell in the sense that his feedback between physical output and aggregate demand unfolded in a cumulative process along a time axis and was a succession of disequilibria: expectations and plans were forever being revised in the light of new experience.

The long run: non-constant returns to scale

Wicksteed was the first to formulate the product-exhaustion theorem but (1894, 1932, p. 33) considered a linear homogeneity of his production function 'of course obvious'. It was left to Wicksell (1901, 1934, pp. 128–9) to examine the stability of a product-exhaustion equilibrium by asking what would happen if, still assuming pure competition, returns to scale were not constant. Wicksell added exit and entry to the picture and thought of the scale of the production function as passing gradually through three domains.

The first domain consisted of relatively low scales on which the returns to scale would be increasing. Here, if every input were paid its marginal value productivity, the entrepreneur would find himself going broke. The slices would be adding up to more than the pie! With such negative profits, there would be exit from the industry, and the number of firms in it would be declining. With fewer firms, each firm would be growing in scale, hence passing out of the first domain and into the second.

The second domain consisted of relatively medium scales on which the returns to scale would be constant. Here, if every input were paid its marginal value productivity, the entrepreneur would find himself just breaking even. The slices would be adding up to just the pie! With such zero profits, there would be neither exit from nor entry into the industry, and the number of firms in it would remain stationary. With a stationary number of firms, each firm would remain stationary in scale and remain in the second domain.

Wicksell's third domain consisted of relatively high scales on which the returns to scale would be decreasing. Here, if every input were paid its marginal value productivity, the entrepreneur would find himself with something left – a distributive share not explained by the marginal-productivity principle. The slices would be adding up to less than the pie! With such positive profits, there would be entry into the industry, and the number of firms in it would be growing. With more firms, each firm would be declining in scale, hence passing out of the third domain and back into the second.

Unlike Marshall, Wicksell was willing to surrender the assumption of pure competition. In (1901, 1934, p. 129) he defined his 'optimum scale' as lying 'at the point of transition from "increasing" to "diminishing" returns" (relative to the scale of production). The firm will here conform to the law of constant returns.' At such an optimum scale firms might still be (1901, 1934, p. 130) 'numerous enough for perfect competition to be maintained', or they might not: 'If the optimum scale of the enterprise is so high, and the number of enterprises consequently so small, that the owners can easily combine in a *ring, trust, or cartel*; then there no longer exists any equilibrium of the kind we are here considering.'

Gustav Cassel (1866–1945)

The long run: microeconomic growth
Gustav Cassel (1923, 1932, pp. 32–41, 137–55) was the first to dynamize general equilibrium into his 'uniformly progressing state', thus inspiring John von Neumann (1937, 1968) who, as Weintraub (1983, pp. 4–5) has pointed out, knew the Walras system only in its Cassel version. In neither Cassel nor von Neumann did prices display any growth, only physical quantities did.

Let there be m physical outputs supplied by industry and demanded by households, on the one hand, and n primary physical inputs supplied by households and demanded by industry, on the other. Cassel set out his dynamic system as follows. Input prices will equalize the given supply of any input with the demand for it. Once such prices are known all incomes are known. Multiply each such price by the technical coefficient for an industry, add such products for that industry, add interest, and find the price of the output of that industry. Once all incomes and such output prices are known consumer demand follows. Output prices will equalize the supply of any output with the demand for it. Once such industry supplies are known, multiply each of them by the technical coefficient for an input, add growth, add such products for that input, and find the aggregate demand for it. Input prices will equalize the given supply of any input with such demand for it. Thus we are back at our point of departure. Unlike Walras, Cassel was a mathematician before he turned to economics. But like Walras, he counted equations and unknowns and merely said (1923, 1932, pp. 140, 145) that equal numbers of them would 'generally' suffice to determine the unknowns – with one reservation.

Like the Walras system, the Cassel system was homogeneous of degree zero in its prices, money expenditures and money incomes. In this sense the system was indeterminate. The job of determining absolute prices, money expenditure, or money incomes would be left, Cassel (1923, 1932, pp. 154–5) said, to monetary policy. Here we see Cassel anticipating Friedman's (1968) dichotomy between nominal and real variables: monetary policy can affect nominal variables but never real ones.

Was Cassel no more and no less than Walras, then? He was at the same time more and less.

Walras asked how a stationary economy would allocate inputs among outputs and outputs among households. Cassel asked how a growing economy would do those things and showed (1923, 1932, p. 153) that in a growing economy the current physical input required per physical unit of current output was a new coefficient that would 'contain, in addition to the elements of the old "technical coefficients", only the rate of progress.' In this sense, Cassel was indeed more than Walras.

Walras thought of utility as a measure of human sensation. Pareto (1906, 1971, pp. 105–33) abandoned the meaning of utility as such a measure and replaced it by a utility index. Infinitely many indices would serve equally well as long as any of them was a monotonic transformation of any other. Here we may ask two questions. First, given a utility function using such a Paretian index, can a demand function always be found by maximizing the utility function subject to a budget constraint? The answer is yes, provided the utility function is differentiable and strictly quasi-concave. Second, given an observed demand function, can a utility function always be found whose maximization subject to a budget constraint will deliver the given demand function? Here the answer is: not necessarily. Antonelli (1886) and Fisher (1892, pp. 86–9) were the first to see this so-called integrability problem.

Cassel may never have heard of the integrability problem; at least he never mentioned it. What he did say was that demand is observable and that utility is not. As a quantitative science economics must deal with observables only, so Cassel (1899; 1923, 1932) purged his system of all references to utility. In this sense, he was less than Walras and the first to use revealed preference, anticipating Samuelson (1938) by twenty years.

So Cassel was at the same time more and less than Walras. Either way his debt to Walras is apparent. Cassel (1899) did mention Walras but merely to scold him for his utility concept. Nowhere in Cassel (1923, 1932) can the name Walras be found. In his autobiography Cassel (1940, p. 435) says: 'When [after 1899] I continued developing economic theory on the foundation I had chosen, I found it unnecessary to occupy myself with Walras and actually never had time to open his works.'

The long run: macroeconomic growth

Thus Cassel had given us a microeconomic growth model. But later in the same volume (1923, 1932, pp. 61–2) he also gave us a macroeconomic one, fully set out in hard algebra identical except for notation to that of Harrod (1948) thirty years later. Exactly as in Harrod the equilibrium rate of growth of output equalled the propensity to save divided by the capital coefficient. Since both were stationary parameters, the rate of growth was stationary: growth was steady-state and balanced, or in Cassel's (1923, 1932, p. 62) own words: 'We . . . come to the conclusion that, in the uniformly progressive exchange economy, the total income as well as both its parts – consumption and capital accumulation – increases in the same percentage as the capital.'

In a Cassel model a higher propensity to save would permit more investment and hence more rapid growth; indeed the steady-state equilibrium rate of growth was in direct proportion to the propensity to save. Saving was a Good Thing! Writing in 1914, Cassel had no Keynesian savings paradox to unlearn, and observed (1923, 1932, pp. 61–2) that 'saving is the chief element in progress'.

Cassel saw his uniformly progressive economy merely as a first, but important, approximation – many other possible patterns were to be found at Stockholm by Lundberg (1937).

The long run: a theory of mining

Sweden was traditionally a major exporter of iron ore and had traditionally applied a conservationist public policy imposing a maximum export quota. Cassel's advice was to do away with the export quota and let the market decide what the optimal depletion of mines should be. What should it be, then? Cassel (1923, 1932, pp. 289–97) showed that in a free market optimal depletion would depend on the rate of interest and the future price of the mineral: Given the rate at which price and cost per ton were inflating, optimal depletion would be the faster the higher the rate of interest. And given the rate of interest,

optimal depletion would be the slower the higher the rate at which price
and cost per ton were inflating.

A comparison

Wicksell and Cassel both came to economics from mathematics. Thus
both had a head start, but Wicksell made more operational, and
therefore more effective, use of his mathematics. Both men had a
remarkable ability to reduce a problem to its essence; both wrote a terse
and lucid German. Both were original thinkers, but Wicksell thought
deeper. Cassel's comparative advantage was his ease with data. Long
before the days of national income accounting, Cassel managed to find
and effectively use the data he needed. One example is his estimate of
the capital coefficient and the propensity to save. Another example is
the massive use of data in his business-cycle theory, to which Wicksell
(1919, 1934, p. 255) paid tribute: 'it is in my opinion incomparably the
best part of his work. Professor Cassel's great gifts for concrete
description based on facts and figures here show to advantage.'

In character Cassel and Wicksell were as different as night and day. A
writer more generous to others than Wicksell would be hard to find. By
contrast, Cassel followed Walras and Pareto, mentioned neither, and
never paid tribute to anybody. Indeed if Cassel's autobiography
(1940–41) and the successive editions and translations of *Theoretische
Sozialökonomie* were marred by a unifying theme it was his lack of
generosity to others and his conviction of his own infallibility, so
irritating to his reader – and so redundant: his work could well have
spoken for itself!

From the vantage point of the thirties, Wicksell's short-run macroeconomic, dynamic, disequilibrium method was exactly what was needed,
and Cassel's long-run dynamic equilibria, whether macroeconomic or
microeconomic, looked less relevant.

From the vantage point of the eighties, Wicksell may still look like the
more profound thinker. But Cassel is not as far behind as he seemed to
be in the early thirties. His microeconomic growth inspired von
Neumann (1937), his optimal depletion of mines came back with
Hotelling (1931) thirteen years later, his revealed preference came back
with Samuelson (1938) twenty years later, his macroeconomic growth
came back with Harrod (1948) thirty years later, and his dichotomy
between nominal and real variables came back with Friedman (1968)
fifty years later.

Notes
1. The author will offer mathematical models of Wicksell and Cassel in two forthcom-
    ing articles, Brems (1989a, 1989b).

References

Åkerman, Gustaf (1923), *Realkapital und Kapitalzins*, Stockholm: Centraltryckeriet.
Antonelli, Giovanni Battista (1886), *Sulla teoria matematica della economia politica*, Pisa, translated by John S. Chipman as 'On the mathematical theory of political economy', in William J. Baumol and S. M. Goldfeld (eds), *Precursors in Mathematical Economics: an anthology*, London, London School of Economics and Political Science, 1968, pp. 33–9.
Böhm-Bawerk, Eugen von (1889), *Positive Theorie des Kapitales*, Innsbruck: Wagner'sche Universitäts-Buchhandlung, translated by William Smart as *Positive Theory of Capital*, London and New York: Macmillan, 1891.
Brems, Hans (1989a), 'Time and interest: Böhm-Bawerk and Åkerman–Wicksell', *Hist. Polit. Econ.*, 22 (forthcoming).
——— (1989b), 'Gustav Cassel Revisited', *Hist. Polit. Econ.*, 22 (forthcoming).
Cassel, Karl Gustav (1899), 'Grundriss einer elementaren Preislehre', *Zeitschrift für die gesamte Staatswissenschaft*, 55, pp. 395–458.
——— (1918), *Theoretische Sozialökonomie*, 1st edition, Leipzig, 3rd edition, Leipzig: Deichertsche Verlagsbuchhandlung, 1923; translated from the 5th edition by S.L. Barron as *The Theory of Social Economy*, New York: Harcourt Brace, 1932.
——— (1940–41), *I förnuftets tjänst* (*In the Service of Reason*), I–II, Stockholm: Natur och Kultur.
Fisher, Irving (1892), *Mathematical Investigations in the Theory of Value and Prices*, New Haven: Yale University Press, reprinted 1925.
Friedman, Milton (1968), 'The role of monetary policy', *Amer. Econ. Rev.*, 58, pp. 1–17.
Harrod, Sir Roy Forbes (1948), *Towards a Dynamic Economics*, London: Macmillan.
Hotelling, Harold (1931), 'The economics of exhaustible resources', *J. Polit. Econ. 39*, pp. 137–75.
Lundberg, Erik Filip (1937), *Studies in the Theory of Economic Expansion*, London, P.S. King.
Neumann, John von (1937), 'Über ein ökonomisches Gleichungssystem und eine Verallgemeinerung des Brouwerschen Fixpunktsatzes', *Ergebnisse eines mathematischen Kolloquiums*, 8, pp. 73–83, translated by G. Morgenstern (Morton) in William J. Baumol and Stephen M. Goldfeld (eds), *Precursors in Mathematical Economics: an anthology*, London: London School of Economics, 1968, pp. 296–306.
Ohlin, Bertil (1934), *Penningpolitik, offentliga arbeten, subventioner och tullar som medel mot arbetslöshet – bidrag till expansionens teori*, Unemployment Report II, 4, Stockholm: P. A. Norstedt & Söner.
Pareto, Vilfredo (1906), *Manuale di economia politica con una introduzione alla scienza sociale*, Milan: Società editrice libraria, translated as *Manual of Political Economy*, New York: Kelley, 1971.
Samuelson, Paul Anthony (1938), 'A note on the pure theory of consumer's behavior', *Economica*, 5, pp. 61–71.
Weintraub, E. Roy (1983), 'On the existence of a competitive equilibrium: 1930–1954', *J. Econ. Lit. 21*, pp. 1–39.
Wicksell, Knut (1893), *Über Wert, Kapital und Rente*, Jena: G. Fischer, translated by S.H. Frohwein as *Value, Capital and Rent*, London: Allen & Unwin, 1954, reprinted in 1970.
——— (1898), *Geldzins und Güterpreise*, Jena: G. Fischer, translated by R.F. Kahn, with an introduction by Bertil Ohlin, as *Interest and Prices*, published on behalf of the Royal Economic Society, London: Macmillan, 1936.
——— (1901), *Föreläsningar i nationalekonomi*, I, Lund: Gleerup, translated as *Lectures on Political Economy*, I, London: Routledge & Kegan Paul, 1934.
——— (1919), 'Professor Cassels nationalekonomiska system', *Ekonomisk Tidskrift, 21*, 195–226, translated as Appendix I, 'Professor Cassel's system of economics', *Lectures on Political Economy*, I, London: Routledge & Kegan Paul, 1934.
——— (1923), 'Realkapital och kapitalränta', *Ekonomisk Tidskrift, 25*, 145–80, translated

as Appendix 2, 'Real capital and interest', *Lectures on Political Economy*, I, London: Routledge & Kegan Paul, 1934.

Wicksteed, Philip H. (1884), *An Essay on the Co-ordination of the Laws of Distribution*, London: Macmillan.

11 Early Italian contributions to the theory of public finance: Pantaleoni, De Viti de Marco, and Mazzola

Orhan Kayaalp[1]

Introduction

This essay re-examines the contributions of Maffeo Pantaleoni, Antonio De Viti de Marco and Ugo Mazzola, the founders of the positive theory of public finance, whose combined effort in the 1880s completely reshaped the Italian doctrine of public finance. In fact, their seminal contributions gave rise to an autonomous economic discipline, *Scienza delle finanze*, which has come to study the economics of the public sector in three sub-disciplines, each focusing on a different set of manifestations of the economic activity of the state. These divisions are Fiscal economics (*Economia finanziaria*), which studies the pure economic proper of the public economy, fiscal politics (*Politica finanziaria*), which investigates the relationships between the public economy and the polity, and fiscal law (*Diritto finanziario*), whose main task is to analyse the relationships between public economy and public law.

Unlike another continental fiscal doctrine also aiming to study the public economy as a whole, *Staatswirtschaft*, however, *Scienza delle finanze* makes individual valuation the central subject matter. As such, it provides invaluable insight not only into the pure economic core of modern public finance – that is, the demand and supply of public goods – but also into the collective choice-related aspects of the discipline, such as voting, individual liberty, fiscal coercion and bureaucracy. This essay aims to present the contributions of Pantaleoni. De Viti and Mazzola in the development of the first, pure economic, sub-discipline of the *Scienza*. The author expresses the hope that, once some misconceptions about this aspect of the Italian fiscal theory are cleared up, the much-needed unification of the continental and Anglo-Saxon fiscal thought will be closer at hand.[2]

The main features of the Italian theory of public goods
If the founders of the first positive theory of public finance were

influenced by classical British political economists it was not accidental.[3] Both the Italian and Anglo-Saxon fiscal doctrines had the same origin: Bentham's utilitarianism. Bentham took it for granted that benefit was measurable for each individual, and J. S. Mill extended this principle directly to the public economy. Mill argued that the benefit principle of taxation, which he traced back to the eighteenth-century continental political philosophers, was preferable over ability to pay since it afforded a *quid pro quo* relationship between the taxpayer and the state. But he ultimately rejected the benefit approach because he found that, paradoxically, it would condone regressive taxation. Mill's assertion that the benefit principle was thus against social justice remained uncontested in England throughout the marginalist revolution, finding its definitive form in Edgeworth's model of the public economy which was built directly upon the ability to pay principle of taxation (1897).

Pantaleoni, De Viti and Mazzola, meanwhile, noted that a theory of fiscal optimum based on ability to pay would be untenable for at least two important reasons. First, such a theory would be tantamount to exempting the state from the rules of economic efficiency (Pantaleoni, 1887; De Viti, 1888). Second, it would conflict with the obvious reality that fiscal optimum could not be obtained otherwise than by a 'collective cooperation between the citizen and the State' (Mazzola, 1890). The point was whether this cooperation could be evaluated 'positively', that is, in conformity with the hypothesis of *homo oeconomicus* as bolstered with 'Walrasian calculus' (Pantaleoni, 1891). In this endeavour, Pantaleoni and De Viti discerned whether the benefit principle – that in Italy was defended as a condition of social justice by Campanella in *La Città del Sole* as early as in 1602 – could be remoulded into a 'condition of fiscal optimum'. De Viti thought that only this principle, not ability to pay, would help guide the statesman to produce an 'economic' solution out of 'the confused mass of fiscal facts' representing conflicting interests and wishes of the citizens and the members of the Parliament (Einaudi, 1937, pp. 25–6).

It was not De Viti's and Pantaleoni's primary intention to offer 'practical' advice to those who governed the public economy. What they wanted:

> was to study, in a logical manner, what would be the actions – and the consequences of the actions – of those who are governed and those who govern, according as the latter are assumed to be bent upon benefiting themselves, on the one hand, and the whole nation, on the other. . .[A 'fiscal'] decision . . . is not . . . a 'political' decision. . . . The student who thinks of the science of public finance solely in terms of politics no longer has a guide when he [attempts] to bring the public economy out of chaos . . .

[For] he would expect inspiration from politics as he proceeds to explain [fiscal] facts by the various changeable, vague, and contradictory reasons which inspire the actions of politicians from time to time. . . . The ..udent must turn his eyes realistically on Jevon's rules, [and] apply them concretely to the budgets presented by. . . . Ministers of Finance. (Einaudi, 1937, pp. 25–7)

Pantaleoni and public expenditures

It was with this aim that the three fiscal economists proceeded to 'discover the positive laws' of the public economy (Pantaleoni, 1883). Pantaleoni set forth the pure economic foundation of the *Scienza* in two essays, *A Contribution to the Theory of Allocation of Public Expenditure (Contributo alla teoria del riparto delle spese pubbliche,* 1883) and *The Theory of Tax Burden (Teoria della pressione tributaria,* 1887). In the first essay, he establishes the first principle of the *Scienza* that taxation must be thought of not only in terms of itself but also in terms of the utility that it produces. As in the private economy, so in the public economy both the burden of the costs (taxes) and the satisfactions derived from (public) goods are felt by the individual (taxpayer). But there is a difference between the two markets: in the latter, the economic agent who decides on what type of tax to levy, how much to levy, and how to allocate the tax revenue among various expenditure items is a member of the government, elected by the majority of voters for a given term. Both the voter who gives the politician a mandate to maximize his utility and the politician who is given the mandate are motivated by rationality and self-interest. What the latter aims to maximize is his tenure. With this goal in mind, he judges the expenditure side of the fiscal account from two points of view. First, he examines each expenditure item from the standpoint of *inherent* utility, on the basis of which he chooses some possible candidates. Second, he ranks these candidates with respect to their *relative* utility, on the basis of which some items qualify as *preferred* expenditure items.

Hence, what the politician does essentially is to assign weights to social wants 'in conformity with public demand' and allocate public revenue according to 'Jevonsian–Walrasian calculus', that is, by equating the 'marginal yields' of alternative public expenditure items (Pantaleoni, 1883). The public economy thus reaches efficient equilibrium, maximizing the interests of both the citizens and the politicians. Fiscal optimum is reached as long as both parties act as '"tribal" egoists', that is, as individuals who identify their own maximum happiness with that of their species.

De Viti and productivity of the state economic activity

In *The Theoretical Character of Fiscal Economics (I carattere teorico dell economia finanziaria* 1888), De Viti reiterates and expands Pantaleoni's premise that public goods are inherently productive. Invoking the benefit approach, he asserts that there is always an economic exchange between the producer of public goods – that is, the state – and the citizens, which would ultimately benefit the latter. These goods are either directly consumed by individual citizens or are employed by them in the production of private goods. Consequently, to each productive service offered by the state must correspond a tax claim. The main concern of public finance, accordingly, must be to help determine the 'correct' amount of tax for each taxpayer.

Like Pantaleoni, De Viti finds that the economic agent in the public economy is not the citizen himself, but a member of the government. De Viti, however, transcends Pantaleoni who envisages a rational state. According to De Viti, the state is sentient (*senziente*), that is, receptive to the public wants emanating from the citizens. According to De Viti, a government that is made up of elected politicians and public administrators might be likened to a corporation's management to which shareholders have delegated the task of running the organization efficiently on their behalf. Like the managerial cadre which must be sentient of shareholders' demands, the government must be sentient of the social wants of the citizens and try to attain a level of performance that in the long run creates maximum total satisfaction for the key coalitions.[4]

De Viti remarks that, over the centuries, larger and larger proportions of citizens have come to participate in fiscal decisions and that this was earned after considerable struggle. As if to anticipate Wicksell, he expresses hope that the struggle will one day culminate into a final stage in which *all* citizens will be able to directly take part in fiscal decisions. This will constitute the 'total cooperation' stage in which the financing of the production of public goods will be achieved at 'net cost'. Unfortunately, however, in contemporary democracies, governments operate within the mandate granted to it only by a majority of citizens; therefore, a minority always remains, to which the budget appears unproductive, that is, overpriced.

In spite of the fact that De Viti summarily delegates to a ruling group the task of allocating public expenditures, he stresses that his theory is nevertheless one of individual valuation. He reminds that fiscal optimum requires two sets of decisions made by the individual citizen. The first concerns the determination of the value of the public good to the *community*. It is through this process that citizens express their judgement, in advance, concerning the advisability of the expenditure side of the budget from the standpoint of collective welfare and thus determine the expenditure side of the budget. At the same time, each citizen determines the value of the public good to himself, that is, to the *individual*, as he compares the marginal utility that he expects to extract from the public good with the marginal disutility of the tax that he will be required to pay for the good. Thus, the problem of the distribution of the tax burden is settled simultaneously, at the time that the decision is made by the citizen with respect to the productivity of public expenditure.[5]

Mazzola and the formalization of the new doctrine

Mazzola, in his *Scientific Elements of Public Finance* (*I dati scientifica della finanza pubblica* 1890), focuses directly on the nature of 'public' ends and 'public' wants, and the capacity of certain (public) goods for satisfying such ends and wants. He expounds:

> There exist, in the first place, the aims of the individual. To attain these, however, it is necessary [that he first] accomplish other aims . . . [Economic] Man does not set as his ultimate or direct aim such things as national defense or general security. He wants to accomplish his material aims in life or his spiritual aims in the field of moral or intellectual improvement. He cannot arrive at these ends, however, unless he is able to live in such a way that he feels secure against his foreign and internal enemies and is prepared to co-operate with other men for the achievement of aims denied to men who live in a state of isolation. Therefore the 'public' aims are distinguished as being 'conditional' to the attainment of the ultimate aims of man and as being attainable only through political co-operation. The voluntary association of private individuals would not serve the purpose; what is needed is rather a political cooperation. (Einaudi, 1936, referring to Mazzola, 1890, p. 23)

Mazzola thus establishes another essential characteristic of the new theory: public goods are *complementary* to private goods. Then he discovers an additional characteristic: public goods, unlike private ones, are *indivisible*. It is precisely because of the latter feature of public goods that price theory cannot be extended 'directly' to the public economy. In Mazzola's usage, the term 'indivisibility' covers also 'non-excludability' and 'non-rivalry'. The following passage may help illustrate this point:

> The utility of most public goods is complementary and indivisible. The services of law and order, public health, etc., are contributory causes to private satisfactions. But although their consumption causes individual satisfaction, the quantities consumed by each individual cannot be divided up and measured. What is known is simply that public goods enter into individual satisfaction in certain proportions. The indivisibility of consumption constitutes the technical reason preventing the formation of a single market price in the public economy. In the case of a private good, anyone

who cannot pay the price is excluded from consumption. But if a public good had a price exceeding its marginal utility for some classes of consumers, their inability to pay the price would not effectively exclude them from consuming the good. To achieve this, the public good must be withdrawn from the market altogether – even from the use of those who are willing to pay the price – for, otherwise, those who wish not to pay would still enjoy the public good. This occurs because the market price is the maximum the consumer would pay for the amount of marginal utility that the good offers. The concept of indivisibility of public goods also explains why the public economy sometimes resorts to a device very similar to private prices – namely, duties or fees – whenever the quantity of a public good consumed can in fact be inputed to the individual. (Mazzola 1890, pp. 171–2) [All excerpts from Mazzola are the author's translation unless otherwise indicated.]

Mazzola postulates that only in some instances can price theory be extended 'directly' to the public economy:

Fees, or fixed charges, as we have had occasion to observe, represent a price phenomenon in the public economy resembling private prices. For example, the delivery of mail may have different marginal utilities for various users, but the price is uniform. The reasons underlying public fees are well known. The fee is a price, and often a monopoly price, fixed by the government in conformity with certain purposes. (1890, p. 178)

The prices of *pure* public goods, meanwhile, are determined by the 'universal law' that regards the allocation of resources:

In the private as well as in the public economy, utility maximizing behaviour dictates that the available resources be allocated among various uses in such a way that marginal utilities of all the goods are, after the allocation, equal. The prices of public goods too are formed in this way, that is, by equating the marginal utilities of public goods after considering the accompanying fiscal burden. This price formation is different from that of the private market, however, since it results [in multiple prices]. (1890, p. 180)

Multiple tax prices
That multiple prices existed in the public economy is by no means an original idea of Mazzola's. Wieser, for example, in referring to Sax's 1883 contribution, observes that one important result of multiple prices (which reflect the degree of intensity that one felt for a given good) is that when they exist wealth ceases to offer any ascendancy and poverty ceases to constitute a hindrance. Wieser remarks, however, that only in the public economy can this phenomenon be observed. In contrast, in the private economy there is gross inequality in the distribution of satisfactions. Wieser is appalled by the spectacle of a society which permits two such conflicting sets of rules, one for its private economy, which is evidently dictated by the laws of political economy, and another

for its public economy, dictated, perhaps, by those of sociology, history, philosophy or law (1889).

Mazzola disagrees with the *second* part of Wieser's conclusion. He replies:

> The analysis of this matter does not lie outside of the limits of theory of value. We do not need historical or philosophical study; we simply need to know why the prices of certain goods are formed in one way and the prices of certain other goods in another way. This is a question of economics pure and simple, and not of philosophy, [history], or jurisprudence. (1890, p. 165)

Mazzola stresses once again that the allocation of resources between private and public goods is governed by the same principle, that is, the principle of utility maximization (1890, p. 180). More specifically, it is the amount of the complementary utility accorded by the individual to the public good that determines the share of the private resources that he would allocate for that good.

He acknowledges that, as in the private economy, so in the public economy differential utility can take place. This occurs either because of faulty valuation on the part of the fiscal administrator or because of his altering the objective scale of utilities. As to the first problem, De Viti remarked that in the private economy too faulty valuations take place since marginal utilities are not always known to the individual. He asked:

> when Jones buys a ticket for a theatrical performance, could it be said that [he knows] the share of utility which he would derive from the performance? Yet no one can doubt that there does exist an economic-exchange relationship between the price of the ticket and the enjoyment that the buyer hopes to derive from its use. (De Viti, 1936, p. 118)

It is just that in the public economy, goods and services of this sort happen to be typical. Consequently, there will always be occasional divergences between the benefits expected from a public good and the price attributed to it. According to Mazzola, the serious problem that the government has to deal with is the latter. For it is quite possible that the Finance Minister, as he prepares the budget, may be tempted to alter the average valuation of public goods to favour a given constituency. He asserts:

> Such a disequilibrium might occur when agencies to which valuation is entrusted choose to serve the interests of a predominating class or person. If they do so, some members of the community would be obliged to allocate a greater part of their private resources to public goods than would correspond to the complementary utility which these goods provide for them, and hence obtain inadequate satisfaction. Some other members, in the meantime, would have at their disposal a larger quantity of private goods, obtained at the expense of other economic units. . . . Apart from these deviations,

however, the law is valid for the entire range of pure public goods. (1890, p. 175)

Fiscal sacrifice, coercion and social justice
In retrospect, Pantaleoni is definitely impervious to the problem of fiscal coercion. Mazzola too circumvents this issue. As to De Viti, he addresses himself to the problem but does not offer a solution that safeguards the interests of a minority of voters that may find the budget overpriced. He reiterates sanguinely that in modern societies individuals are called upon to give their judgement *in advance* concerning the advisability of the state's economic acts, very much like when they are buying a season ticket. There is no force that would make the purchaser of the ticket attend any and every performance. The analogy between the management of a corporation and the government still holds, with the exception that the latter group has at its disposal the power of compulsion. The citizens are aware of the eventuality that they will be penalized by the government if they failed to honour their fiscal obligation that was duly determined through a legitimate process.

Many contemporaries of Pantaleoni, De Viti and Mazzola found this aspect of the Italian theory of public goods particularly objectionable. According to Wicksell, for example, it is a flagrant injustice to force someone to contribute to the financing of a public activity which did not enhance his own interest. Implicating Mazzola, he remarks:

> [The 'law' that] the imposition of taxes is just and applies without arbitrariness and error when each taxpayer succeeds in distributing his resources in such a manner that his utility is maximized . . . is really meaningless. If the individual is to spend his money for private and public uses so that his satisfaction is maximized, he will obviously pay nothing whatsoever for public purposes. . . . Of course, if everyone were to do the same, the State would soon cease to function. . . . Equality between the marginal utility of public goods and their price cannot, therefore, be established by the single individual, but must be secured by consultation between him and all other individuals or their delegates. How is such consultation to be arranged so that the goal may be realized? On this point Mazzola does not say a word, as 'I see it, [although] this is precisely the question which ought to be decided. (Musgrave and Peacock, 1958, pp. 81–2)

From there on, Wicksell proceeds to develop his own theory of public goods, which ingeniously provides an escape from the free-rider dilemma. He thus demonstrates that a 'pure' theory of demand and supply of public goods can be formulated in such a way that it also affords justice for *all*.[6]

Conclusion
Admittedly, Mazzola's, De Viti's and Pantaleoni's shares in the deve-

lopment of modern public finance have been an indirect one, one that reached the American soil through Sweden via the works of Wicksell and Lindahl who applied their effort to place the Italian doctrine on a normative foundation. Therefore, it would be unfair to compare the contributions of the Italian founders of public finance with those of the Scandinavians who proceeded to improve them. But when the contributions of Pantaleoni, De Viti and Mazzola are compared with those of Marshall, Edgeworth and Sidgwick – in whose eyes public finance was 'little more than utiliarian ethics applied to certain economic problems' (Whittaker, 1962, p. 311) – then the true stature of the classical Italian theory of public goods can be discerned.

It should be also borne in mind that the Italian fiscal doctrine is relevant only within the framework of the marginalist framework. Evidently, a second revolution that came about in the 1930s has restricted the whole concept of utility, regardless of to which sphere of economic activity it is applied (Cooter and Rappoport, 1984). This paper has attempted to present the Italian theory of public goods in relation to the first, the marginalist, revolution. And within that framework, the Italian corpus certainly displays much strength that Marshalian–Pigovian-oriented contemporary fiscal theories still lack.

Appendix

In an attempt to render the contributions of classical Italian fiscal scientists more accessible to students of modern public finance, this appendix presents a mathematical exposition of the Italian theory of public goods.

According to Pantaleoni, the complementary character of public goods requires that

$B^1 = B^1 (X^1_1, X^1_2)$ where
B^1 : total benefit of individual 1;
X^1_1 : benefit of private good to individual 1;
X^1_2 : benefit of public good to individual 1.
    Similarly, the total cost to the individual:
$C^1 = C^1 (X^1_1, X^1_2)$ where X^1_1 and X^1_2

represent tax prices for the individual 1 of the private and public good, respectively.

As expounded by Pantaleoni, the Finance Minister must apply 'marginal calculus in the allocation of public expenditures in such a way that marginal yields from equivalent units are equalized' (1883, p. 11). Thus:

$$\frac{\dfrac{\partial B^1}{\partial X^1_1}}{\dfrac{\partial B^1}{\partial X^1_2}} - \frac{\dfrac{\partial C^1}{\partial X^1_1}}{\dfrac{\partial C^1}{\partial X^1_2}} = 0$$

where the ratio on the left is the marginal rate of substitution between the public good and the private good for individual 1, and the ratio on the right the marginal rate of transformation between the public good and the private good for the same individual.

Because of the summative nature of the benefit emanating from the public good – as discussed by Mazzola in great detail [1890] – taking two individuals together:

$$\frac{b^1_{x_2}}{b^1_{x_1}} + \frac{b^2_{x_2}}{b^2_{x_1}} = \frac{c_{x_2}}{c_{x_1}}$$

where lower-case b's and c's indicate partial derivatives. This shows that the sum of the marginal rates of substitution between the public and private good is equal to the goods' marginal cost. Hence, it can be demonstrated that the Italian theory of public goods preceded the seminal contributions of Samuelson (1954) and Buchanan (1968) by at least sixty years.

Notes

1. The author is Associate Professor of Economics at Lehman College of The City University of New York.
2. See three other essays of mine for a more detailed discussion of the views of Pantaleoni and De Viti (1985) and Mazzola (1987a). A three-way comparison of Italian, Scandinavian and Anglo-Saxon fiscal doctrines is in my 1987b essay.
3. It should be remarked at this point that Italy also provided a few splendid names. For instance, Pantaleoni, De Viti and Mazzola learned from Ferrara – who expounded fifteen years before Jevons (1871) – that the value of a good was derived from its 'perceived utility' (1934). Ferrara was aware of the important contributions of Briganti (1780), who almost a century before Jevons defined economics as 'mechanics of pleasure, or hedonism', and of Ortes (1790), who earnestly investigated the link between subjective utility and the market value. But Ferrara was a step ahead of Briganti and Ortes: he maintained that utility constituted the basis of the prices of *all* goods, private or public.
4. That a descriptive postulate lay at the heart of De Viti's otherwise positive theory of public goods threw off many competent Anglo-Saxon public finance specialists.

Henry Simons, for one, labelled De Viti's assertion 'individuals *demand* public goods and taxes are the *prices* against which people set the utilities of these goods' as 'a mass of intellectual confusion and of dangerous half-truths which, along with other vestiges of continental thought, are likely to plague us still for many years' (1937, p. 717). In retrospect, however, it seems that Simons' criticism stems from an unswerving allegiance to the principle of ability to pay.

5. De Viti's construct of 'determination of the value from the standpoint of the *community* and the *individual*' clearly parallels Sax's construct of the determination of *absolute taxes* and *relative taxes* in the purely public goods proper (1883).

6. It should be noted that Wicksell's solution, which is based on the assumptions of unanimity of votes and free agreement among voters, is considered by De Viti as a special case, namely, the 'total cooperation' stage. Lindahl's 'cooperative democracy construct' too can be traced back to De Viti. Although Lindahl: '. . . avoids Wicksell's improbable condition of unanimity, there is still . . . nothing in Lindahl's requirement of "free agreement," reasonably interpreted, which can guarantee the achievement of the fiscal optimum through "government" any more than that of [De Viti or] Mazzola'. (Head, 1974, p. 145)

References

Briganti, Filippo (1780), *L'esame economico del sistema civile,* reprinted in *Economici classici Italiani,* Milano: Destefani, 1804.

Buchanan, James M. (1968), *The Demand and Supply of Public Goods,* Chicago: Rand-McNally.

Cooter, Robert and Rappoport, Peter (1984), 'Were Ordinalists wrong about welfare economics?' *Journal of Economic Literature* (June), pp. 507–30.

De Viti de Marco, Antonio, Marchese (1936), *First Principles of Public Finance,* London: Johnathan Cape, which is the English translation of De Viti's *I primi principii dell'economia finanziaria,* Roma: A. Sampolesi (1928), which, in turn, is based on his 1888 book *Carattere teorico dell'economia finanziaria,* Roma: Pasqualicci.

Einaudi, Luigi (1936), 'Introduction' to De Viti de Marco's *First Principles* . . . (1936) cited.

Ferrara, Francesco (1934), *Lezioni di economia politica,* Bologna: Nicola Zanichelli. This edition is based on the lectures that Ferrara delivered intermittently between 1856 and 1873. Incidentally, pp. 551–765 of this work includes Ferrara's lectures in Public Finance.

Head, John J. (1974), *Public Goods and Public Welfare,* Durham, North Carolina: Duke University Press.

Jevons, William S. (1871), *The Theory of Political Economy,* reprinted in New York: Kelley and Millman (1957).

Kayaalp, Orhan (1988), 'Ugo Mazzola and the Italian Theory of Public Goods', *History of Political Economy,* Vol. 20, No. 1 (Spring), pp. 15–25.

Kayaalp, Orhan (1987b), 'Political tradition and national fiscal doctrines: a taxonomical note', *Rivista di diritto finanziario e scienza delle finanze,* Vol. XLVI, No. 1 (March), pp. 130–41.

Kayaalp, Orhan (1985), 'Public-choice elements of the Italian theory of public goods'. *Public Finance/Finances Publiques,* Vol. XXXX, No. 3, pp. 395–410.

Lindahl, Erik R. (1919), *Die Gerechtigkeit der Besteureung,* Lund.

Mazzola, Ugo (1890), *I dati scientifici della finanza pubblica,* Roma: Ermanno Loescher. Chapter IX of this book, translated as 'The formation of the prices of public goods', is in Musgrave and Peacock's *Classics* . . . (1958), pp. 37–47.

Musgrave, Richard A. and Peacock, Alan T. (1958), *Classics in the Theory of Public Finance,* New York: Macmillan.

Ortes, Giammaria (1790), *Calcolo sopra il valore delle opinioni e sopra i piaceri e i dolori,* reprinted in *Scrittori classici italiani di economia politica,* Milano (1894), Vol. 24, pp. 257–318.

Pantaleoni, Maffeo (1891), 'Cenni sul concetto di massimi edonistici individuali e collettiv.', *Giornale degli economisti,* Vol. IV. Reprinted in Pantaleoni's *Erotemi di economica,* Bari: Laterza e figli (1925), Vol. II, pp. 1–44.

Pantaleoni, Maffeo (1887), 'Teoria della Pressione tributaria'. Reprinted in Pantaleoni's *Scritti varii di economia,* Palermo (1904).

Pantaleoni, Maffeo (1883), 'Contributo alla teoria del riparto delle spese pubbliche', *Rassegna Italiana,* October 15.

Samuelson, Paul (1954), 'The pure theory of public expenditure', *Review of Economics and Statistics,* Vol. 36, November, pp. 387–9.

Sax, Emil (1993), *Grundlegung der theoretischen Staatswirtschaft,* Vienna.

Simons, Henry C. (1937), 'Book review: *First Principles of Public Finance* by Antonia De Viti de Marco', *Journal of Political Economy,* Vol. XLV, October, pp. 712–17.

Whittaker, E. (1962), *Schools and Streams of Economic Thought,* Chicago: The University of Chicago Press.

Wicksell, Knut (1896), 'Ein neues Prinzip der gerechten Besteuerung', *Finanztheoretische Untersuchungen,* Jena. Pp. iv–vi, 76–87, and 101–59 of this work, translated as 'A New Principle of Just Taxation', is in Musgrave and Peacock's *Classics . . .* (1958), pp. 73–118.

Wieser, Friedrich Von (1889), *Der natürliche Wert,* Vienna: A. Holder.

12 Nicolaas Gerard Pierson

Arnold Heertje[1]

Life history

Nicolaas Gerard Pierson was born on 7 February 1839 in Amsterdam, where he died on 24 December 1909. During his long and active life, he was President of the Dutch Central Bank, professor of economics, author of many articles and several books, Minister of Finance and, last but not least, Prime Minister of the Netherlands. In all these different capacities, he exercised an enormous influence on the development of Dutch banking, on theoretical economics and on the Dutch financial and social policies.

From 1845 until 1852, Pierson studied at the French school in Amsterdam. After the final exam he stayed in Brussels to attend the English school, where he applied himself mainly to modern languages. As he was interested in commerce, this was important to him. Many years later, when he had become a theoretical economist, his profound knowledge of the international literature was one of his most striking qualities. Before he had reached the age of eighteen, Pierson had studied the works of key economists such as Adam Smith and J.B. Say thoroughly. From 1855 until 1857 he attended evening classes in the principles of economics at the commercial school in Amsterdam. As Pierson had a keen interest in the cotton trade, he started to work with the Dutch commissioners Bleckman & Co. Soon, however, he left for Liverpool, at the time the most important centre for cotton trade in Europe. It was in this commercial town, while working with Campbells, that he acquired his practical experience. He studied the trade closely, gathering extensive statistical data, and at night he studied Danish and Italian and continued his economic studies.

On the advice of the cotton trader Campbell, Pierson undertook a journey to the US in order to expand his knowledge of the cotton trade. After his daily duties in an office in New Orleans, he continued to gather statistical material on the trade. He noticed that banking in Lousiana was very well organized and after studying the subject closely his first economic publication on the trade and banking of this state appeared, in 1859. An extraordinary achievement for a twenty-year old who had learned the basic principles of economics by self-education!

In 1859 Pierson returned to Amsterdam to work in his father's glassworks. And his activities in the cotton trade were reduced to a limited scale. On 25 February 1861, he established, together with H.B. Wiardi Beckman, 'Beckman and Pierson', commissioners in cotton and colonial goods. On 1 January 1865, Pierson was appointed President of the Surinam Bank in Amsterdam and he resigned from the firm. What tipped the scale was his important 1863 publication on the future of the Dutch Central Bank.

In 1864 Pierson was invited to become a teacher at the same school he had attended as a youth, the commercial school in Amsterdam. By that time, he had written several economic papers, but nevertheless was not qualified to teach economics. Consequently, he began preparing himself for the necessary degree in political economy and statistics, which in 1864 could be obtained for the first time. There were just three candidates, and Pierson was the only one who passed. In September of the same year, he took up his appointment and set to work with much enthusiasm. He wrote a secondary education textbook, which was proposed as a standard school text. However, Pierson refused, as he considered the book too limited for a larger public.

Until 1868, Pierson combined the posts of President of the Surinam Bank and secondary school teacher. In the same year he published the text of the magnificent papers on the 'Cultural System'[2] which he had given during the winter of 1866—67. In this work he warmly advocated the application of classic English liberal thought to the system of production in Java. For ethical and economic reasons, he was opposed to the system of exploitation imposed by his own country. Because of his well-founded and enlightened opinions on important contemporary topics, which were always based on a profound knowledge of the various economic views, Pierson became a public figure.

On 1 July 1868, at the age of twenty-nine, he was appointed managing director of the Dutch Central Bank. In those days, managing the Dutch financial affairs took only a few hours a day. Nevertheless, Pierson resigned both as President of the Surinam Bank and as a teacher of economics. He was very active as a publicist, and carried out many social functions. As a theoretical economist, he was becoming successful and his social and political influence was increasing. In 1870 he was offered a government post, but he refused. In 1875 the University of Leiden appointed him to doctoris honoris causa in law. Shortly thereafter, his book *Elements of Economics*, originally written for secondary schools, was published enhancing his reputation as a leading economist still further.

When in 1877 the University of Amsterdam was founded, a chair of Political Economy and Statistics was established. Pierson was offered the chair and accepted. With the consent of the Amsterdam municipality, he combined this job with his post at the Dutch Central Bank, after he had agreed to waive the salary related to his professorial duties. On 27 October 1877, he read his oration, 'Retrospect on the History of Political Economy since Adam Smith'.

In January 1885 he resigned his professorship, because he was appointed President of the Dutch Central Bank. During the years of his professorship, he had begun to write a book which was to become very famous – his *Textbook of Political Economy*. The first part was published in 1884 and the second part in 1890. From 1887 to 1891 he was also chairman of the editorial staff of the Dutch magazine *The Economist*.

More than once, Pierson had declined to become Minister of Finance. In 1891, however, when there was a liberal cabinet, he accepted this portfolio. During his term of office, which lasted until 1894, he had the opportunity to realize his ideas to reform the Dutch tax system. After the overthrow of the cabinet, he returned to political science, and until 1897 was again chairman of the editorial staff of *The Economist*. He also became chairman of the Dutch Society for Political Economy and Statistics.

In 1897 the cabinet of Pierson–Goeman Borgesius was established, in which Pierson was not only Minister of Finance, but also Prime Minister. Because of its progressive policy, this cabinet became known as 'the cabinet of social justice'. It introduced a number of important social reforms regarding education, health care and child labour. After the cabinet resigned in 1901, Pierson returned once again to political science and until his death in 1909 was again chairman of the editorial staff of *The Economist*.

This brief outline gives the impression of an extremely gifted man, who possessed enormous talents in the field of commerce and banking, science, administration and legislation. Indeed, in all these different fields he reached the top – in banking and politics, not driven by personal ambition but invited by others; in political science, driven from his early youth by an unbridled longing for a theoretical, statistical and institutional understanding of the economic process and by the desire to report, in writing and lectures, his growing knowledge. Throughout his life he used the opportunities he was given extremely well. He exploited his talent in a manner which reflected his belief and trust in people, his belief in their progress and his trust in their ability to develop themselves freely.

Pierson and the changing economics scene

When Pierson was born in 1839, David Ricardo (1772–1823) had been dead sixteen years. The French mathematician, statistician and economist Augustin A. Cournot (1801–77) was already thirty-eight, John Stuart Mill (1806–73), the prodigy of the classic school, was thirty-three, and Karl Marx (1818–83) had just reached maturity, Hermann Heinrich Gossen (1810–58), the eccentric forerunner of the ultimate utility theory, was then a young man of twenty-eight, Alfred Marshall (1842–1924) was not yet born, and Jean-Baptiste Say (1768–1832 had been dead seven years.

In 1859, when Pierson published his first article on the commerce and banking of the American state Louisiana,[3] the most important economic papers by Cournot[4] and Gossen[5] had been published, but had so far passed unnoticed.[6] The standard work of John Stuart Mill[7] had been popular for some time, but until 1875 there was no Dutch translation.[8] The sensational price-theoretic works of Jevons,[9] Menger[10] and Walras[11] had not yet been written. The *Communist Manifesto*,[12] by Marx and Engels, on the other hand, had appeared in 1848, but the first edition of the first part of *Das Kapital*[13] was to come out much later.

In 1884, when the first edition of Pierson's *Textbook*[14] was published, economic theory was developing very rapidly. The works of Cournot and Gossen had been saved from oblivion. Marx was dead, but his thoughts were subject to much theoretical and social debate. On 20 February 1885, Alfred Marshall delivered his oration in Cambridge, in which he compared the inductive method with the deductive method.[15] In Austria, F. von Wieser[16] published a paper in which he expounded the Austrian version of price theory. Long before, F.Y. Edgeworth had published his stimulating book,[17] which, because of the introduction of the idea of 'the core of an economy', still serves as a starting point for the theory of general equilibrium. In Lausanne, Léon Walras was very active in the field of mathematical economics.[18] In 1884, Schumpeter and Keynes were both only one year old.

When Pierson died in 1909, the analysis of the marginal utility school had become common knowledge; the theories of Marx were being subjected to many exchanges of views and Marshall's *Principles of Economics*,[19] the first edition of which had been published in 1890, had begun its triumphal march. Schumpeter had just finished his first important book,[20] and a few years later Keynes appeared on the scene.[21]

Pierson's work to 1871

Whoever studies Pierson's articles and pamphlets up to 1871 is impressed by their broad scope and depth. Three articles deal with the object and methodology of economics; two are about the history of economic ideas. Two others are devoted to public finance, two bear an historical character and one is about phenomena in the financial market. Of particular interest is his brochure on the future of the Dutch Central Bank, in which the President-to-be strongly defended the idea that the right to issue banknotes should remain the monopoly of the Bank.[22] His lectures on the 'Cultural System' were published in book form.

If we consider the rather low state of economics in Holland at that time, the merit of the young, self-made Pierson becomes even more estimable. It is also the reason why he referred principally to foreign rather than to Dutch scholars. Right from the beginning he was opposed to so-called 'practical political economy' and advocated a much more theoretical approach.

Pierson adhered to the deductive method along the lines of John Stuart Mill, but did not exclude the importance of inductive aspects. At twenty years of age he did not want to restrict himself entirely to the rigid laws of logic: 'for the progress of science, one needs more.'[23] His interest in the importance of the inductive element was not only expressed in his historical-economic publications, but also in his statement: 'Without progress in statistics, no progress in political economy.'[24] As to history he observed: 'combined with speculative thinking it is of the utmost importance.'[25] His plea for the integration of history, statistics and deduction in the study of economics, would make him, like Schumpeter, a founding father of the Econometric Society.

Whoever reads Pierson's essay on wealth from 1864[26] can hardly escape the sense of witnessing him struggle with the refractory theoretical material on this subject. Some years earlier, several other Dutch economists had tried their hand at this theme, but Pierson, although very well read, did not seem to pay any attention to what his predecessors had to say. Starting from the relatively simple question: 'What is wealth?', Pierson became entangled in a confused dispute which finally resulted in an extremely vague conclusion: wealth is the normal economic situation of the social organism.[27] The emphasis is on the word 'organism'. According to Pierson an organism is characterized by continual development and movement. By movement, Pierson means exchange, as an indispensable condition for creating wealth. Hence development and movement are identified with wealth. In his later work Pierson underlined the importance of exchange in this respect even further.[28]

In connection with his criticism on the individualistic approach of Adam Smith, Pierson repeatedly referred to what nowadays would be called the aggregation problem.[29] In his opinion, Adam Smith regarded our society as a large family, thus underestimating the mutual dependence of the members of this society, in particular that of producers and consumers. Pierson's reproach seems groundless, if we take into account that Smith used individualism as a method for analysis and as a cornerstone for the coordinating role of the market mechanism.

Pierson's depiction of society as a living organism, in which consumers and producers are mutually dependent and which is characterized by continual movement and development, does not clash with Adam Smith's vision or with his statement that 'consumption is the sole end and purpose of all production'.[30] In fact, Pierson's organistic view on society boils down to the same as Smith's.[31]

Pierson declared that his experiences in trade were not compatible with 'orthodox economics', in so far as this meant that 'all so-called unproductive use is harmful to society'.[32] To Pierson, trade is an indispensable source of wealth. Wealth is the normal economic situation of the social organism, and without it,[33] there is no development or movement, in short no normal situation. Consequently, wealth will decline. If asked, Pierson might have said that his concept of wealth had a concrete meaning, adopted from reality, while his concept of economics should be understood in an abstract sense.[34] Wealth is not the sum of material objects, a specification of wealth remains abstract, as this sum means nothing without the incentive role of trade.[35] It is peculiar that Pierson holds to his essential distinction between making goods and trading goods, thus blocking the way to a broader view on the concept of welfare.

In his 1866 article in *The Economist* on value and costs of production[36], Pierson made a sharp distinction between cost of production in general and necessary production costs – necessary because they are determined by the state of technology and 'the economic state of society'.[37] In this respect, he proved to be a forerunner of the so-called Amsterdam School in business economics. In emphasizing the importance of the costs that are necessary at the most efficient level, he was referring to the concept of opportunity costs later to be developed by Austrians.[38]

In accordance with the value theory of Adam Smith and David Ricardo, Pierson made a distinction between market equilibrium in the long and short run. Pierson argued that long-run market prices are mainly determined by necessary production costs and are temporary by concrete circumstances, especially on the demand side of the market. It is important that Pierson also made a distinction between durable goods and goods 'for daily use', because it draws him to the conclusion that long-term prices do not always have to be the same as production costs. 'Value is no slave, who goes where its masters want it to go; it also obeys other masters, whose voice may be decisive.'[39] With regard to short-term influences on prices, Pierson designed a model in which factors such as the purchasing power and needs of consumers and profit margins all play a part.

Pierson's articles on the history of economic ideas are impressive. In 1866 he published an article in *The Economist* on the Italian economic ideas of the seventeenth and eighteenth centuries,[40] based on the famous edition of P. Custodi[41] which contains the works of A. Serra, M. Gioja, F. Galiani, P. Verri, G. Ortes, A. Genovesi and C. B. Beccaria. His excellent knowledge of Italian enabled him to go into great detail. It is to Pierson's credit that he acknowledged the importance of the Italian writers at such an early date. It was almost another hundred years before Schumpeter, in his turn, turned the spotlight on these Italian economists, who, since then have fallen into oblivion once more.[42]

In 1866 he published another article on the German iconoclast F. List[43] and again showed an incredibly detailed knowledge of his subject matter. He did not agree with List's proposal to introduce protective duties, because 'protection undermines the entrepreneurial spirit',[44] but he nevertheless had a great deal of admiration for List. Two articles, written around the same time, show the enormous scope of Pierson's knowledge and his wide interest. In the first, he discussed the development of the economic system in Russia, in order to illustrate the so-called anti-individualistic creed in cultural history.[45] The second describes the economic state of Athens, a few centuries before Christ.[46]

After 1865, Pierson regularly wrote articles for *The Economist* on monetary and financial issues.[47] His great interest in public finance was also expressed in an article of 1870 on income tax, in which he came to the conclusion that an income tax is not advisable.[48] In respect to his later political appointment as Minister of Finance, it is important that Pierson rejected the idea of income tax on theoretical grounds.

Pierson's work after 1871

After 1871, Pierson continued as a prolific and successful writer on many aspects of economics. He vehemently defended his methodological insights against Levy, who in a publication on katheder-socialism, had tried to refute a critical essay on the subject by Pierson.[49] Pierson again emphasized the explanatory task of economics and rejected the idea that science should exercise an advisory role for the government.

Pierson can amaze us by raising a question which, even now, is very advanced: 'can cutting the working-day offer a solution in the fight against unemployment? I think I can demonstrate that he who doesn't acknowledge it and he who denies it, are both in error, the first as he overlooks the fact that cutting working hours, under certain conditions, may indeed be a means to overcome unemployment; the other as he ignores these conditions'.[50]

Pierson's article of 1902 on valuation in a centrally planned socialist economy deserves special mention.[51] For the first time, he raised the question of how in a society without a market and price system one can value the factors of production, consumer goods and the methods of production. Later, Hayek expressed his admiration for Pierson's work and included Pierson's contribution in his well-known book on *Collectivist Economic Planning*:[52]

> This article is the first important contribution to the modern discussion of the economic aspects of socialism, and although it remained practically unknown outside of Holland and was only made accessible in a German version after the discussion had been started independently by others, it remains of special interest as the only important discussion of these problems published before the War. It is particularly valuable for its discussion of the problems arising out of the international trade between several socialist communities.

These words, written more than twenty-five years after Pierson's death, illustrate the international fame of this Dutch economist.

Pierson's great interest in the history of economics remained keen throughout his entire life. His article on the physiocrats[53] offers a much better insight than much that has been written on this subject since. Apart from his keen interest in the history of economics, his inquiring mind was exercised by empirical issues and economic history. This becomes evident when one reads his articles on the Irish land law of 1881,[54] on the Sicilian riots of 1893[55] and on the plague which beset Europe in 1348.[56] Again and again, Pierson's striking ability to elucidate so many themes is notable.

Pierson was also active in the sphere of international economic relations, monetary questions and the theory and practice of public finance. In 1864, for example, he translated Goschen's book on exchange rates into Dutch.[57] On the same topic he wrote an article, meant for *The Economic Journal*, which was, however, not accepted as it was considered too long, and was therefore not published until 1911.[58] He was a strong defender of free trade and very much opposed to protection in international trade.[59]

Pierson is also known for being in favour of bimetallism, although he did not defend it for reasons of scarcity of gold,[60] referring instead to the advantage of the stability of exchange rates between countries with a golden and silver standard.[61] Pierson's view on the internal value of money is related to Carl Menger's distinction in the internal and external exchange value of money, expressed in the second edition of his book in 1923.[62] Pierson's analysis of money and inflation foreshadows the theory of neutral money.

Of all Pierson's many contributions to the theory of public finance, it was his contributions on the progressive income tax that led to the famous thesis written by A.J. Cohen Stuart,[63] which was noted in the international literature.[64] After 1870, Pierson reflected more and more upon this theme and argued for a proportional relation between sacrifice and utility in a subjectivist sense. It is clear that the marginal utility theory was indispensable to the evolution in his thinking. Notwithstanding his earlier rejection of income tax, he arranged, as Minister of Finance, for a tax reform based on a mix of taxes and also on income tax based on the sacrifice principle.

Pierson's *Textbook on Economics*

As we have seen above, volume I of Pierson's *Textbook* appeared in 1884 and volume II in 1890.[65] Teaching at Dutch universities was governed by this book for several decades. It was also renowned in international circles and has been translated into English, French and Italian.[66] From the English edition, several parts were also translated into Japanese.[67] Schumpeter observed that Pierson 'founded a school that, supported by leaders such as Verrijn Stuart and de Vries, lasted well into the 1920's'.[68] While in Austria, it was Eugen von Böhm-Bawerk who gave Pierson's book a positive evaluation.[69]

The *Textbook* starts with a fascinating overview of the history of economic thought.[70] Pierson's emphasis on material welfare, on the practical aim and normative task of economics, is intriguing to today's reader, who perceives Pierson's appreciation of the Austrian view and approves his statement: 'It is never the task of science to set rules; it is even less the task of economics, for it is concerned with merely material interests, and as soon as those come into conflict with superior interests, the first, naturally, have to step aside.'[71] Pierson realized, however, that it is not appropriate to make normative statements: 'Its only vocation is to illuminate obscure matters. It may never tell the government: do this or do that.'[72] Pierson was, on the other hand, convinced that science is obliged to provide the knowledge that the government demands.

In Pierson's view the solution to economic problems is closely related to exchange. A considerable part of the *Textbook* is set within this framework. Themes such as the exchange value of goods, the prices of production factors, the analysis of the general price level, monetary and banking affairs and the international economic relations, are all dealt with. But when, in the third part, we are confronted with sections on socialism and the wants and needs of the workers, and in the fourth part with public finance, the reader sees that Pierson has not become the victim of his own dogma. To a certain extent, it confirms Pierson's view that general economic laws always have a conditional character.

His value theory, which is the subject of the first part of the *Textbook*, is mainly based on Jevons' version of the marginal utility theory, although Pierson also shows evidence of appreciating Menger.[73] He observes that value is determined by the 'the utility of the final increment', in other words, by what Jevons calls final utility.[74] Apart from the concept of value, Pierson also goes into detail on the cost-price. Notable in this respect is his distinction between entrepreneurial costs and costs in a social context. To the entrepreneur, it is of no importance at all whether declining costs are brought about by declining wages or by new production methods, but it is important to society.[75] Declining wages imply less income for the workers. New production methods, however, imply an increasing amount of useful goods.

Also, while establishing a relationship between value and cost price, Pierson applies the marginal productivity theory to labour and then relates the relative prices of goods to the quantity of labour, incorporated in the goods, which is a direct link to Ricardo's relative labour theory of value. Ricardo also comes to mind when Pierson writes that things do not have value because they require labour, but that labour is allocated because they have value, as Ricardo once said with respect to rent. Without saying so explicitly, Pierson introduces subjective value in use against objective value in exchange: the first is determined by marginal utility and the second by costs. Subsequently, the distinction between market prices in the short run and in the long run is entirely left out. It has to be assumed that Pierson has perfect competition in mind, but this becomes less clear than in his publications on value and production costs.

Pierson's treatment of the prices of goods is followed by production factors. Rent, rental value, capital interest, entrepreneurial profits, as distinguished from entrepreneurial wages and wages are all discussed in detail. On rent, Pierson follows Ricardo and in doing so he also appreciates Menger, as Ricardo's theory on rent can be seen as a forerunner of the Austrian vision.[76] The discussion on rental value is illustrated by many practical examples. The detailed treatment of interest, however, indicating a market equilibrium determined by demand and supply, fails to provide a clear account of the underlying accessory factors. Pierson further argues that entrepreneurial wages and labourers' wages are determined by similar laws.[77] Entrepreneurial profits offer a reward for the risk of the entrepreneur has to run. Only when discussing wages does Pierson explicitly return to the theory on 'the final increment'.[78] Wages are determined by the produce of the workers, who are working under extremely unfavourable conditions. Pierson raises the question whether a strike might help them to improve their wages, but according to him, they should not raise their hopes too high.

Pierson finishes his treatment of price theory with a chapter on the prices of goods. It then becomes clear that supply and demand in a situation of perfect competition play an important role and that Pierson also acknowledges the existence of monopoly. The discussion on money prices forms a natural bridge to the second part on exchange, in which the focus is on national and international monetary questions. These trains of thought, richly illustrated with statistical and historical information, result in a plea for an introduction of the double standard. To Pierson, bimetallism is an important tool in the struggle against inflation and deflation.[79]

The third part of the *Textbook* is concerned with production and consumption. For the reader who remembers Pierson's sympathy for the principles of the marginal utility theory and his references to the Austrian economists Menger and Böhm-Bawerk, his restriction of production to 'material' or 'tangible' goods[80] is hard to explain. It is my opinion that Pierson did not notice this inconsistency, as he did not relate his thoughts on production to the allocation of scarce resources, which can be seen as the typical economic aspect. Pierson devotes ample attention to the allocation of means of production in connection with the 'capitalistic production method'. He argues that an entrepreneur is punished if he exploits the means of production carelessly, and that he receives a bonus if he perceives in time, which goods or services are going to be demanded.[81] To Pierson, the price mechanism is a compass with regard to the functioning of supply and demand. It is the cornerstone of an economic order, and forms the best possible help for solving the enormous social problem of allocation. He believes this type of economic order can secure an efficient capital formation.

Yet Pierson does not forget the role of self-interest. 'There is no profit in founding hospitals, schools for the poor, libraries and public parts. Yet all these things are necessary. However, if one waits until they are brought about by self-interest, one will wait in vain'.[82] It is possible for social profits to exceed the gain of the producer. Pierson cites the example of transport, from which the external positive effects are undeniable. It is therefore wrong to follow the compass of price mechanism blindly, as it does not always forecast 'what direction one should take in order to serve the interest of humanity and society'.[83] Every public work that supplies a need, is economically productive. However, as Pierson adds, its production should possess 'the highest possible degree of productivity'.[84] Government subsidies are only justified if the benefits to the population convincingly exceed the profits that the entrepreneurs may appropriate by capitalistic methods of production. Pierson provides a fully modern account of what should be left to private enterprise and what to public enterprise: 'One can be sure that much useful work would remain undone' if a country adhered to the principle of *laisser-faire*.[85] Depressions and crises also demonstrate to Pierson the imperfection of a society in which self-interest is allowed full play. He again advocates a monopolistic position for the Central Bank, as a means 'to temper disasters'.[86]

Pierson pays a lot of attention to the interest of the employees, who may be harmed by the entrepreneur's arbitrary attitude. Trade unions are very important in the fight against the many existing abuses of power. But the government has an essential role to play in combating many unjust practices so Pierson shows himself to be a warm defender of social legislation. One sees here a relationship between his theoretical analysis and his conduct as a politician, in particular as Prime Minister of a 'cabinet of social justice'. The principal element in Pierson's criticism of a society based on self interest is the enormous inequality in welfare, which it brings about'.[87] We must know better than to identify the present order with the 'natural order'. 'It is no more natural than any other society. It is based on the right of property, brought into being by the law, and protected by a strong defence. Purely scientifically speaking, one can only regard it as one of many possible orders, and every sincere economist should ask himself whether it is the best.'[88] This quotation would not be out of place in a modern introduction to the economic analysis of property rights.[89]

In his subsequent treatment of socialism, Pierson does Karl Marx little justice when he says that he is an author whose feelings run high and who one 'can hardly call a strict scientific scholar'.[90] In Pierson's account of the advantages and disadvantages of socialism, it is note-worthy that inequality remains, though 'some of the causes from which it follows' have been removed.[91] He does not recommend an experiment with socialism, which, in his opinion, had been justly compared with a religion. The present imperfect order is not to be abandoned until socialists have succeeded in solving the considerable disadvantages of their system. Pierson discusses the disadvantages in more detail in his study on a centrally planned system.

In the fourth part of his *Textbook*, Pierson shows himself to be a master of the theory and policy of taxation and loans. There is a paragraph in which he argues that the burden of taxation can actually be reduced by shifting it on to other groups or by introducing technical innovations.[92] When discussing policy on loans, he distinguishes between permanent and temporary ones. In his view, permanent loans should be allowed only if they contribute to income at least equal to the interest on the loan.[93] Only in exceptional cases can one borrow on a permanent basis, as there is great uncertainty about the question of whether public activity can produce the interest. Temporary loans, however, 'if used in an efficient manner, can be very useful'.[94] In the second edition of his book, these themes are dealt with more thoroughly. With respect to economic laws, much attention is paid to A. Marshall.[95] Gossen is mentioned, not as a forerunner of the marginal utility theory, but as one of those authors who uses mathematical figures for economic analysis. A separate paragraph is devoted to the origin of capital interest, in which he explains and defends Böhm-Bawerk's theory.

No less a scholar than F.Y. Edgeworth wrote on the occasion of the second printing of part II: 'His solid sense and weighty learning move steadily along the main lines of economic reasoning like those vast engines which rolling over our material highroads render them more smooth, compact, and serviceable'.[96] This evaluation justly throws light on the synthetic character of Pierson's *Textbook*.

Pierson and the marginal utility theory
In the Appendix to Pierson's article on Ricardo's sytem,[97] there is no trace of his accepting a subjectivistic specification of value and costs. Pierson is true to the line of thought he had advocated in his 1864 article on wealth. Two years later he published an article in *The Economist* on value and production costs, and it is here that a subjectivist element can be acknowledged, although the concept of marginal utility is entirely omitted. Whether an increase of production costs is followed by an increased price depends, according to Pierson, just on the question whether the product concerned satisfies essential needs or not; and secondly how fast the stock of the products will be used.

It is evident that Pierson must have had a change of mind during the period prior to the publication of the *Textbook*. In the magnificent biographical notice from 1911 J. d'Aulnis de Bourouill,[98] describes how Pierson introduced him to the work of Jevons.

> In the spring of 1873, when I was a student at the University of Leiden, I made contact with Pierson through my honoured lecturer Professor Buys. The earliest publications by Pierson in *The Gids* had stirred my longing to try

my hand at a thesis on theoretical economics. But that was not easy. Soon I was tangled in a series of contradictory reasonings. In my despair I consulted Buys, my professor in constitutional law, who had taught economics in Amsterdam for several years and who had treated my fellow students and myself to several severe lectures on political economy at the meetings of the Student Debating Club in Leiden. Buys declared that he could not help me either. 'Go and see Pierson in Amsterdam' he said, 'if the present state of science allows an answer to your questions, Pierson will be able to give it to you'.

Thus I went to Amsterdam, equipped with an introductory letter of Buys. Pierson received me . . . and . . . supplied the answer. The solution to the riddles, he said, can be found in a new theory on value, lately discovered by an English author, William Stanley Jevons, professor in political economy in Manchester, who, in 1871, had written a book titled *The Theory of Political Economy*. I returned to Leiden and studied the difficult book. I extended the theory of Jevons a little and completed my dissertation. Initially, the novel theory was rather strange to my promotor, Professor Vissering, but soon he acknowledged that it meant a great improvement. For it had not escaped his keen insight how much confusion the older political economy entailed. He had followed the earlier attacks by Pierson in *The Gids* with much interest and welcomed the fact that there was a new foundation from which one could move on. A new theory on value had to be the basis for a regeneration.

And so it was to be. Economic theory of the last forty years, for example the Austrian view on capital and capital interest, has Jevons's theory as a basis. Pierson's sharp insight had traced the method in an English book, which was full of mathematics. In the book there was an application of differential calculus, inaccessible for the average economist. Pierson, however, was an exception.[99]

It is odd that d'Aulnis de Bourouill does not mention Pierson at all in his dissertation of 1874,[100] although he points out in his preface that he takes his stand entirely on Jevons. He does refer, however, to his correspondence with Walras and Jevons. All in all, the impression was kept alive that d'Aulnis de Bourouill had introduced the new theory on value in Holland. From the correspondence between Jevons and Walras it is clear that d'Aulnis de Bourouill played an important role.[101] In a letter of 1 June 1874 to Walras, d'Aulnis de Bourouill says: 'Pierson a fixé mon attention sur le livre de M. Jevons comme indispensable pour tout étudiant d'économie politique.'[102] Other passages from this letter also prove that d'Aulnis de Bourouill regarded Pierson as an authority. This attitude is once more confirmed in a letter of 29 June 1874, in which he approached Jevons for the first time and from which it is evident that Pierson actually should be seen as d'Aulnis de Bourouill's mentor.[103] Only one week later, Jevons replied that, although his theory had received little attention in his home country, he remained convinced 'of its substantial truth, though I have feared that it would take a long time to obtain for it any reception'.[104]

In Leiden, in November 1874, d'Aulnis de Bourouill obtained a doctor's degree for a dissertation on the income of society in which he displayed a detailed knowledge of the work of Jevons and Walras. His expositions are nevertheless largely based on Jevons' theory both as far as the attitude of individual subjects as demanders of goods, and providers of labour and capital, are concerned. His concise 22nd theorem runs as follows: 'Utility is the basis of value.' The behaviour of producers is discussed neither by Jevons nor by d'Aulnis de Bourouill.[105]

Pierson had briefly referred to Jevons' marginal utility theory of the behaviour of the consumer in the first edition of volume II of his *Principles*[106] which was published in 1876. He discusses his version of the marginal utility theory more elaborately in his *Textbook*. Like Jevons, Pierson discusses value first of all, independent of exchange, and concludes that it is determined by the utility of the last increment, which Jevons calls, from the point of view of the consumer, final utility. After that, Pierson follows Jevons in discussing the question how much labour an owner of this factor of production will expend. Labour is regarded as production effort. The distribution of this effort on the production of various goods is determined by the utility of the last increment. Pierson concludes that the amount of goods demanded is lower as the price is higher, and he points out the declining marginal utility of goods, as well as the 'inequality' in the appreciation of the sacrifices.[107]

When Pierson discusses the prices of factors of production, like Menger[108] but unlike Jevons, he takes the view of the entrepreneur into account. In particular, when discussing labour, there are traces of the marginal utility theory when analysing the price level in an industry.[109] The prices of the goods are established in market equilibrium, founded on collective schedules of supply and demand. Pierson did not provide a subjectivist interpretation of supply, so one should not be surprised that he repeatedly returns to Ricardo.

In 1889, in *The Economist*, Pierson discussed the work of Böhm-Bawerk.[110]

> A few years ago, Professor Wieser brought a term into vogue, for which one would wish to be able to find a Dutch equivalent, as it comprises the entire theory within one single word: *Grenznutzen*. By that he understands what Jevons call *Final Utility*, namely the utility of the last increment to a supply. It is this utility which governs the value of things, and Von Böhm will demonstrate that it provides the key for explaining the interest rate.

One year later, Pierson cited Jevons and Menger as those who gave another turn to the value theory after 1870.[111] In his review, Pierson referred further to the work of Alfred Marshall, who, at that time, had recently been published. He immediately acknowledged the great importance of Marshall[112] and pays much attention to his work in his review of 1891.[113] Pierson shows much appreciation for Marshall, but also makes some criticisms, especially on the composition of Marshall's masterpiece. It is striking, however, that he did not refer to Marshall's rendering of the marginal utility theory, or the introduction of the term marginal utility and the application of the subjectivist line of thought on labour, as is implicit from the term 'marginal disutility of labour'.[114]

Pierson visited Marshall during the first half of the 1890s.[115] In 1896, when a second edition of volume I of Pierson's *Textbook* appeared, Pierson mentioned the term marginal utility as an equivalent to final utility, but there is no reference to Marshall,[116] yet he adopts the terms himself. Pierson approaches the marginal productivity theory closest while discussing the wages of labour. 'It is now most important that the general law, which governs the value, is acknowledged to govern the wages also. The value of services depends upon their marginal utility.' If one takes into consideration that by 1896 three editions of Marshall's *Principles* had been published, in which the prices of products and factors of production were discussed thoroughly, one can only conclude that Pierson missed the chance to revise his book with respect to price theory.

It was Pierson who, via his pupil J. d'Aulnis de Bourouill, made the marginal utility theory accessible in the Netherlands. He himself certainly helped to propagate the theory there although his treatise is sometimes hampered by a lack of precise terminology, a somewhat superficial analysis and by a rather fragmentary application of the principle of marginal utility. Pierson stays true to the material concept of welfare and consequently to the ideas of the classics, and this blocked his formation of an unprejudiced view on the subjectivist way of thinking.

Pierson and Ricardo

There are many similarities between Pierson and Ricardo. They were both self-made men and had acquired a profound knowledge of economics by intense self-education. Both were gifted theorists and had a talent for practical application in the field of commerce and exchange. Both entered economics by way of monetary issues and the policy of the Central Bank. Both recorded their theories in textbooks and had an active political career. Both combined a liberal attitude to life with a warm interest in social changes.[117] We should not be surprised, then, that Pierson frequently turned to the work of Ricardo, which he praised

repeatedly, especially as far as Ricardo's deductive method is concerned. Pierson was fascinated by Ricardo throughout his life and he
devoted several important studies to his fellow economist. In particular,
in his article of 1864,[118] published in *de Gids*, the twenty-five-year-old
Pierson discussed the third edition of Ricardo's *Principles*.[119] In this
article, Pierson's extensive knowledge is obvious and it also shows his
keen analytical insight and judgement. There are many passionate
discussions on how to interpret Ricardo's system of the functioning of
the economic process.[120] Pierson seems to have foreseen the extraordinary position which Ricardo was to occupy in economic science:
'Nobody ever believed the importance of Ricardo as a political economist to be contestable, though his theories were often fought fiercely
and he will be entitled to this importance, as long as political economics
will be studied.'[121] And: 'any theorem Ricardo ever defended is even
now subjected to many debates.'[122] Nevertheless, it is Pierson's opinion
that Ricardo's efforts did not yield much, as science responded to them
with disdain. Today's debates on Ricardo's theories illustrate his
influence on the development of economic thinking.

It was Pierson's opinion that Ricardo's system is determined by two
issues, namely the theory on rent and the theory on value. Just as in
modern discussions, Pierson raised the question whether Ricardo
considered the costs of production as the sole determinant of value, or
whether he also took the demand side and the utility of goods into
account. Pierson pointed out that Ricardo's labour theory of value is
founded on two conditions: utility and reproduction of goods. With
respect to value, Pierson throws light on Ricardo's distinction in
reproducible and non-reproducible goods. This distinction is very
important for a full understanding of the interpretations of Ricardo
which are based on Sraffa. Pierson points out that Ricardo puts the
emphasis on value, as it is determined in the long run by cost of
production, so that incidental factors on the supply and demand side of
the market have to be abandoned.

Pierson also appreciated Ricardo's opinion that value is determined
by labour which, under unfavourable conditions, that is, at the margin,
is necessary for production. This point of view was important with
respect to Ricardo's theory. Rent is not an element but a result of price,
because of the determination of the value of goods by the application of
labour under unfavourable conditions. Pierson carefully discussed the
different objections which had been put forward against Ricardo's
theory of rent and finally came to the conclusion that Ricardo's theory,
in principle, was just, though it needed to be refined.[123] In this
sophisticated essay, Pierson vigorously defended Ricardo's deductive

method. It is, in particular, Ricardo's methodology which won Pierson's admiration.

> With respect to the method, it is Ricardo who is the master. And that is why it is not too daring to assume that there will be a time, when all the results, with which we are filling our textbooks now, will be looked upon in a manner similar to our appreciation of the publications of, for instance, Pieter de la Court and John Locke. Then, a future Wilhelm Roscher will write about some peculiar man who lived in the beginning of the nineteenth century and who wrote a book on political economy and taxation; and with much interest one will notice that several principles of that science were already extant in that book. But when that time comes, and if political economy is not doomed to strand at the present stage of development, she will – I am quite positive – be indebted to no one, after Adam Smith, so much as to David Ricardo.[124]

Fifteen years later, when Pierson again discussed Ricardo, he expressed his deep admiration once more. 'Ricardo possessed an extremely interesting mind; not all he has written may be just, but it is always certainly worthwhile. He seldom followed an old trail; mostly, he chooses his own way and leads us to a point which pre-eminently provides the opportunity to become acquainted with the phenomena he wants to explain.'[125]

The theory that Pierson had in mind was recorded in Ricardo's first publication.[126] In this pamphlet, Ricardo challenges the accepted theory according to which metals will be exported when there is an unfavourable balance of payments, and imported when the balance is favourable. According to him, metals are ordinary goods, the dispersion of which is controlled in different countries by similar economic considerations. Metals, as set against identical goods, possess a similar value, and thus the exchange rate reflects the parity of purchasing power. After an impressive argument, in which he mainly compares Ricardo's version with that of Goschen, Pierson comes to the conclusion that Ricardo is right in the end, but not that any import or export of metal can be explained by an identification with ordinary goods. Pierson returned to this subject in 'Foreign Exchanges', an essay written in English, and which was intended for publication in *The Economic Journal*.[127] Once more, he goes into great detail with respect to Ricardo's theories.

With this background it is quite understandable that Pierson introduced Ricardo into several of the subjects of his *Textbook*; in particular, while discussing the influence of technology on the position of works and capitalists. Without acknowledging it, Pierson was obviously influenced by Ricardo in the second volume of his book, when he stated: an 'economic law, by which manual labour is replaced by machinery, which is, after a period of adaptation, to the advantage of the labourer, is only extant in the minds of a few optimists.'[128] One hears the echo of

Ricardo's famous statement in the third edition of his *Principles*: 'Machinery and labour are in constant competition',[129] when Pierson says: 'Machinery is indeed the competitor of the labourer, but if the profits which it yields are taken into account, it supplies him with a strong ally.'[130]

We can conclude that Pierson showed, by his great appreciation for the work of Ricardo, his liking for an independent, deductive and analytical study of economics. He also acknowledged the importance of the essential basic questions that Ricardo's theory implies and which are still the subject of many important discussions.

And then . . .

In the summer of 1904, Pierson's international fame was acknowledged when he was appointed doctoris honoris causa by the University of Cambridge. Pierson was once called a 'moderate member of both the classic and the Austrian–American school'. There certainly is some truth in this statement, for Pierson agreed with several essential elements in the theories of important representatives of both schools. And yet it clashes with Pierson's way of weighing one theory against another, with the evolution in his thinking and with his desire to study all theories and keep what is worthwhile. Although Pierson sometimes voiced severe criticism, he was absolutely averse to dogmatics. D'Aulnis de Bourouill said that: 'If one compares the state of affairs of economics when Pierson was a youth, to the state to which he has been able to develop his beloved science, one may gratefully acknowledge that by his efforts political economy in Holland has gained in depth, scope and objectivity.'[131] It is true that this mainly applies to the Netherlands, but Pierson nevertheless belongs to a small coterie of great economists who will always be above any arbitrary classification.

Pierson did not leave many traces in the international literature on economics. One of the most important is his article which was included in Hayek's book (1935) on central planning. Viner refers to the English edition of Piersons *Textbook* twice in 1937.[132] Between the two world wars, one finds many references to his work in Dutch lectures, textbooks and articles. The years 1926–36, the 'years of high theory' as Shackle described them,[133] meant a break with Pierson's inheritance, especially in the field of price theory and macro economics. Gradually, the interest in Pierson declined.

Pierson is honoured in one more publication on economics. In his classic study on the economic motive and economic principle, the Dutch economist Hennipman frequently refers warmly to Pierson.[134] There is, however, a fundamental difference with respect to the interpretation of the concept of welfare remains, as Hennipman – inspired by the Austrian school – chooses the formal subjectivistic approach, while Pierson has a material and objectivistic interpretation. From that publication until the present, Pierson has been infrequently mentioned. Only on special occasions does he now appear in the economics literature.

Notes

1. The author wishes to thank Prof. Dr. P. Hennipman for his helpful critical notes.
2. N.G. Pierson (1868), *The Cultural System* (Hert Kultuurstelsel), Amsterdam. A revised version, *Colonial Politics* (Koloniale Politiek) was published in 1877.
3. N.G. Pierson (1859), 'Trade and commerce in the State of Louisiana' (De handel en het bankwezen van de staat Louisiana), *Journal of Political Economy and Statistics* (Tijdschrift voor staathuishoudkunde en statistiek), pp. 177–93.
4. A.A. Cournot (1838), *Recherches sur les principes mathématiques de la théorie des richesses*, Paris.
5. H.H. Gossen (1854), *Entwickelung der Gesetze des menschlichen Verkehrs und der daraus fliessenden Regeln für menschliches Handeln*, Braunschweig.
6. See the preface of the second edition of Jevons' (1879), *The Theory of Political Economy*, London, in which he says that he bought Gossen's book only in 1872 and declares: 'The eminent and learned economist of Amsterdam, Professor N.G. Pierson, writes to me: "Gossen's book is totally unknown to me".'
7. J.S. Mill (1848), *Principles of Political Economy*, London.
8. J. Oppenheim (1875–1876), *John Stuart Mill's Staathuishoudkunde*, Groningen.
9. W.S. Jevons (1871), *The Theory of Political Economy*, London.
10. C. Menger (1871), *Grundsätze der Volkswirtschaftslehre*, Vienna.
11. L. Walras (1874–1877), *Eléments d'économie politique pure*, Lausanne.
12. K. Marx and F. Engels (1848), *Das Kommunistisch Manifest*, Berlin.
13. K. Marx (1867), *Das Kapital*, Hamburg.
14. N.G. Pierson *Textbook of Political Economy*, volume I, (Leerboek der staathuishoudkunde, deel I) 1884; the second volume was published in 1890.
15. A. Marshall (1925), *The Present Position of Economics*, London, 1885; see also *Memorials of Alfred Marshall*, ed. A.C. Pigou, London.
16. F. von Wieser (1884), *Über den Ursprung und die Hauptgesetze des wirtschaftlichen Wertes*, Vienna.
17. F.Y. Edgeworth (1881), *Mathematical Psychics*, London.
18. L. Walras (1883), *Théorie mathématique de la richesse sociale*, Lausanne.
19. A. Marshall (1890), *Principles of Economics*, London the fifth edition was published in 1907 and the sixth in 1910.
20. J. Schumpeter (1908), *Das Wesen und der Hauptinhalt der theoretischen Nationalökonomie*, Leipzig.
21. J.M. Keynes (1913), *Indian Currency and Finance*, London.
22. N.G. Pierson (1863), *The Future of the Dutch Central Bank* (De toekomst der Nederlandsche Bank), Haarlem. For a modern discussion on the same subject, see F.A. Hayek, (1976), *Denationalisation of Money*, London.
23. *Economic Papers of N.G. Pierson* (1910), volume I (Verspreide economische geschriften van Mr. N.G. Pierson, deel I), ed. C.A. Verrijn Stuart, Haarlem, p.10.
24. Ibid., p.10.
25. Ibid., p.11.
26. N.G. Pierson *The Concept of Wealth* (Het begrip van volksrijkdom), published as a pamphlet in Amsterdam in 1864; see also *Economic Papers*, volume I, pp. 14–103.
27. Ibid., p. 88.
28. N.G. Pierson (1884), *Textbook of Political Economy*, Haarlem, pp. 25–30.

29. P. de Wolff (1941), Income Elasticity of Demand, *The Economic Journal*, pp. 140–5; see also J.A. Schumpeter (1954), *History of Economic Analysis*, London, p. 993.
30. A. Smith (1784), *An Inquiry into the Nature and Causes of the Wealth of Nations*, third edition, London p. 515.
31. Ibid., p. 86.
32. Ibid., p. 39.
33. Ibid., p. 62.
34. Ibid., p. 49.
35. Ibid., p. 85.
36. N.G. Pierson (1866), Value and Production Costs (Waarde en produktiekosten), *The Economist*, pp. 385–402; see also *Economic Papers*, volume I, pp. 104–25.
37. Ibid., p. 106.
38. See J. Schumpeter (1954), *History of Economic Analysis*, New York, p. 917.
39. N.G. Pierson, *Economic Papers*, volume I, p. 113.
40. N.G. Pierson (1910), Contribution to the History of Economic studies in Italy during the 17th and 18th century (Bijdrage tot de geschiedenis der economische studiën in Italië gedurende de 17e en 18e eeuw), *The Economist*, 1866, pp. 451–558; see also *Economic Papers*, volume II, pp. 1–130.
41. *Scrittori Classici Italiani di Economia Politica* (1803–1816), published by P. Custodi, 50 volumes, Milan.
42. J.A. Schumpeter (1954), *History of Economic Analysis*, London.
43. N.G. Pierson (1910), Friedrich List and his time (Friedrich List en zijn tijd), *De Gids*, 1866; see also *Economic Papers*, volume II, pp. 257–88.
44. Ibid., p. 279.
45. See *Economic Papers*, volume III, pp. 58–98.
46. See *Economic Papers*, volume III, pp. 1–57.
47. N.G. Pierson (1865), *Banking* (Bankwezen), *The Economist*, pp. 224–44; it is his first contribution in this field.
48. N.G. Pierson (1871), 'Income tax' (De inkomstenbelasting), *De Gids*, see also *Economic Papers*, volume V, pp. 20–56.
49. N.G. Pierson (1878), 'Katheder-Socialism' (Het katheder-socialisme), *De Gids*; see also *Economic Papers*, volume I, p. 211–47.
50. See *Economic Papers*, volume I, p. 308.
51. N.G. Pierson (1902), 'The problem of value in a socialist society' (Het waardeprobleem in een socialistische maatschappij), *The Economist*, pp. 423–56; see also *Economic Papers*, volume I, pp. 333–7.
52. *Collectivist Economic Planning, Critical Studies on the Possibilities of Socialism by N.G. Pierson, Ludwig von Mises, Georg Halm, and Enrico Barone*, ed. F.A. Hayek, London, 1935.
53. N.G. Pierson (1880), 'Physiocratism' (Het Physiocratisme), *The Economist*, pp. 673–777; see also *Economic Papers*, volume II, pp. 131–208.
54. N.G. Pierson (1882), 'The Irish Landlaw' (De Iersche landwet), *De Gids*; see also *Economic Papers*, volume III, pp. 99–172.
55. N.G. Pierson (1895), 'Sicilian situations' (Siciliaanse toestanden), *The Economist*, pp. 473–532; see also *Economic Papers*, Volume III, pp. 173–235.
56. N.G. Pierson (1910), 1348, *The Economist*, pp. 617–38; see also *Economic Papers*, volume III, pp. 236–59.
57. G.J. Goschen (1864), De Wisselkoersen, translated from the English by N.G. Pierson, Haarlem; the English edition *Theory of the Foreign Exchanges* is of 1861.
58. N.G. Pierson, 'Foreign exchanges', *Economic Papers*, volume IV, pp. 114–77.
59. N.G. Pierson (1888), 'The relation between import and export', *The Economist*, pp. 1–18; see also *Economic Papers*, volume IV, pp. 193–209.
60. N.G. Pierson (1895), 'Index numbers and appreciation of gold', *The Economic Journal*, pp. 329–35; see also *Economic Papers*, volume IV, pp. 352–9, and Further Considerations on Index Numbers, *The Economic Journal*, 1896, pp. 127–31.

61. N.G. Pierson (1884), *Textbook of Political Economy*, volume I, Haarlem, p. 548; third edition, Haarlem 1912, p. 671.
62. C. Menger (1923), *Grundsätze der Volkswirtschaftslehre*, Vienna, pp. 299–313.
63. N.G. Pierson (1880), 'New literature on taxes' (Nieuwe literatuur over belastingen), *De Gids*, and Progressive Income tax (De progressieve inkomstenbelasting), *The Economist*, 1888, pp. 745–52. For the last article see also *Economic Papers*, volume V. pp. 175–82. A.J. Cohen Stuart (1889), *Contribution to the Theory on Progressive Income Tax* (Bijdrage tot de theorie der progressieve inkomstenbelasting), The Hague. In 1958 several important paragraphs were published in *Classics in the Theory of Public Finance*, ed. R.A. Musgrave and A.T. Peacock (1958), London. Musgrave (1959); pays attention to Cohen Stuart in his book *The Theory of Public Finance*, Tokyo, pp. 95–101.
64. Compare F.Y. Edgeworth (1897), 'The pure theory of taxation', *The Economic Journal*, pp. 46–70, 226–38 and 550–71; see also *Papers Relating to Political Economy*, volume II, London 1925, p. 107.
65. N.G. Pierson (1884), *Textbook of Political Economy*, volume I, Haarlem, volume II, Haarlem 1890; the second edition was published in 1896 and the third in 1912.
66. N.G. Pierson (1902–1912), *Principles of Economics*, translated by A.A. Wotzel, London; *Traité d'Economie Politique*, translated by L. Suret (1916–1917), Paris, *Trattato di Economica Politica*, translated by E. Malagoli (1905), Turijn.
67. N.G. Pierson (1911), *Kachizon*, Tokyo, translated by S. Kawada and H. Kawakami from the English.
68. J.A. Schumpeter (1954), *History of Economic Analysis*, New York, pp. 861–2.
69. E. von Böhm-Bawerk (1914), *Geschichte und Kritik der Kapitalzins-Theorien*, third edition, Innsbrück, p. 627.
70. Ibid., p. 15.
71. Ibid., p. 23.
72. Ibid., p. 23.
73. R. Zuckerkandl (1889), *Zur Theorie des Preises*, Leipzig, p. 120.
74. Ibid., p. 55.
75. Ibid., p. 61.
76. H.H. Behrens (1969), *The Development in Economic Thinking* (De ontwikkeling in het economisch denken), Utrecht, p. 406.
77. Ibid., p. 228.
78. Ibid., p. 243.
79. Ibid., first edition, volume I, p. 555.
80. N.G. Pierson (1890), *Textbook of Political Economy*, volume II, Haarlem, p. 30.
81. Ibid., p. 45.
82. Ibid., p. 51.
83. Ibid., p. 55.
84. Ibid., p. 57.
85. Ibid., p. 59.
86. Ibid., p. 74.
87. Ibid., p. 87.
88. Ibid., p. 88.
89. See for example R. Sugden (1986), *The Economics of Rights, Co-operation and Welfare*, Oxford.
90. Ibid., p. 91.
91. Ibid., p. 97.
92. Ibid., volume II, p. 386–90.
93. Ibid., volume II, p. 584.
94. Ibid., volume II, p. 596.
95. Pierson shows much appreciation for Marshall and yet he underestimates him when he discusses his *Principles of Economics* and says: 'There have been greater scholars; Marshall is no genius', *The Economist*, 1891, p. 207; see also *Economic Papers*, volume II, p. 544.

96. F.Y. Edgeworth (1925), *Papers relating to Political Economy*, London; earlier published in *The Economic Journal*, 1891.
97. N.G. Pierson (1864), Appendix, *De Gids*; see also *Economic Papers*, volume I, pp. 205–10.
98. J. d'Aulnis de Bourouill (1911), *Biography of N.G. Pierson* (Levensbericht van Mr N.G. Pierson), Amsterdam.
99. Ibid., pp. 14 and 15.
100. J. d'Aulnis de Bourouill (1874), *The Income of Society* (Het inkomen der maatschappij), Leiden.
101. See *Papers and Correspondence of William Stanley Jevons*, R.D. Collison Black (1977), in particular volume IV, London, and *Correspondence of Léon Walras and Related Papers*, W. Jaffé (1965), in particular volume I, Amsterdam.
102. *Correspondence of Léon Walras and Related Papers* (1965), volume I, Amsterdam, p. 404.
103. *Papers and Correspondence of William Stanley Jevons*, volume IV, R.D. Collison Black, London, p. 57.
104. *Papers and Correspondence of William Stanley Jevons*, volume IV, R.D. Collison Black (1977), London, 61–2.
105. T.W. Hutchison (1953), *A Review of Economic Doctrines, 1870–1929*, Oxford, p. 44–5.
106. N.G. Pierson (1875), *Principles of Political Economy*, volume I, (Grondbeginselen der Staathuishoudkunde, deel I), Haarlem; volume II, Haarlem 1876.
107. Ibid., p. 72.
108. C. Menger (1871), *Grundsätze der Volkswirtschaftslehre*, Vienna, pp. 136–42.
109. Ibid., pp. 241–3.
110. N.G. Pierson (1889), Review of von Böhm, Kapital und Kapitalzins, *The Economist*, p. 199; see also *Economic Papers*, volume I, p. 412–46.
111. N.G. Pierson (1890), Economic Overview (Economisch overzicht), *The Economist*, pp. 607–39; see also *Economic Papers*, volume II, p. 502.
112. Recently P. Groenewegen discovered a letter of Marshall, in which he praised Pierson's *Principles* and in which he also says: 'it has gradually established itself as the book for our students'. P. Groenewegen, An Unpublished Letter of Alfred Marshall (1985), *Australian History of Economic Thought Newsletter*, pp. 27–30.
113. N.G. Pierson (1891) Economic Overview, *The Economist*, pp. 177–207; see also *Economic Papers*, volume II, pp. 516–44.
114. A. Marshall (1890), *Principles of Economics*, volume I, London, pp. 155 and 188.
115. J.M. Keynes (1933), *Essays in Biography*, London, p. 237. 'I particularly remember meeting in this way Adolf Wagner and N.G. Pierson, representatives of a generation of economists which is now almost past.' Keynes says he met Pierson: 'When I was first old enough to be asked out to luncheon or to dinner.'
116. Ibid., p. 65.
117. *The Works and Correspondence of David Ricardo, volume X*, P. Sraffa (1951), Cambridge; A. Heertje (1970), Some Notices on the Life of David Ricardo (Enkele opmerkingen over het leven van David Ricardo), *The Economist*, p. 589–97; D. Weatherall (1976), *D. Ricardo, A Biography*, The Hague.
118. N.G. Pierson (1864), 'The principles of Ricardo's system' (De grondslagen van Ricardo's stelsel), *De Gids*; see also *Economic Papers*, volume I, pp. 126–211.
119. D. Ricardo (1821), *On the Principles of Political Economy and Taxation*, third edition, London; the first edition was published in 1817.
120. Compare for example *The Legacy of Ricardo*, ed. G.A. Caravale (1985), Oxford.
121. Ibid., p. 126.
122. Ibid., p. 127.
123. Ibid., p. 183.
124. Ibid., p. 204.
125. N.G. Pierson (1879), 'A theory of Ricardo' (Eene theorie van Ricardo), *The Economist*, pp. 561–776; see also *Economic Papers*, volume IV, Haarlem, 1911.

126. D. Ricardo (1810), *The High Price of Bullion, a Proof of the Depreciation of Bank Notes*, London.
127. N.G. Pierson, *Economic Papers*, volume IV, pp. 114–77.
128. N.G. Pierson (1896), *Textbook of Political Economy*, volume I, second edition, Haarlem, pp. 343–4.
129. D. Ricardo (1821), *On the Principles of Political Economy and Taxation*, third edition, London, p. 479.
130. Ibid., p. 344.
131. J. d'Aulnis de Bourouill (1911), *Biography of N.G. Pierson*, Amsterdam, p. 31.
132. J. Viner (1937), *Studies in the Theory of International Trade*, New York, pp. 503 and 507.
133. G.L.S. Shackle (1967), *The Years of High Theory*, Cambridge.
134. P. Hennipman (1945), *Economic Motive and Economic Principle*, (Economisch motief en economisch principe), Amsterdam.

13 Marshall's and Pigou's policy prescriptions on unemployment, socialism and inequality

Nahid Aslanbeigui[1]

John Maynard Keynes once praised Arthur Cecil Pigou for having shown 'what a powerful engine for cutting a way in tangled and difficult country the Marshall analysis affords in the hands of one who has been brought up to understand it well.[2] In this statement, identifying Pigou as an embodiment and an extension of Marshall, Keynes, is not alone (see for example, Solow, 1980). Keynes, Solow and others are not mistaken in finding a continuity between the analytical thoughts of Marshall and Pigou. Pigou's analysis of the labour markets and of the laws of return (and the tax-bounty proposals) follow those of Marshall very closely. Striking similarities can also be identified with respect to the two economists' social similarities and can also be identified with respect to the two economists' social philosophy and approach to economics.

Keynes' and Solow's diagnosis, however, cannot be extended to the policy prescriptions of the two economists. Marshall's pronouncements reflect a strong belief that economic freedom leads to growth and progress, i.e., eradication of poverty, and that government intervention creates so many disincentives that it might and probably will do more harm than good.[3] Marshall's policy proposals are hence to reinforce the smooth operation of the markets. Pigou does not share Marshall's optimism. In a free market economy, resource allocation is wasteful because it leads to the satisfaction of the less urgent wants as opposed to more urgent ones.[4] Fairness is only to be achieved by extensive government intervention without creating strong disincentive effects. Pigou's policy proposals are therefore non- or at time even anti-Marshallian.

Pigou himself attributed these differences in 'emphasis and outloook' to the 'difference between the setting' in which the inter-war and the pre-World War I economists worked. Marshall's writings reflected the general optimism created by the end of the 'Hungry Forties', the long-term trends of internal stability, expanding markets, and the prospects of permanent world leadership for England. As a result, 'problems of transition or the great evils of fluctuating employment', even though not ignored, occupied a secondary place on Marshall's agenda relative to 'the underlying forces by which production and distribution [were] governed'. On the other hand, Pigou's ideas were the 'natural' and 'inevitable, consequence' of the turbulent inter-war period when econ-omists faced the 'aftermath of ruin . . . unbalanced Budgets and astronomical inflations; the slow readjustment; the terrible relapse of the great depression and the political tensions that accompanied it'. Short-run, and to Pigou transitory, phenomena presented themselves 'with far greater urgency' relative to the long run. 'In calm weather', said Pigou, 'it is proper to reckon the course of a ship without much regard for the waves. But in a storm the waves may be everything. The problems of transition are the urgent problems. For, if they are not solved, what happens is not transition, but catastrophe; the long run never comes.'[5] Pigou's policy proposals were hence a lot closer to those of Keynes than Marshall's.[6]

Historians of thought have emphasized the differences between Pigou and his contemporaries (Keynes) but have ignored those between him and his teacher, Marshall. This paper, therefore, exposes the latter differences by comparing and contrasting Marshall and Pigou on matters of policy. Remedies to unemployment, poverty and/or inequa-lity will be emphasized since it is in these areas that the disparities are most pronounced. Further discussed are their views on socialism because in their remedies to the above problems, both Marshall and Pigou comment on the merits of socialism as an alternative to the free market economy.

Marshall
'In spite of his youthful and recurring anxiety "to do good" . . . Marshall's conscientious concern for scientific discipline rendered him highly cautious and restrained in his public pronouncements on policy.'[7] His policy proposals were, therefore, scattered in minor writings or letters some of which were kept confidential until his death.[8] None the less it is not impossible to find Marshall's various policy prescriptions on unemployment and poverty.

Unemployment
Unemployment, for Marshall, was a 'symptom of several distinct social maladies, which require different treatment'. The 'occasional unem-ployment of capable energetic workers of all grades', said Marshall, was a 'wholly different disease from systematic unemployment'. 'A large

part of the . . . unemployment [at the time]', he wrote in 1903, was of the latter kind – a symptom of the disease rather than the disease itself, it was caused by the 'existence of large numbers of people, who will not or cannot work steadily or strongly enough to make it possible that they should be employed regularly'.[9] This 'residuum' was itself the product of various factors: bad harvests, inappropriate government intervention (the poor laws) and the workers' irresponsible behaviour (for producing multitudes of children). Another factor was people's inability to manage properly that 'unshackled monster', competition; a relatively recent phenomenon. This led the often 'harsh and ignorant' employers to create such working conditions and 'the manufacturing population had been crushed down to such hard, unwholesome work, that their lives were full of disease and misery'.[10]

The size of this group was fortunately not 'one-half as great' as that of the previous fifty years and the worst evils of the 'dark times' were gone never to return. For this we had many factors to thank: (i) cheap basic necessities due to economic progress; (ii) increased investment in human capital; (iii) reformed poor laws, repealed corn laws and the Factory Acts; (iv) a more effective management of competition; and (v) the British working class's courage and self-reliance.[11]

Marshall was not satisfied with these positive developments, however. 'The system of economic freedom is probably the best from both a moral and material point of view for those who are in fairly good health of mind and body. But the "Residuum" cannot turn it to account.'[12] Since 'society at large, [was] responsible for the existence of this disease', society had to take part in 'removing or lessening the causes' of it through 'very large expenditure of public and private funds'.[13] Public funds were to be spent cautiously, however.

> Works that are not in themselves necessary, but are undertaken in order to give employment, should be such as can be suspended at any time. The pay should be enough to afford the necessaries of life, but so far below the ordinary wages of unskilled labour in ordinary trades that people will not be contented to take it for long, but will always be on the look-out for work elsewhere. I for one can see no economic objection to letting public money flow freely for relief works on this plan.[14]

Other very paternalistic measures that Marshall proposed ranged from the de-urbanization of life 'in the sense in which urbanized life is enfeebled life' to a kindly but 'severe discipline of those who are bringing up children under physical and moral conditions which will make them recruits to the great army of the habitually unemployed'.[15]

The unemployment of the 'capable energetic workers of all grades' was discounted, on the other hand, because it was only occasional, diminishing in size and mainly due to the existence of imperfect information. The occasionally unemployed were so because they were 'beings of finite intelligence' unable to 'forecast coming economic needs and opportunities with perfect precision'.[16] By this Marshall meant people's inability to forecast 'trade fluctuations and changes' a good example of which was the depression of 1873–95. The depression was partly due to the relative decline of Britain in the world market (the challenge of Germany worried Marshall tremendously).[17] This relative decline, in turn, had its reasons in the new militant trade unionist movement among other things.

> The balance against us, allowing for the superior weight of American locomotives, comes out at about 3 : 1, i.e. 3 Glasgow men needed to do the work of 1 American. I should put (say) a quarter of this to account for our employers, a half to account of new-unionism, and the remaining quarter to no account at all.[18]

The Marshall who was sympathetic enough to advocate efficiency wages for the workers,[19] found 'the dominance in some unions of the desire to "make work"' and 'unmixed evil for all', and a 'threat to national well-being':

> I have often said that T.U.'s are a greater glory to England than her wealth. But I thought then of T.U.'s in which the minority, who wanted to compel others to put as little work as possible into the hour, were overruled. Latterly they have, I fear, completely dominated the Engineers' union. I want these people to be beaten at all costs: the complete destruction of Unionism would be as heavy a price as it is possible to conceive: but I think not too high a price.[20]

Short of this harsh measure, the problem of unions was to be resolved by 'preventing the use of collective bargaining as a means of hindering new men and new machines from coming into work for which they are needed'. The information problem, on the other hand, was to be alleviated by 'a better understanding of the causes of trade fluctuations and changes',[21] and by 'further research . . . and . . . development of economic forecasting'.[22]

Despite his worries, Marshall was quite optimistic about the future of Britain as a free market economy. This optimism was nowhere more apparent than in his *Industry and Trade* where he stated: 'After 1873 various signs of weakness were perceived; and later on some exaggerated alarms arose.' But the 'national character is again showing itself in a resolute facing the difficulties'.[23] Progress 'towards the distant goal on an ideally perfect, social organization' had occurred.[24]

Socialism
In response to the growing influence of the Fabian Socialists, Marshall

emphasized the negative aspects of this alternative to capitalism.[25] The remedy to poverty and/or unemployment did not lie in the 'ill-considered' measures of socialism or 'collectivism'. Socialism implied the 'assumption and ownership by government of all the means of production'. Even if brought about gradually and slowly, it 'might cut deeper into the roots of social prosperity than appears at first sight'. Since inventions and the accumulation of capital had always taken place either directly by the private sector or indirectly by borrowing from it, there was 'strong *prima facie* cause for fearing that collective ownership of the means of production would deaden the energies of mankind, and arrest progress'.[26]

For Marshall, new extensions of government work which needed 'ceaseless creation and initiative' were to be regarded as '*prima facie anti-social*', because they retarded 'the growth of that knowledge and those ideas which [were] incomparably the most important form of collective wealth'.[27] The 'self-reliant and inventive faculties',[28] the ability to make spontaneous decisions, and motivation were part of this collective wealth threatened by socialism.[29] Socialists thought 'too much of competition as the exploiting of labour by capital, of the poor by the wealthy, and too little of it as the constant experiment by the ablest men for their several tasks, each trying to discover a new way in which to attain some important end'.[30]

Income distribution

Marshall's scepticism towards socialism did not prevent him from expressing extreme concern for the artisans and masses of unskilled workers who worked hard for long hours, and provided 'for others the means of refinement and luxury' but obtained 'neither for themselves nor their children the means of living a life' that was worthy of man.[31] But he was quick to caution people against exaggerating the existing ills. After all, similar and worse evils had existed in earlier ages.[32] Furthermore, inequality was not as significant as people thought it to be. The proportional return to the income of the rich was very small. 'Take the case of Sir Thomas Brassey, who, on contracts amounting to 78,000,000 made a total profit of 2,500,000 or 1/2d. in the shilling. What small shopkeeper would do his business at that return?'[33]

Marshall urged people to take account of the improvements in the conditions of the working class brought about by the forces of the free market economy. The 'social and economic forces already at work are changing the distribution of wealth for the better . . . they are persistent and increasing in strength; and . . . their influence is for the greater part cumulative'.[34]

He also advised them to accept that *Natura non facit saltum* and that 'there cannot be a great sudden improvement in man's conditions of lige'.[35] This was because: (i) human nature did not change very fast; (ii) since economic institutions were the product of human nature they did not and could not change much faster than human nature; and (iii) human nature was to be found in government as elsewhere.

The best hope of the poor was, therefore, 'not in violent interruption of property rights, or large-scale government intervention'[36] *but in the voluntary actions of the workers and employers within the existing social order.* On the one hand, the poor were advised to control the number of births in their families, to educate their children, to be hard-working and thrifty, to have a higher sense of duty and stay away from excessive drinking and crime.[37] On the other hand, the rich were invited to see the social possibilities of *economic chivalry* or *voluntary* transferences of income. Governments were to perform functions that did not interfere with the market system but instead guaranteed its efficient operation. They were to help inform, educate and train the poor and their children. These coupled with the inherent long-run growth tendencies of capitalism were going to get rid of the 'worst evils of poverty from the land'.[38]

Pigou

Pigou clearly broke away from Marshall in his willingness to prescribe policies and to engage in controversies.[39] In his case, social enthusiasm won over 'objectivity' and caution. In fact, Hutchison blames 'Pigou for having introduced a shift following which 'the conception of a disciplined positive economics, as pronounced by Sidgwick, Marshall and J.M. Keynes, was to be further eroded, and then abandoned, in pursuit of much more fundamental and "revolutionary" aims and claims'.[40]

Unemployment

Even though armed with the Marshallian tools, Pigou did not share Marshall's optimism about the possibilities of growth within a free-market economy. The inter-war period had eroded the growth outlook that Marshall had believed in so optimistically. Economists encountered a new problem: stagnation, and consequently *systematic unemployment of the able-bodied workers.* Not only had this not diminished over time, as Marshall had predicted, it had also become very persistent. In Pigou's own words, what 'before 1914 was a malaise, only on occasions becoming virulent, had been transformed into a devastating endemic disease'.[41]

Perhaps because of this, Pigou addressed the problem of unemployment much more extensively than Marshall (1933 and 1945). But the theoretical model remained Marshallian as did the specific factors causing unemployment. Pigou found, for instance, that the unemployment of the early 1920s was due to the over-optimistic expectations created during the boom of 1919–20 (imperfect information).[42] Or the high unemployment figures of the great depression indicated that money wages had not fallen to match the fall of prices. Real wages, then, were 'substantially above that proper to nil unemployment, and . . . a substantial part of post-war unemployment [was] attributable to that fact.' But they also showed a change in the institutional structure of the economy, that is, the combined action of government and trade unions.[43] The system of unemployment insurance, argued Pigou, decreased the fear of creating unemployment to the trade unions since it removed the cost of such problems from their shoulders. 'I am inclined to attribute a substantial part of the differences between the average level of unemployment in the inter-war and in the pre-1914 period to this circumstance.'[44]

For Marshall, the occasional unemployment of the able-bodied was mainly caused by imperfect information, the provision of information, of course, being the remedy. Pigou's remedies were much more interventionist. 'For prosperity to be restored either money costs must fall or money prices must rise.' Pigou did not favour a wage cut, however. 'The practical difficulties in the way of the former solution have proved so serious and the friction to be overcome so great that the main body of instructed opinion has turned toward the latter', viz. a deliberate policy of reflation. This was to be achieved by import restrictions (to increase prices), by monetary expansion (much more effective if adopted by all nations) or through public work projects.[45]

It is true, argued Pigou, that in normal times (full employment), 'State action designed to stimulate employment in any particular field will . . . merely divert labour from more productive to less productive occupations.' This argument 'whether in pure form or wrapped up in the customary trappings, would provide good reasons for deprecating State action designed to reduce unemployment . . . provided that there were no unemployment to reduce!' It is important, however, to 'be sure that our presuppositions are adjusted not to imaginary but to actual conditions'.[46] The real world was faced with 'an enormous mass of unemployment', the existence of which necessitated government intervention and the artificial creation of employment.[47] Unlike Marshall, Pigou did not limit the wages of those working on the public work projects to the subsistence level. In fact, he implicitly assumed that they would be paid wages higher than the minimum provided through unemployment insurance.[48] Pigou insisted on the benefits to society of

198 Classical and neoclassical economic thought

the public work projects by claiming that 'If an enterprise is likely to fall short by only a little of being directly remunerative to the investor, it is sure to be remunerative in a substantial degree to the community as a whole. When in doubt, therefore, do not suspend judgment; above all do not contract. *When in doubt, expand*'.[49]

The reader will immediately recognize the non- (or anti-) Marshallian nature of this statement. *When in doubt*, the cautious Marshall would have argued, *do not adopt the policy*!

Socialism
Contrary to Marshall, Pigou was quite sympathetic to socialism. This is apparent in his reviews of Hayek's *Road to Serfdom* (1944) and of the Webbs' *Soviet Communisn: A New Civilization?* (1936) where

> Pigou may be seen to distance himself distinctly further, in general philosophy, from Hayek than from the Webbs. Pigou of course, accepts Hayek's condemnation of central planning in the case of the regimes of Hitler and Mussolini, but claims that central planning is simply a means, and rejects Hayek's 'historical thesis' that its tendency is to destroy liberty and personal responsibility.[50]

Holding a much more critical view, Pigou found capitalism to be wasteful in satisfying the less urgent wants. The productive resources of the economy were devoted to 'satisfying the whims of the rich' while 'large numbers of people [were] inadequately fed, clothed, housed and educated'.[51] In contrast, he admired the Stalinist Russia for having enshrined in its policy the doctrine that 'the approaches to civilisation should be free to all not a privilege of a few'.[52]

Pigou discounted Marshall's concern with reduced incentives under socialism. Since the 'accumulation of capital is cared for directly by the State', there was 'no longer need to rely on the ability and the willingness of private persons to provide it'. The incentive to work hard was enhanced, said Pigou, since the workers did not face the worst ills of capitalism: *unemployment* and *exploitation*. There was no doubt that socialism had evoked 'tremendous enthusiasm for work on the part of manual wage-earner'.[53]

Socialism necessitated extensive government intervention but Pigou was not worried about that either. State action, he argued, depended partly on the willingness of the public but also on the 'quality of the body that would be called upon to act'. If Adam Smith believed in *laissez-faire*, it was not out of a theoretical conviction that 'if you leave things alone, they are almost bound to work out right'. Rather, it was out of the practical experience that 'if you interfere in the sort of way in which governing authorities, as he knew them in his day, did interfere, they are almost bound to work out wrong'. The quality of the governing bodies had improved tremendously since Adam Smith's time. This had even impressed Marshall, said Pigou.[54] But Marshall had also believed that the more the government spreads itself over work that can be done by the private sector, the 'less energies it will have to spare for and the less efficiently it will perform . . . its proper tasks'. On this account, Pigou called our attention to the then recent development of independent, publicly managed organizations of which Marshall 'had had practically no experience and which, had he been able to reckon with it, might perhaps have made him less unbending'.[55] In sum and compared to Marshall, Pigou did not see any *inherent anti-social nature to government intervention*. There was no general rule. *The merits of government intervention*, he argued, *should be judged on a case-by-case basis*.

Income distribution

Despite the arguments in favour of socialism, Pigou was reluctant to choose it over capitalism because there was not enough information to justify such a move. Having dismissed socialism as a viable alternative, Pigou shifted his attention towards the redistribution of income. Marshall had 'insisted strongly on the . . . possible damaging effects of redistribution on production,[56] and had therefore advocated voluntary transferences of income. Pigou was more concerned with the *inadequacy* of *economic chivalry*.

> Unfortunately, it is quite certain that, in present conditions, voluntary transference will fall much below the aggregate of transferences from relatively well-to-do people which the general sense of the community demands. *A considerable amount of coercive transference is, therefore, also necessary.*[57]

Pigou did share Marshall's concern about redistributive policies. The transference was justified unless 'aggregate real income is damaged as a consequence of the transfer'. He admitted that the *expectation* and the *fact* of redistribution were likely to decrease the size of the national dividend in the present and in the future. It was for this reason that he objected to food subsidies in 1948: the 'process of raising the money to finance these transfers is . . . likely in present conditions indirectly to bring about a considerable cut in the size of the cake that we are trying to distribute more evenly.'[58]

This, however, suggested caution and not inaction. A circular saw, Pigou argued, may easily cut the hands of a bungler, or more importantly, the hands of other people. But in the hands of an expert, it may do wonders. Even at his most cautious moment Pigou was much more willing to allow for redistributive measures than Marshall.

> It is generally agreed that a substantial measure of egalitarian policy can be carried through without producing injurious side effects that outweigh the direct gain. The live issue is not whether *any* transfer can be made with advantage, but at what point the net benefit from further transfers ceases.[59]

For Pigou, redistributive measures promoted fairness in a capitalist economy. It was true that they were likely to lead to 'a reduction of the incentive to work and enterprise among people capable of earning high incomes; . . . a reduction of the incomes of rich people, who are especially likely to invest a large proportion of their incomes; and . . . a reduction for those people of the incentive to invest'.[60] But this was less of a problem then than during Marshall's time. People cared about their relative income as well as the absolute levels and were not likely to be too discouraged if their friends were getting less as well. Furthermore, the reduction in the incomes of the rich would not reduce investment much since the voluntary savings of the rich was not as important a source of investment as before.[61] Besides, governments could compensate for the decreased investment by means of 'compulsory savings engineered through taxation or forced loans or through the price and wage policy of State-controlled industries'.[62]

Having in mind that gradually moulding and transforming was a better and more viable alternative than violently uprooting, Pigou proposed the following measures: (i) heavily graduated death duties and graduated incomes taxes to diminish the inequalities of 'fortune and opportunity'; (ii) increased investment in the 'health, intelligence and character of the people'; (iii) public supervision and control of industries which are affected by a public interest or are capable of wielding monopoly power; (iv) nationalization of such big industries as coal and railway; (v) demand management to reduce the impact of business fluctuations; (vi) nationalization of other more important industries using central government planning to allocate the 'country's annual investment in new capital'.[63] It is obvious that aside from the second and perhaps the first policies, Marshall would have objected to the rest for the extent of government intervention they required.

Conclusion

Pigou's economic writings are often viewed as natural extensions of Marshall's theories. A careful comparison of the two with respect to their views and policies on unemployment, socialism and inequality indicates otherwise. Marshall was extremely optimistic about the possibilities of growth in the context of a free-market economy. The ideal society was one where *economic chivalry* took care of the poor and the needy and the government informed and educated the individuals. He was very apprehensive of socialism and/or government intervention and of their impact on the incentives to work hard, save, invest and accumulate.

Pigou, on the other hand, called for major compulsory redistributive measures which resembled the Attlee government's programme of 1945–50. Taking a 'leaf from the book of Soviet Russia',[64] he advocated increasing the areas of government intervention to the takeover of some industries, regulation of others, and even went as far as planning for investment for the future generations. He was aware of the possible reduced incentives under socialism and/or government intervention. But he warned economists against dressing this argument as a bogy. 'The offset to increased fairness in distribution is . . . likely to be, not a catastrophe for production, but at the worst, some slowing down in its rate of increase, and that is not a disaster.'[65]

Notes
1. The author would like to thank Celia Capule, John Edwards, John Newman and Adele Wick for helpful comments on earlier versions of the paper.
2. In Pigou, 1925, p. 44.
3. Marshall, 1920b, pp. 675–713.
4. Pigou, 1937, p. 21.
5. Pigou, 1939, p. 217.
6. See Hutchison, 1978, p. 194. The differences can also be attributed to Marshall's cautious nature, his distaste for change, and also his distrust of governments as opposed to Pigou.
7. Hutchison, 1981, p. 57.
8. See for example his letter to Edward Caird in regard to the Engineers' strike, in Pigou, 1925, pp. 398–9.
9. In Pigou, 1925, p. 446.
10. In Stigler and Coase, 1969, pp. 197, 189.
11. Marshall, 1920b, pp. 675–87; see also Stigler and Coase, 1969, pp. 189–90.
12. In Hutchison, 1978, pp. 109–10.
13. In Pigou, 1925, p. 447.
14. Marshall, 15 February 1886.
15. In Pigou, 1925, p. 447.
16. Ibid.
17. See Marshall, 1920a, pp. 92–3.
18. In Pigou, 1925, pp. 399–400.
19. See Harrison, 1963; also see Petridis, 1973.
20. In Pigou, 1925, pp. 399–400.
21. Ibid., pp. 401, 446.
22. Hutchison, 1978, p. 111. By the 1920s, Marshall came to accept that 'fluctuations in the rate of progress seem likely to continue' (Marshall, 1923, p. 245). Remedies, however, remained for informing and educating the public.
23. Marshall, 1920a, p. 92.
24. In Tullberg, 1975, p. 111.
25. In fact, one reason for Marshall's condemnation of the trade unions was that they were under the influence of the socialists. He went on to say: 'I think the Engineers

have been under exceptional temptations, and have yielded to the seductions of those semi-socialists who have captured them' (in Pigou, 1925, pp. 403, 400).

26. Marshall, 1920b, pp. 712–13.
27. In Pigou, 1925, p. 339.
28. In Whitaker, 1975, p. 342.
29. Tullberg, 1975, p. 85.
30. In Pigou, 1925, p. 283.
31. Marshall, 1892, p. 361. The concern was based on moral but also on economic grounds. Extreme poverty created the greatest 'waste product' of the world's history: 'the latent, the undeveloped, the choked-up and wasted faculties for higher work, that for the lack of opportunity have come to nothing' (In Pigou, 1925, p. 228). It decreased industrial efficiency and the production of material wealth which affected the 'health and strength, physical, mental and moral of the human race' (Marshall, 1892, p. 131), hence creating a vicious circle.
32. In Pigou, 1925, p. 361.
33. In Stigler and Coase, 1969, p. 198.
34. Marshall, 1920b, pp. 675–87 and 712.
35. Ibid., p. 665.
36. Whitaker, 1975, p. 343.
37. In Stigler and Coase, 1969, pp. 198–210.
38. Marshall, 1920b, p. 719.
39. See his letters to the editor of *The Times* with respect to the unemployment problem of the early 1930s.
40. Hutchison, 1981, p. 65.
41. Pigou, 1952, p. 88.
42. Pigou, 1923, pp. 38–40.
43. Pigou, 1933, p. 256. Surprisingly, in the era of General Strike, Pigou did not have much to say about trade unions. He did not show 'much interest or anxiety regarding what Marshall had seen as Britain's 'greatest danger': that is the way in which trade unions were exercising their power' (Hutchison, 1981, p. 66).
44. Pigou, 1952, p. 103.
45. Pigou, 6 January 1933.
46. Pigou, 6 June 1930.
47. In a letter to *The Times*, Pigou, Keynes and others agreed that increased savings were not 'patriotic' under the circumstances. Private economy, as they called it, 'instead of enabling labour-power, machine power and shipping power to a different and more important use . . . it throws them into idleness' (MacGregor et al., 17 October 1932). Aside from rescuing people from 'soul-destroying idleness' public work projects had the advantage of saving in the amount of unemployment benefits paid out. But perhaps more importantly, 'by indirect psychological reactions' confidence would be stimulated and 'a cumulative movement toward expansion started' (21 February 1933).
48. This is apparent from the following argument where Pigou tries to prove the economic benefits of such projects. 'It may well be that, when they come in, they will not be worth the wage paid to them. But this does not imply a waste of national resources. So long as they are worth more than the excess of their wage over what they would otherwise have received in unemployment benefit and so on, there is not a loss to the rest of the community, but a gain' (6 June 1930).
49. Pigou, 6 June 1930, emphasis added.
50. Hutchison, 1981, p. 69.
51. Pigou, 1937, p. 21.
52. Pigou, 1936, p. 94.
53. Pigou, 1937, pp. 29, 67, 98 and 99.
54. Pigou, 1935, pp. 125–6.
55. Pigou cited the 'three most recent and largest organiztions for public management – the Coal Board, the British Transport Commission and. . .Steel Corporation'. Even

though subject to the control of ministers in the last resort, they were 'in their day-to-day working, independent bodies for whose operations ministers can disclaim responsibility' (1953, p. 62).
56. Hutchinson, 1981, p. 65.
57. Pigou, 1932, p. 713, emphasis added.
58. Pigou, 1952, p. 127.
59. Ibid., pp. 77 and 160.
60. Pigou, 1955, pp. 85–6.
61. According to Pigou, saving, investment and capital accumulation came from the undistributed profits of companies, insurance companies, etc. rather than from the rich individuals (1953, p. 55).
62. Pigou, pp. 86–7.
63. Pigou, 1937, pp. 135–8.
64. Ibid., p. 138.
65. Pigou, 1955, p. 87.

References

Ashworth, W. (1960), *An Economic History of England 1870–1939*, Methuen, London.
Barou, N. (1947), *British Trade Unions*, Victor Gollancz, London.
Clark, K. (1969), *Marshall, Marx and Modern Times*, Cambridge University Press, Cambridge.
Flanders, A. (1952). 'Great Britain', in W. Galenson (ed.), *Comparative Labor Movements*, Prentice-Hall, New York.
Hutchison, T. W. (1978), *On Revolutions and Progress in Economic Knowledge*, Cambridge University Press, London.
Hutchison, T. W. (1981), *The Politics and Philosophy of Economics*, Basil Blackwell, Oxford.
Kirby, M. W. (1981), *The Decline of British Power Since 1870*, George Allen and Unwin, London.
Levine, H.J. (1956), 'Standards of welfare in economic thought', *Quarterly Journal of Economics*, (February).
MacGregor, D. H. et al. (1932), 'Private spending: money for productive investment', *The Times* (17 October).
Marshall, A. (1886), 'Political economy and outdoor relief', *The Times* (15 February).
Marshall, A. (1892), *Elements of Economics of Industry*, Macmillan, London.
Marshall, A. (1920a), *Industry and Trade*, Macmillan, London.
Marshall, A. (1920b), *Principles of Economics*, 8th edn, Macmillan, London.
Marshall, A. (1923), *Money Credit and Commerce*, Macmillan, London.
Marshall, A. and Marshall, M. P. (1879), *The Economics of Industry*, Macmillan, London.
Petridis, A. (1973), 'Alfred Marshall's attitudes to and economic analysis of trade unions: a case of anomalies in a competitive system', *History of Political Economy*, vol. 5, no. 1 (Spring), pp. 165–98.
Pigou, A. C. (1923), *Essays in Applied Economics*, P.S. King and Son, London.
Pigou, A. C. (ed.) (1925), *Memorials of Alfred Marshall*, Macmillan, London.
Pigou, A. C. (1927), 'Wage policy and unemployment', *Economic Journal*, vol. 37, no. 147 (September), pp. 355–68.
Pigou, A. C. (1930), 'Unemployment policy', *The Times* (6 June).
Pigou, A. C. (1932), *The Economics of Welfare,* 4th edn, Macmillan, London.
Pigou, A. C. (1933), *The Times* (21 February).
Pigou, A. C. (1933), 'Price Policy: sterling and its task – A possible lead to the world', *The Times* (6 January).
Pigou, A. C. (1933), 'Public works: earnings, direct and indirect', *The Times* (28 July).
Pigou, A. C. (1933), *The Theory of Unemployment*, Macmillan, London.
Pigou, A. C. (1935), *Economics in Practice*, Macmillan, London.

Pigou, A. C. (1936), 'The Webbs on soviet communism', *Economic Journal*, vol. 46, no. 181 (March), pp. 88–97.
Pigou, A. C. (1937), *Socialism Versus Capitalism*, Macmillan, London.
Pigou, A. C. (1939), 'Presidential address', *Economic Journal*, vol. 49, no. 194 (June), pp. 215–21.
Pigou, A. C. (1944), 'Review of Hayek's *The Road to Serfdom*', *Economic Journal*, vol. 56, no. 214 (June), pp. 217–19.
Pigou, A. C. (1945), *Lapses from Full Employment*, Macmillan, London.
Pigou, A. C. (1946), *Income, An Introduction to Economics*, Macmillan, London.
Pigou, A. C. (1952), *Essays in Economics*, Macmillan, London.
Pigou, A. C. (1953), *Alfred Marshall and Current, Thought*, Macmillan, London.
Pigou, A. C. (1955), *Income Revisited*, Macmillan, London.
Solow, R. M. (1980), 'On theories of unemployment', *The American Economic Review*, vol. 70, no. 1 (March), pp. 1–11.
Stigler, G. and Coase, R. (1969), 'Alfred Marshall's lectures on progress and poverty', *Journal of Law and Economics*, vol. 12, no. 1 (April), pp. 181–226.
Tullberg, R. (1975), 'Marshall's tendency to socialism', *History of Political Economy*, vol. 7, no. 1 (Spring), pp. 75–111.
Whitaker, J. K. (ed.) (1975), *The Early Economic Writings of Alfred Marshall, 1867–1890*, The Free Press, New York.
Winch, D. (1970), *Economics and Policy*, Walker and Company, New York.

Subject index

absolute equilibrium of buyer and seller (Canard) 44–5, 46
accumulation 106, 128
of capital and profit rate 73, 76
agriculture
productive labour in 92–3
in Soviet national income accounting 97–100
allocation of resources 65, 101, 141
Anglo-Irish school 7
apparent abundance of commodity 59
apprenticeship system, Smith on 26–7, 32
applied economics 135
artificial monopolies, suppression of (Walras) 141

balance
of payments 56
of trade, 17th–18th c. 6, 13
bimetallism 177
budget constraint 137–8, 140
bullion debate 13

calculus 55
capacity to produce (Canard) 45
capital
accumulation and profit rate 73, 76
circulating (Wicksell) 145–7
circulation of (Marx) 92, 94–5
fixed 145–7
and hired-for-profit labour 88
reorganization of stock 125
vs revenue 88–9
wealth 83
capitalist economy and GE theory 133
capitalist as productive worker

(Smith) 85
capitalist production (Marx) 90–96
circulating capital (Wicksell) 145–7
circulation of capital (Marx) 92,94–5
classical economic thought
pre-19th c. 3–67
19th c. 69–130
classical equilibrium and law of demand 115–17
collective ownership 136
commercial revulsions preventing stationary state 75
commodity prices 127
commodity standard 53, 55–6
common law, Coke on 20, 22–5, 31–2, 35
commutative justice (Walras) 141–3
comparative statics 55–6, 59, 60, 62
competition
Canard on 40, 43–4, 46
demand and 110
mid-18th c. ideas on 14
Smith on 26–31, 33, 73
Walras on 136–41
comprehensive production concept 82
constant-outlay demand curve 53, 59
constant returns to scale 123–4, 128
consumer preferences 123
consumption, Pierson on 177–8
continuity in classical economic thought 104–13
Ricardo's invariable measure of value 104–9
role of demand conditions 109–11
Sraffa's Standard Commodity 104–9
corn model (Ricardo) 104–8, 117–23
corporation law, 17th–18th c. 19, 28

Author index

Agnati, A. 65, 66
Akerman, Gustaf 146, 153
Allen, William R. 80, 81
Allix, Edgar 48, 49, 50, 51, 52
Anderson, G. M. 28, 36
Antica, P. de 65
Antonelli, Giovanni Battista 150, 153
Ashley, William 6, 17
Aslanbeigui, Nahid ix, x, 191–204
Augello, M. 66
Aulnis de Bourouill, J. d' 180, 182, 185, 189, 190

Bailey, S. 117, 129
Baranzini, M. 113
Baron, S. L. 153
Baumol, William J. 38, 49, 50, 51, 153
Beccaria, Cesare B. 53, 58–9, 63, 64, 65, 66, 173
Becker, J. 26, 36
Behrens, H. H. 188
Bentham, Jeremy 156
Bernard, Sir John 11
Bertrand, J. 50
Bianchini, Marco viii, x, 53–67
Billet, L. 31, 36
Black, R. D. C. 16
Blanqui, Jerome Adolphe 52
Blaug, Mark 16
Blewitt, George 7
Bliss, C. 114, 129
Böhm-Bawerk, Eugen von 145–7, 153, 175, 177, 179, 182, 188
Bortkewitsch, L. von 144
Bousquet, G.-H. 51
Boven, Pierre 49, 50, 51
Boyd, Walter 3

Bradley, I. 112
Brandis, Royall viii, x, 71–81
Brems, Hans ix, x, 145–54
Breton, Yves 52
Briganti, Filippo 165
Broggia, Carlo Antonio 53
Buchanan, D. 117, 129
Buchanan, James M. 36, 165
Burmeister, E. 112

Cajori, Florian 50
Campanella, Tommaso 156
Campbell, R. H. 17
Campbell, William 35
Canard, Nicholas-Francois viii, 38–52
Canciani, Gottardo 53, 59, 66
Cannan, Edwin 83, 101–2, 103
Cantillon, Richard 17, 49
Capule, Celia 201
Caravale, Giovanni viii, x, 104–13, 190
Carli, Gianrinaldo 53
Cassel, Gustav ix, 149–54
Cesarano, F. 65, 66
Ceva, Giovanni 53, 55–7, 65, 66
Chailley, Joseph 52
Child, Sir Josiah 4, 26
Chipman, John S. 153
Cirillo, R. 135, 144
Coase, R. 201, 204
Cohen Stuart, A. J. 175, 188
Coke, Sir Edward viii, 19–26, 31–6
Coleman, D. C. 35, 36
Cooke, C. A. 36
Cooter, Robert 163, 165
Cournot, Augustin 40, 41, 48–9, 50, 51, 52, 170, 186

212